The Oregon Trail

FRANCIS PARKMAN

THE OREGON TRAIL

Sketches of Prairie and Rocky Mountain Life

Lino-cuts by PETER PENDREY

Cover by Wendell Minor

HART PUBLISHING COMPANY, INC.
NEW YORK CITY

Contents

Introduction

In 1846, barely recovered from a long and painful struggle with illness, Francis Parkman enthusiastically embarked upon a trip to the Far West. The trip was to serve a dual purpose for Parkman: as a diversion from his arduous study of the law, and as potential research on Indians for a history he hoped to write about the "old French War."

Such determination and refusal to yield to the dictates of his feeble body were typical of Francis Parkman. The son of a wealthy New England merchant, and educated at Harvard College, Parkman had suffered from physical ailments—indigestion, acute pains in the head, severe problems with his eyes—from his earliest years. A lesser man living constantly with such anguish might have simply settled down at home to enjoy his inherited wealth; but the series of difficulties Parkman constantly had to overcome seems only to have motivated him all the more.

Parkman was, of course, not ignorant of the Far West. No educated man could have been unacquainted with the doctrine of "manifest destiny" which had captured the imaginations of all Americans of that era. No son of a Bostonian merchant could be indifferent to the struggle between American and English investors for control of the Oregon and Rocky Mountain fur trade. Parkman must also have been aware of the impending territorial war with Mexico.

But to report on the progress of these dramas was not Parkman's intention in *The Oregon Trail*. The book was based on the journal notations he made throughout the trip. Upon examining Parkman's journal and earlier editions of *The Oregon Trail*, the author's purpose becomes clear: opinions, analysis, and predictions were deleted from the journal; observations and adventure were retained.

During his long trek across the American continent, Parkman again grew ill. His condition remained poor even after his journey home and, being too ill to write, he was forced to dictate the first draft of *The Oregon Trail*. Between the years of 1847 and 1849, portions of the book appeared in *Knickerbocker Magazine*. A complete, revised edition appeared in 1849, under the long title *The California and Oregon Trail: Being Sketches of Prairie and Rocky Mountain Life*. Putman, the book's publisher, reprinted it in 1852, under the title *The Oregon Trail as Prairie and Rocky Mountain Life; Or, the California and Oregon Trail*. Twenty years later, Parkman revised it again, and it was issued in 1873 by Little, Brown and Company as *The Oregon Trail*.

This version of the book was reprinted many times until 1891, when Parkman initiated still another revision. Although each previous revision had improved the book in style and clarity, in his final version of the book Parkman showed his awareness of the new role his book was to play for its readership. The American West had changed dramatically in the 45 years since his trip: *The Oregon Trail* had to serve, not as a description of the contemporary American West, but as a narration of how it once was. Recognizing this fact, Parkman wrote in his preface to the final edition:

The buffalo is gone, and of all his millions nothing is left but bones. Tame cattle and fences of barbed wire have supplanted his vast herds and boundless grazing lands ... The wild Indian is turned into an ugly caricature of his conqueror; and that which made him romantic, terrible, and hateful, is in large measure scourged out of him. The slow cavalcade of horsemen armed to the teeth has disappeared before parlor cars and the effeminate comforts of modern travel. The rattlesnakes have grown bashful and retiring . . . The Wild West is tamed, and its savage charms have withered. If this book can help to keep their memory alive, it will have done its part.

NANCY GOLDBERG

1. The Frontier

Last spring, 1846, was a busy season in the city of St Louis. Not only were emigrants from every part of the country preparing for the journey to Oregon and California, but an unusual number of traders were making ready their wagons and outfits for Santa Fé. The hotels were crowded, and the gunsmiths and saddlers were kept constantly at work in providing arms and equipments for the different parties of travellers. Steamboats were leaving the levee and passing up the Missouri, crowded with passengers on their way to the frontier.

In one of these, the 'Radnor,' since snagged and lost, my friend and relative Quincy Adams Shaw, and myself left St Louis on the 28th of April, on a tour of curiosity and amusement to the Rocky Mountains. The boat was loaded until the water broke alternately her guards. Her upper-deck was covered with large wagons a peculiar form, for the Santa Fé trade, and her hold was ammed with goods for the same destination. There were also the equipments and provisions of a party of Oregon emigrants, a band of mules and horses, piles of saddles and harness, and a multitude of nondescript articles, indispensable on the prairies. Almost hidden in this medley was a small French cart, of the sort very appropriately called a 'mule-killer' beyond the frontiers, and not far distant a tent, together with a miscellaneous assortment of boxes and barrels. The whole equipage was far from prepossessing in its appearance; yet, such as it was, it was destined to a long and arduous journey, on which the persevering reader will accompany it.

The passengers on board the 'Radnor' corresponded with her freight. In her cabin were Santa Fé traders, gamblers, speculators, and adventurers of various descriptions, and her steerage was crowded with Oregon emigrants, 'mountain men,' negroes, and a party of Kanzas Indians, who had been on a visit to St Louis.

Thus laden the boat struggled upward for seven or eight days against the rapid current of the Missouri, grating upon snags, and hanging for two or three hours at a time upon sand-bars. We entered the mouth of the Missouri in a drizzling rain, but the weather soon became clear, and showed distinctly the broad and turbid river, with its eddies, its sand-bars, its ragged islands, and forest-covered shores. The Missouri is constantly changing its course,—wearing away its banks on one side, while it forms new ones on the other. Its channel is continually shifting. Islands are formed, and then washed away; and while the old forests on one side are undermined and swept off, a young growth springs up from the new soil upon the other. With all these changes the water is so charged with mud and sand that, in spring, it is perfectly opaque, and in a few minutes deposits a sediment an inch thick in the bottom of a tumbler. The river was now high; but when we descended in the autumn it was fallen very low, and all the secrets of its treacherous shallows were exposed to view. It was frightful to see the dead and broken trees, thick-set as a military abattis, firmly imbedded in the sand, and all pointing down stream, ready to impale any unhappy steamboat that at high water should pass over them.

In five or six days we began to see signs of the great western movement that was taking place. Parties of emigrants, with their tents and wagons, were encamped on open spots near the bank, on their way to the common rendezvous at Independence. On a rainy day, near sunset, we reached the landing of this place, which is some miles from the river, on the extreme frontier of Missouri. The scene was characteristic, for here were represented at one view the most remarkable features of this wild and enterprising region. On the muddy shore stood some thirty or forty dark, slavish-looking Spaniards, gazing stupidly out from beneath their broad hats. They were attached to one of the Santa Fé companies, whose wagons were crowded together on the banks above. In the midst of these, crouching over a smouldering fire, was a group of Indians, belonging to a remote Mexican tribe. One or two French hunters from the mountains, with their long hair and buckskin dresses, were looking at the boat; and seated on a log close at hand were three men, with rifles lying across their knees. The foremost of these, a tall, strong figure, with a clear blue eye and an open, intelligent face, might very well represent that race of restless and intrepid pioneers whose axes and rifles have opened a path from the Alleghanies to the western prairies. He was on his way to Oregon, probably a more congenial field to him than any that now remained on this side of the great plains.

Early on the next morning we reached Kanzas, about five hundred miles from the mouth of the Missouri. Here we landed, and leaving our equipments in charge of Colonel Chick, whose log-house was the substitute for a tavern, we set out in a wagon for Westport, where we hoped to procure mules and horses for the journey.

It was a remarkably fresh and beautiful May morning. The woods, through which the miserable road conducted us, were lighted by the bright sunshine and enlivened by a multitude of birds. We overtook on the way our late fellow-travellers, the Kanzas Indians, who adorned with all their finery were proceeding homeward at a round pace; and whatever they might have seemed on board the boat, they made a very striking and picturesque feature in the forest landscape.

Westport was full of Indians, whose little shaggy ponies were tied by dozens along the houses and fences. Sacs and Foxes, with shaved heads and painted faces, Shawanoes and Delawares, fluttering in calico frocks and turbans, Wyandots dressed like white men, and a few wretched Kanzas wrapped in old blankets, were strolling about the streets or lounging in and out of the shops and houses.

As I stood at the door of the tavern I saw a remarkable-looking personage coming up the street. He had a ruddy face, garnished with the stumps of a bristly red beard and moustache; on one side of his head was a round cap with a knob at the top, such as Scottish laborers sometimes wear; his coat was of a nondescript form, and made of a gray Scotch plaid, with the fringes hanging all about it; he wore trousers of coarse homespun, and hob-nailed shoes; and to complete his equipment, a little black pipe was stuck in one corner of his mouth. In this curious attire, I recognized Captain C——, of the British army, who, with his brother, and Mr R——, an English gentleman, was bound on a hunting expedition across the continent. I had seen the Captain and his companions at St Louis. They had now been for some time at Westport, making preparations for their departure, and waiting for a reinforcement, since they were too few in number to attempt it alone. They might, it is true, have joined some of the parties of emigrants who were on the point of setting out for Oregon and California; but they professed great disinclination to have any connection with the 'Kentucky fellows.'

The Captain now urged it upon us that we should join forces and proceed to the mountains in company. Feeling no greater partiality for the society of the emigrants than they did, we thought the arrangement a good one, and consented to it. Our future fellow-travellers had installed themselves in a little log-house, where we found them surrounded by saddles, harness, guns, pistols, telescopes, knives, and in short their complete appointments for the prairie. R——, who had a taste for natural history, sat at a table stuffing a woodpecker; the brother of the Captain, who was an Irishman, was splicing a trail-rope on the floor. The Captain pointed out, with much complacency, the different articles of their outfit. 'You see,' said he, 'that we are all old travellers. I am convinced that no party ever went upon the prairie better provided.' The hunter whom they had employed, a surly-looking Canadian, named Sorel, and their muleteer, an American ruffian from St Louis, were lounging about the building. In a little log stable close at hand were their horses and mules, selected with excellent judgment by the Captain.

We left them to complete their arrangements, while we pushed our own to all convenient speed. The emigrants, for whom our friends professed such contempt were encamped on the prairie about eight or ten miles distant, to the number of a thousand or more, and new parties were constantly passing out from Independence to join them. They were in great confusion, holding meetings, passing resolutions, and drawing up regulations, but unable to unite in the choice of leaders to conduct them across the prairie. Being at leisure one day, I rode over to Independence. The town was crowded. A multitude of shops had sprung up to furnish the emigrants and Santa Fé traders with necessaries for their journey; and there was an incessant hammering and banging from a dozen blacksmiths' sheds, where the heavy wagons were being repaired, and the horses and oxen shod. The streets were thronged with men, horses, and mules. While I was in the town, a train of emigrant wagons from Illinois passed through, to join the camp on the prairie, and stopped in the principal street. A multitude of healthy children's faces were peeping out from under the covers of the wagons. Here and there a buxom damsel was seated on horseback, holding over her sunburnt face an old umbrella or a parasol, once gaudy enough, but now miserably faded. The men, very sober-looking countrymen, stood about their oxen; and as I passed I noticed three old fellows, who, with their long whips in their hands, were zealously discussing the doctrine of regeneration. The emigrants, however, are not all of this stamp. Among them are some of the vilest outcasts in the country. I have often perplexed myself to divine the various motives that give impulse to this migration; but whatever they may be, whether an insane hope of a better condition in life, or a desire of shaking off restraints of law and society, or mere restlessness, certain it is that multitudes bitterly repent the journey, and, after they have reached the land of promise, are happy enough to escape from it.

In the course of seven or eight days we had brought our preparations nearly to a close. Meanwhile our friends had completed theirs, and, becoming tired of Westport, they told us that they would set out in advance, and wait at the crossing of the Kanzas till we should come up. Accordingly R——— and the muleteer went forward with the wagon and tent, while the Captain and his brother, together with Sorel and a trapper named Boisverd, who had joined them, followed with the band of horses. The commencement of the journey was ominous, for the captain was scarcely a mile from Westport, riding along in state at the head of his party,

leading his intended buffalo horse by a rope, when a tremendous
thunder-storm came on and drenched them all to the skin. They
hurried on to reach the place, about seven miles off, where R——
was to have had the camp in readiness to receive them. But this
prudent person, when he saw the storm approaching, had selected
a sheltered glade in the woods, where he pitched his tent, and was
sipping a comfortable cup of coffee while the Captain galloped for
miles beyond through the rain to look for him. At length the
storm cleared away, and the sharp-eyed trapper succeeded in
discovering his tent. R—— had by this time finished his coffee,
and was seated on a buffalo-robe smoking his pipe. The Captain
was one of the most easy-tempered men in existence, so he bore
his ill-luck with great composure, shared the dregs of the coffee
with his brother, and lay down to sleep in his wet clothes.

We ourselves had our share of the deluge. We were leading a
pair of mules to Kanzas when the storm broke. Such sharp and
incessant flashes of lightning, such stunning and continuous
thunder I had never known before. The woods were completely
obscured by the diagonal sheets of rain that fell with a heavy
roar, and rose in spray from the ground, and the streams swelled
so rapidly that we could hardly ford them. At length, looming
through the rain, we saw the log-house of Colonel Chick, who
received us with his usual bland hospitality; while his wife, who,
though a little soured and stiffened by a long course of camp-
meetings, was not behind him in good-will, supplied us with the
means of bettering our drenched and bedraggled condition. The
storm clearing away at about sunset opened a noble prospect
from the porch of the Colonel's house which stands upon a high
hill. The sun streamed from the breaking clouds upon the swift
and angry Missouri, and on the vast expanse of forest that
stretched from its banks back to the distant bluffs.

Returning on the next day to Westport we received a message
from the Captain, who had ridden back to deliver it in person,
but finding that we were in Kanzas, had intrusted it to an
acquaintance of his, named Vogel, who kept a small grocery and
liquor shop. Whiskey, by the way, circulates more freely in Westport than is altogether safe in a place where every man carries a
loaded pistol in his pocket. As we passed this establishment we
saw Vogel's broad German face thrust from his door. He said he
had something to tell us, and invited us to take a dram. Neither
his liquor nor his message was very palatable. The Captain had

returned to give us notice that R——, who assumed the direction of his party had determined upon another route from that agreed upon between us; and instead of taking the course of the traders, had resolved to pass northward by Fort Leavenworth, and follow the path marked out by the dragoons in their expedition of last summer. To adopt such a plan without consulting us, we looked upon as a high-handed proceeding; but suppressing our dissatisfaction as well as we could, we made up our minds to join them at Fort Leavenworth, where they were to wait for us.

Accordingly, our preparation being now complete, we attempted one fine morning to begin our journey. The first step was an unfortunate one. No sooner were our animals put in harness than the shaft-mule reared and plunged, burst ropes and straps, and nearly flung the cart into the Missouri. Finding her wholly uncontrollable, we exchanged her for another, with which we were furnished by our friend Mr Boone, of Westport, a grandson of Daniel Boone, the pioneer. This foretaste of prairie experience was very soon followed by another. Westport was scarcely out of sight when we encountered a deep muddy gully, of a species that afterward became but too familiar to us, and here for the space of an hour or more the cart stuck fast.

2. Breaking the Ice

Emerging from the mud-holes of Westport, we pursued our way for some time along the narrow track, in the checkered sunshine and shadow of the woods, till at length, issuing into the broad light, we left behind us the farthest outskirts of the great forest that once spread from the western plains to the shore of the Atlantic. Looking over an intervening belt of bushes, we saw the green, ocean-like expanse of prairie, stretching swell beyond swell to the horizon.

It was a mild, calm spring day,—a day when one is more disposed to musing and reverie than to action, and the softest part of his nature is apt to gain the upper hand. I rode in advance of the party as we passed through the bushes, and as a nook of green grass offered a strong temptation, I dismounted and lay down

there. All the trees and saplings were in flower, or budding into
fresh leaf; the red clusters of the maple-blossoms and the rich
flowers of the Indian apple were there in profusion; and I was half
inclined to regret leaving behind the land of gardens, for the rude
and stern scenes of the prairie and the mountains.

Meanwhile the party came in sight out of the bushes. Foremost
rode Henry Chatillon, our guide and hunter, a fine athletic figure,
mounted on a hardy gray Wyandot pony. He wore a white
blanket-coat, a broad hat of felt, moccasins, and trousers of deer-
skin, ornamented along the seams with rows of long fringes. His
knife was stuck in his belt; his bullet-pouch and powder-horn
hung at his side, and his rifle lay before him, resting against the
high pommel of his saddle, which like all his equipments had seen
hard service and was much the worse for wear. Shaw followed
close, mounted on a little sorrel horse and leading a larger animal
by a rope. His outfit, which resembled mine, had been provided
with a view to use rather than ornament. It consisted of a plain,
black Spanish saddle, with holsters of heavy pistols, a blanket
rolled up behind, and the trail-rope attached to his horse's neck
hanging coiled in front. He carried a double-barrelled smooth-
bore, while I had a rifle of some fifteen pounds' weight. At that
time our attire, though far from elegant, bore some marks of
civilization, and offered a very favorable contrast to the inimitable shabbiness of our appearance on the return journey. A red
flannel shirt, belted around the waist like a frock, then constituted
our upper garment; moccasins had supplanted our failing boots;
and the remaining essential portion of our attire consisted of an
extraordinary article manufactured by a squaw out of smoked
buckskin. Our muleteer, Deslauriers, brought up the rear with his
cart, wading ankle-deep in the mud, alternately puffing at his
pipe and ejaculating, in his prairie patois, 'Sacré enfant de garce!'
as one of the mules would seem to recoil before some abyss of unusual profundity. The cart was of the kind that one may see by
scores around the market-place at Quebec, and had a white covering to protect the articles within. These were our provisions and
a tent, with ammunition, blankets, and presents for the Indians.

We were in all four men with eight animals; for besides the
spare horses led by Shaw and myself, an additional mule was
driven along with us as a reserve in case of accident.

After this summing up of our forces it may not be amiss to
glance at the characters of the two men who accompanied us.

Deslauriers was a Canadian, with all the characteristics of the
true Jean Baptiste. Neither fatigue, exposure, nor hard labor
could ever impair his cheerfulness and gayety, or his politeness to
his *bourgeois*; and when night came he would sit down by the fire,
smoke his pipe, and tell stories with the utmost contentment. The
prairie was his element. Henry Chatillon was of a different stamp.
When we were at St Louis, several gentlemen of the Fur Company had kindly offered to procure for us a hunter and guide
suited for our purposes; and on coming one afternoon to the office,
we found there a tall and exceedingly well-dressed man, with a
face so open and frank that it attracted our notice at once. We
were surprised at being told that it was he who wished to guide us
to the mountains. He was born in a little French town near St
Louis, and from the age of fifteen years had been constantly in
the neighborhood of the Rocky Mountains, employed for the most
part by the company, to supply their forts with buffalo meat. As
a hunter, he had but one rival in the whole region, a man named
Simoneau, with whom, to the honor of both of them, he was on
terms of the closest friendship. He had arrived at St Louis the day
before, from the mountains, where he had been for four years;
and he now asked only to go and spend a day with his mother,
before setting out on another expedition. His age was about
thirty; he was six feet high, and very powerfully and gracefully
moulded. The prairies had been his school; he could neither read
nor write, but he had a natural refinement and delicacy of mind,
such as is rare even in women. His manly face was a mirror of
uprightness, simplicity, and kindness of heart; he had, moreover,
a keen perception of character, and a tact that would preserve
him from flagrant error in any society. Henry had not the restless
energy of an Anglo-American. He was content to take things as he
found them; and his chief fault arose from an excess of easy
generosity, not conducive to thriving in the world. Yet it was
commonly remarked of him that, whatever he might choose to do
with what belonged to himself, the property of others was always
safe in his hands. His bravery was as much celebrated in the
mountains as his skill in hunting; but it is characteristic of him
that, in a country where the rifle is the chief arbiter between man
and man, he was very seldom involved in quarrels. Once or twice,
indeed, his quiet good-nature had been mistaken and presumed
upon, but the consequences of the error were such that no one
was ever known to repeat it. No better evidence of the intrepidity

of his temper could be asked than the common report that he had killed more than thirty grizzly bears. He was a proof of what un-aided nature will sometimes do. I have never, in the city or in the wilderness, met a better man than my true-hearted friend, Henry Chatillon.

We were soon free of the woods and bushes, and fairly upon the broad prairie. Now and then a Shawanoe passed us, riding his little shaggy pony at a 'lope,' his calico shirt, his gaudy sash, and the gay handkerchief bound around his snaky hair, fluttering in the wind. At noon we stopped to rest not far from a little creek, replete with frogs and young turtles. There had been an Indian encampment at the place, and the framework of the lodges still remained, en-abling us very easily to gain a shelter from the sun, by merely spreading one or two blankets over them. Thus shaded, we sat upon our saddles, and Shaw for the first time lighted his favorite Indian pipe, while Deslauriers was squatted over a hot bed of coals, shading his eyes with one hand, and holding a little stick in the other, with which he regulated the hissing contents of the frying-pan. The horses were turned to feed among the scattered bushes of a low, oozy meadow. A drowsy spring-like sultriness per-vaded the air, and the voices of ten thousand young frogs and insects, just awakened into life, rose in varied chorus from the creek and the meadows.

Scarcely were we seated when a visitor approached. This was an old Kanzas Indian,—a man of distinction, if one might judge from his dress. His head was shaved and painted red, and from the tuft of hair remaining on the crown dangled several eagle's-feathers, and the tails of two or three rattlesnakes. His cheeks, too, were daubed with vermilion; his ears were adorned with green glass pendants; a collar of grizzly bears' claws surrounded his neck, and several large necklaces of wampum hung on his breast. Having shaken us by the hand with a grunt of salutation, the old man, dropping his red blanket from his shoulders, sat down cross-legged on the ground. We offered him a cup of sweetened water, at which he ejaculated, 'Good!' and was beginning to tell us how great a man he was, and how many Pawnees he had killed, when suddenly a motley concourse appeared wading across the creek toward us. They filed past in rapid succession, men, women and children: some were on horseback, some on foot, but all were alike squalid and wretched. Old squaws, mounted astride of shaggy, meagre, little ponies, with perhaps one or two

snake-eyed children seated behind them, clinging to their tattered
blankets; tall, lank young men on foot, with bows and arrows in
their hands; and girls whose native ugliness not all the charms of
glass beads and scarlet cloth could disguise, made up the procession; although here and there was a man who, like our visitor,
seemed to hold some rank in this respectable community. They
were the dregs of the Kanzas nation, who, while their betters were
gone to hunt the buffalo, had left the village on a begging expedition to Westport.

When this ragamuffin horde had passed, we caught our horses,
saddled, harnessed, and resumed our journey. Fording the creek,
the low roofs of a number of rude buildings appeared, rising from
a cluster of groves and woods on the left; and riding up through
a long lane amid a profusion of wild roses and early spring flowers,
we found the log-church and schoolhouses belonging to the Metho-
dist Shawanoe Mission. The Indians were on the point of gathering to a religious meeting. Some scores of them, tall men in half-
civilized dress, were seated on wooden benches under the trees,
while their horses were tied to the sheds and fences. Their chief,
Parks, a remarkably large and athletic man, had just arrived from
Westport, where he owns a trading establishment. Besides this,
he has a large farm and a considerable number of slaves. Indeed
the Shawanoes have made greater progress in agriculture than
any other tribe on the Missouri frontier; and both in appearance
and in character form a marked contrast to our late acquaintance
the Kanzas.

A few hours' ride brought us to the banks of the river Kanzas.
Traversing the woods that lined it, and ploughing through the
deep sand, we encamped not far from the bank, at the Lower
Delaware crossing. Our tent was erected for the first time, on a
meadow close to the woods, and the camp preparations being
complete, we began to think of supper. An old Delaware woman,
of some three hundred pounds' weight, sat in the porch of a little
log-house, close to the water, and a very pretty half-breed girl
was engaged, under her superintendence, in feeding a large flock
of turkeys that were fluttering and gobbling about the door. But
no offers of money, or even of tobacco, could induce her to part
with one of her favorites; so I took my rifle, to see if the woods or
the river could furnish us anything. A multitude of quails were
plaintively whistling in the meadows; but nothing appropriate
to the rifle was to be seen, except three buzzards, seated on the

spectral limbs of an old dead sycamore, that thrust itself out over
the river from the dense sunny wall of fresh foliage. Their ugly
heads were drawn down between their shoulders, and they seemed
to luxuriate in the soft sunshine that was pouring from the west.
As they offered no epicurean temptations, I refrained from disturbing their enjoyment; but contented myself with admiring
the calm beauty of the sunset,—for the river, eddying swiftly in
deep purple shadows between the impending woods, formed a
wild but tranquillizing scene.

When I returned to the camp I found Shaw and an old Indian
seated on the ground in close conference, passing the pipe between
them. The old man was explaining that he loved the whites and
had an especial partiality for tobacco. Deslauriers was arranging
upon the ground our service of tin cups and plates; and as other
viands were not to be had, he set before us a repast of biscuit and
bacon, and a large pot of coffee. Unsheathing our knives, we
attacked it, disposed of the greater part, and tossed the residue
to the Indian. Meanwhile our horses, now hobbled for the first
time, stood among the trees with their fore-legs tied together, in
great disgust and astonishment. They seemed by no means to
relish this foretaste of what awaited them. Mine, in particular,
had conceived a mortal aversion to the prairie life. One of them,
christened Hendrick, an animal whose strength and hardihood
were his only merits, and who yielded to nothing but the cogent
arguments of the whip, looked toward us with an indignant
countenance, as if he meditated avenging his wrongs with a kick.
The other, Pontiac, a good horse, though of plebeian lineage,
stood with his head drooping and his mane hanging about his
eyes, with the grieved and sulky air of a lubberly boy sent off to
school. His forebodings were but too just; for when I last heard
from him, he was under the lash of an Ogillallah brave, on a war-
party against the Crows.

As it grew dark and the voices of the whippoorwills succeeded
the whistle of the quails, we removed our saddles to the tent to
serve as pillows, spread our blankets upon the ground, and prepared to bivouac for the first time that season. Each man selected
the place in the tent which he was to occupy for the journey. To
Deslauriers, however, was assigned the cart, into which he could
creep in wet weather, and find a much better shelter than his
bourgeois enjoyed in the tent.

The river Kanzas at this point forms the boundary line between the country of the Shawanoes and that of the Delawares. We crossed it on the following day, rafting over our horses and equipments with much difficulty, and unloading our cart in order to make our way up the steep ascent on the farther bank. It was a Sunday morning; warm, tranquil, and bright; and a perfect stillness reigned over the rough inclosures and neglected fields of the Delawares, except the ceaseless hum and chirruping of myriads of insects. Now and then an Indian rode past on his way to the meeting-house, or, through the dilapidated entrance of some shattered log-house, an old woman might be discerned enjoying all the luxury of idleness. There was no village bell, for the Delawares have none; and yet upon that forlorn and rude settlement was the same spirit of Sabbath repose and tranquillity as in some New England village among the mountains of New Hampshire, or the Vermont woods.

A military road led from this point to Fort Leavenworth, and for many miles the farms and cabins of the Delawares were scattered at short intervals on either hand. The little rude structures of logs, erected usually on the borders of a tract of woods, made a picturesque feature in the landscape. But the scenery needed no foreign aid. Nature had done enough for it; and the alternation of rich green prairies, and groves that stood in clusters, or lined the banks of the numerous little streams, had all the softened and polished beauty of a region that has been for centuries under the hand of man. At that early season, too, it was in the height of its freshness. The woods were flushed with the red buds of the maple; there were frequent flowering shrubs unknown in the East; and the green swells of the prairie were thickly studded with blossoms.

Encamping near a spring, by the side of a hill, we resumed our journey in the morning, and early in the afternoon were within a few miles of Fort Leavenworth. The road crossed a stream densely bordered with trees, and running in the bottom of a deep woody hollow. We were about to descend into it when a wild and confused procession appeared, passing through the water below and coming up the steep ascent toward us. We stopped to let them pass. They were Delawares, just returned from a hunting expedition. All, both men and women, were mounted on horseback, and drove along with them a considerable number of pack-mules, laden with the furs they had taken, together with the buffalo-robes, kettles, and other articles of their travelling equip-

ment, which, as well as their clothing and their weapons, had a
worn and dingy look, as if they had seen hard service of late. At
the rear of the party was an old man, who, as he came up, stopped
his horse to speak to us. He rode a tough, shaggy pony, with
mane and tail well knotted with burs, and a rusty Spanish bit in
its mouth, to which, by way of reins, was attached a string of
raw hide. His saddle, robbed probably from a Mexican, had no
covering, being merely a tree of the Spanish form, with a piece of
grizzly bear's skin laid over it, a pair of rude wooden stirrups
attached, and, in the absence of girth, a strap of hide passing
around the horse's belly. The rider's dark features and keen snaky
eye were unequivocally Indian. He wore a buckskin frock, which,
like his fringed leggings, was well polished and blackened by
grease and long service, and an old handkerchief was tied around
his head. Resting on the saddle before him lay his rifle, a weapon
in the use of which the Delawares are skilful, though, from its
weight, the distant prairie Indians are too lazy to carry it.

'Who 's your chief?' he immediately inquired.

Henry Chatillon pointed to us. The old Delaware fixed his eyes
intently upon us for a moment, and then sententiously remarked,—

'No good! Too young!' With this flattering comment he left us
and rode after his people.

This tribe, the Delawares, once the peaceful allies of William
Penn, the tributaries of the conquering Iroquois, are now the
most adventurous and dreaded warriors upon the prairies. They
make war upon remote tribes, the very names of which were unknown to their fathers in their ancient seats in Pennsylvania, and
they push these new quarrels with true Indian rancor, sending
out their war-parties as far as the Rocky Mountains, and into
the Mexican territories. Their neighbors and former confederates,
the Shawanoes, who are tolerable farmers, are in a prosperous
condition; but the Delawares dwindle every year, from the number of men lost in their warlike expeditions.

Soon after leaving this party we saw, stretching on the right,
the forests that follow the course of the Missouri, and the deep
woody channel through which at this point it runs. At a distance
in front were the white barracks of Fort Leavenworth, just
visible through the trees upon an eminence above a bend of the
river. A wide green meadow, as level as a lake, lay between us and
the Missouri, and upon this, close to a line of trees that bordered

a little brook, stood the tent of the Captain and his companions, with their horses feeding around it; but they themselves were invisible. Wright, their muleteer, was there, seated on the tongue of the wagon, repairing his harness. Boisverd stood cleaning his rifle at the door of the tent, and Sorel lounged idly about. On closer examination, however, we discovered the Captain's brother, Jack, sitting in the tent, at his old occupation of splicing trail-ropes. He welcomed us in his broad Irish brogue, and said that his brother was fishing in the river, and R—— gone to the garrison. They returned before sunset. Meanwhile we pitched our own tent not far off, and after supper a council was held, in which it was resolved to remain one day at Fort Leavenworth, and on the next to bid a final adieu to the frontier, or, in the phraseology of the region, to 'jump off.' Our deliberations were conducted by the ruddy light from a distant swell of the prairie, where the long dry grass of last summer was on fire.

3. Fort Leavenworth

On the next morning we rode to Fort Leavenworth. Colonel, now General Kearney, to whom I had had the honor of an introduction when at St Louis, was just arrived, and received us at his quarters with the courtesy habitual to him. Fort Leavenworth is in fact no fort, being without defensive works, except two block-houses. No rumors of war had as yet disturbed its tranquillity. In the square grassy area, surrounded by barracks and the quarters of the officers, the men were passing and repassing, or lounging among the trees; although not many weeks afterwards it presented a different scene; for here the off-scourings of the frontier were congregated for the expedition against Santa Fé.

Passing through the garrison, we rode toward the Kickapoo village, five or six miles beyond. The path, a rather dubious and uncertain one, led us along the ridge of high bluffs that border the Missouri; and, by looking to the right or to the left, we could enjoy a strange contrast of scenery. On the left stretched the prairie, rising into swells and undulations, thickly sprinkled with groves, or gracefully expanding into wide grassy basins, of miles in extent, while its curvatures, swelling against the horizon, were often surmounted by lines of sunny woods,—a scene to which the freshness of the season and the peculiar mellowness of the atmosphere gave additional softness. Below us, on the right, was a tract of ragged and broken woods. We could look down on the tops of the trees, some living and some dead; some erect, others leaning at every angle, and others piled in masses together by the passage of a hurricane. Beyond their extreme verge the turbid waters of the Missouri were discernible through the boughs, rolling powerfully along at the foot of the woody declivities on its farther bank.

The path soon after led inland; and as we crossed an open meadow we saw a cluster of buildings on a rising ground before us, with a crowd of people surrounding them. They were the storehouse, cottage, and stables of the Kickapoo trader's establishment. Just at that moment, as it chanced, he was beset with half the Indians of the settlement. They had tied their wretched, neglected little ponies by dozens along the fences and out-houses, and were either lounging about the place, or crowding into the trading-house. Here were faces of various colors,—red, green, white, and black,—curiously intermingled and disposed over the visage in a variety of patterns. Calico shirts, red and blue blankets, brass ear-rings, wampum necklaces, appeared in profusion. The trader was a blue-eyed, open-faced man, who neither in his manners nor his appearance betrayed any of the roughness of the frontier; though just at present he was obliged to keep a lynx eye on his customers, who, men and women, were climbing on his counter, and seating themselves among his boxes and bales.

The village itself was not far off, and sufficiently illustrated the condition of its unfortunate and self-abandoned occupants. Fancy to yourself a little swift stream working its devious way down a woody valley; sometimes wholly hidden under logs and fallen trees, sometimes spreading into a broad, clear pool; and on its banks, in little nooks cleared away among the trees, miniature log-houses, in utter ruin and neglect. A labyrinth of narrow, ob-

structed paths connected these habitations one with another.
Sometimes we met a stray calf, a pig, or a pony, belonging to some
of the villagers, who usually lay in the sun in front of their
dwellings, and looked on us with cold, suspicious eyes as we approached. Farther on, in place of the log-huts of the Kickapoos,
we found the *pukwi* lodges of their neighbors, the Pottawattamies,
whose condition seemed no better than theirs.

Growing tired at last, and exhausted by the excessive heat and
sultriness of the day, we returned to our friend, the trader. By this
time the crowd around him had dispersed, and left him at leisure.
He invited us to his cottage,—a little white-and-green building,
in the style of the old French settlements,—and ushered us into
a neat, well-furnished room. The blinds were closed, and the heat
and glare of the sun excluded; the room was as cool as a cavern.
It was neatly carpeted, too, and furnished in a manner that we
hardly expected on the frontier. The sofas, chairs, tables, and
a well-filled bookcase, would not have disgraced an eastern city;
though there were one or two little tokens that indicated the
rather questionable civilization of the region. A pistol, loaded
and capped, lay on the mantel-piece; and through the glass of
the bookcase, peeping above the works of John Milton, glittered
the handle of a very mischievous-looking knife.

Our host went out, and returned with iced water, glasses, and
a bottle of excellent claret,—a refreshment most welcome in the
extreme heat of the day; and soon after appeared a merry, laughing woman, who must have been, a year or two before, a very rich
specimen of creole beauty. She came to say that lunch was ready
in the next room. Our hostess evidently lived on the sunny side
of life, and troubled herself with none of its cares. She sat down
and entertained us while we were at table with anecdotes of fishing parties, frolics, and the officers at the fort. Taking leave at
length of the hospitable trader and his friend, we rode back to the
garrison.

Shaw passed on to the camp, while I remained to call upon
Colonel Kearney. I found him still at table. There sat our friend
the Captain, in the same remarkable habiliments in which we saw
him at Westport; the black pipe, however, being for the present
laid aside. He dangled his little cap in his hand and talked of
steeple-chases, touching occasionally upon his anticipated exploits in buffalo-hunting. There, too, was R——, somewhat more
elegantly attired. For the last time we tasted the luxuries of

civilization, and drank adieus to it in wine good enough to make us regret the leave-taking. Then, mounting, we rode together to the camp, where everything was in readiness for departure on the morrow.

4. 'Jumping Off'

Our transatlantic companions were well equipped for the journey.
They had a wagon drawn by six mules, and crammed with provisions for six months, besides ammunition enough for a regiment, spare rifles and fowling-pieces, ropes and harness, personal
baggage, and a miscellaneous assortment of articles, which produced infinite embarrassment. They had also decorated their persons with telescopes and portable compasses, and carried English
double-barrelled rifles of sixteen to the pound calibre, slung to
their saddles in dragoon fashion.

By sunrise on the twenty-third of May we had breakfasted; the
tents were levelled, the animals saddled and harnessed, and all
was prepared. '*Avance donc!* get up!' cried Deslauriers to his mule.
Wright, our friends' muleteer, after some swearing and lashing,

got his insubordinate train into motion, and then the whole party
filed from the ground. Thus we bade a long adieu to bed and
board, and the principles of Blackstone's Commentaries. The day
was a most auspicious one; and yet Shaw and I felt certain misgivings, which in the sequel proved but too well founded. We had
just learned that though R—— had taken it upon him to adopt
this course without consulting us, not a single man in the party
knew the way; and the absurdity of the proceeding soon became
manifest. His plan was to strike the trail of several companies of
dragoons, who last summer had made an expedition under
Colonel Kearney to Fort Laramie, and by this means to reach the
grand trail of the Oregon emigrants up the Platte.

We rode for an hour or two, when a familiar cluster of buildings appeared on a little hill. 'Hallo!' shouted the Kickapoo trader
from over his fence, 'where are you going?' A few rather emphatic
exclamations might have been heard among us, when we found
that we had gone miles out of our way, and were not advanced an
inch toward the Rocky Mountains. So we turned in the direction
the trader indicated; and with the sun for a guide, began to trace
a 'bee-line' across the prairies. We struggled through copses and
lines of wood; we waded brooks and pools of water; we traversed
prairies as green as an emerald expanding before us mile after
mile, wider and more wild than the wastes Mazeppa rode over.

> 'Man nor brute,
> Nor dint of hoof, nor print of foot,
> Lay in the wild luxuriant soil;
> No sign of travel; none of toil;
> The very air was mute.'

Riding in advance, as we passed over one of these great plains,
we looked back and saw the line of scattered horsemen stretching
for a mile or more; and far in the rear, against the horizon, the
white wagons creeping slowly along. 'Here we are at last!' shouted
the Captain. And, in truth, we had struck upon the traces of a
large body of horse. We turned joyfully and followed this new
course, with tempers somewhat improved, and towards sunset
encamped on a high swell of the prairie, at the foot of which a lazy
stream soaked along through clumps of rank grass. It was getting
dark. We turned the horses loose to feed. 'Drive down the tent-
pickets hard,' said Henry Chatillon, 'it is going to blow.' We did
so, and secured the tent as well as we could; for the sky had

changed totally, and a fresh, damp smell in the wind warned us that a stormy night was likely to succeed the hot, clear day. The prairie also wore a new aspect, and its vast swells had grown black and sombre under the shadow of the clouds. The thunder soon began to growl at a distance. Picketing and hobbling the horses among the rich grass at the foot of the slope where we encamped, we gained a shelter just as the rain began to fall; and sat at the opening of the tent, watching the proceedings of the Captain. In defiance of the rain, he was stalking among the horses, wrapped in an old Scotch plaid. An extreme solicitude tormented him, lest some of his favorites should escape, or some accident should befall them; and he cast an anxious eye towards three wolves who were sneaking along over the dreary surface of the plain, as if he dreaded some hostile demonstration on their part.

On the next morning we had gone but a mile or two when we came to an extensive belt of woods, through the midst of which ran a stream, wide, deep, and of an appearance particularly muddy and treacherous. Deslauriers was in advance with his cart; he jerked his pipe from his mouth, lashed his mules, and poured forth a volley of Canadian ejaculations. In plunged the cart, but midway it stuck fast. He leaped out knee-deep in water, and by dint of *sacrés* and a vigorous application of the whip, urged the mules out of the slough. Then approached the long team and heavy wagon of our friends; but it paused on the brink.

'Now my advice is,'—began the Captain, who had been anxiously contemplating the muddy gulf.

'Drive on!' cried R——.

But Wright, the muleteer, apparently had not as yet decided the point in his own mind; and he sat still in his seat, on one of the shaft-mules, whistling in a low, contemplative strain to himself.

'My advice is,' resumed the Captain, 'that we unload; for I 'll bet any man five pounds that if we try to go through we shall stick fast.'

'By the powers, we shall stick fast!' echoed Jack, the Captain's brother, shaking his large head with an air of firm conviction.

'Drive on! drive on!' cried R——, petulantly.

'Well,' observed the Captain, turning to us as we sat looking on, much edified by this by-play among our confederates, 'I can only give my advice, and if people won't be reasonable, why, they won't, that 's all!'

Meanwhile Wright had apparently made up his mind; for he suddenly began to shout forth a volley of oaths and curses, that, compared with the French imprecations of Deslauriers, sounded like the roaring of heavy cannon after the popping and spluttering of a bunch of Chinese crackers. At the same time he discharged a shower of blows upon his mules, who hastily dived into the mud, and drew the wagon lumbering after them. For a moment the issue was doubtful. Wright writhed about in his saddle, and swore and lashed like a madman; but who can count on a team of half-broken mules? At the most critical point, when all should have been harmony and combined effort, the perverse brutes fell into disorder, and huddled together in confusion on the farther bank. There was the wagon up to the hub in mud, and visibly settling every instant. There was nothing for it but to unload; then to dig away the mud from before the wheels with a spade, and lay a causeway of bushes and branches. This agreeable labor accomplished, the wagon at length emerged; but as some interruption of this sort occurred at least four or five times a day for a fortnight, our progress towards the Platte was not without its obstacles.

We travelled six or seven miles farther, and 'nooned' near a brook. On the point of resuming our journey, when the horses were all driven down to water, my home-sick charger, Pontiac, made a sudden leap across, and set off at a round trot for the settlements. I mounted my remaining horse and started in pursuit. Making a circuit, I headed the runaway, hoping to drive him back to camp, but he instantly broke into a gallop, made a wide tour on the prairie, and got by me again. I tried this plan repeatedly with the same result,—Pontiac was evidently disgusted with the prairie; so I abandoned it and tried another, trotting along gently behind him, in hopes that I might quietly get near enough to seize the trail-rope which was fastened to his neck, and dragged about a dozen feet behind him. The chase grew interesting. For mile after mile I followed the rascal with the utmost care not to alarm him, and gradually got nearer, until at length old Hendrick's nose was fairly brushed by the whisking tail of the unsuspecting Pontiac. Without drawing rein I slid softly to the ground; but my long, heavy rifle encumbered me, and the low sound it made in striking the horn of the saddle startled him, he pricked up his ears and sprang off at a run. 'My friend,' thought I, re-mounting, 'do that again and I'll shoot you!'

Fort Leavenworth was about forty miles distant, and thither I determined to follow him. I made up my mind to spend a solitary and supperless night, and then set out again in the morning. One hope, however, remained. The creek where the wagon had stuck was just before us; Pontiac might be thirsty with his run and stop there to drink. I kept as near him as possible, taking every precaution not to alarm him again; and the result proved as I had hoped, for he walked deliberately among the trees and stooped down to the water. I alighted, dragged old Hendrick through the mud, and with a feeling of infinite satisfaction picked up the slimy trail-rope, and twisted it three times round my hand. 'Now let me see you get away again!' I thought as I remounted. But Pontiac was exceedingly reluctant to turn back; Hendrick, too, who had evidently flattered himself with vain hopes, showed the utmost repugnance, and grumbled in a manner peculiar to himself at being compelled to face about. A smart cut of the whip restored his cheerfulness; and, dragging the recovered truant behind, I set out in search of the camp. An hour or two elapsed, when, near sunset, I saw the tents, standing on a swell of the prairie, beyond a line of woods, while the bands of horses were feeding in a low meadow close at hand. There sat Jack C——, cross-legged in the sun, splicing a trail-rope; and the rest were lying on the grass, smoking and telling stories. That night we enjoyed a serenade from the wolves, more lively than any with which they had yet favored us; and in the morning one of the musicians appeared, not many rods from the tents, quietly seated among the horses, looking at us with a pair of large gray eyes; but perceiving a rifle levelled at him, he leaped up and made off in hot haste.

I pass by the following day or two of our journey, for nothing occurred worthy of record. Should any one of my readers ever be impelled to visit the prairies, and should he choose the route of the Platte (the best, perhaps, that can be adopted), I can assure him that he need not think to enter at once upon the paradise of his imagination. A dreary preliminary, a protracted crossing of the threshold, awaits him before he finds himself fairly upon the verge of the 'great American desert,'—those barren wastes, the haunts of the buffalo and the Indian, where the very shadow of civilization lies a hundred leagues behind him. The intervening country, the wide and fertile belt that extends for several hundred miles beyond the extreme frontier, will probably answer tolerably well to his preconceived ideas of the prairie; for this it is from which

picturesque tourists, painters, poets, and novelists, who have
seldom penetrated farther, have derived their conceptions of the
whole region. If he has a painter's eye, he may find his period of
probation not wholly void of interest. The scenery, though tame,
is graceful and pleasing. Here are level plains too wide for the eye
to measure; green undulations, like motionless swells of the
ocean; abundance of streams, followed through all their windings
by lines of woods and scattered groves. But let him be as en-
thusiastic as he may, he will find enough to damp his ardor. His
wagons will stick in the mud; his horses will break loose; harness
will give way; and axle-trees prove unsound. His bed will be a soft
one, consisting often of black mud of the richest consistency. As for
food, he must content himself with biscuit and salt provisions;
for strange as it may seem, this tract of country produces very
little game. As he advances, indeed, he will see, mouldering in the
grass by his path, the vast antlers of the elk, and farther on the
whitened skulls of the buffalo, once swarming over this now
deserted region. Perhaps, like us, he may journey for a fortnight,
and see not so much as the hoof-print of a deer; in the spring, not
even a prairie-hen is to be had.

Yet, to compensate him for this unlooked-for deficiency of game,
he will find himself beset with 'varmints' innumerable. The wolves
will entertain him with a concert at night, and skulk around him
by day just beyond rifle-shot; his horse will step into badger-holes;
from every marsh and mud-puddle will arise the bellowing, croak-
ing and trilling of legions of frogs, infinitely various in color, shape,
and dimensions. A profusion of snakes will glide away from under
his horse's feet, or quietly visit him in his tent at night; while the
pertinacious humming of unnumbered mosquitoes will banish
sleep from his eyelids. When, thirsty with a long ride in the
scorching sun over some boundless reach of prairie, he comes at
length to a pool of water and alights to drink, he discovers a troop
of young tadpoles sporting in the bottom of his cup. Add to this
that, all the morning, the sun beats upon him with a sultry, penetrating heat, and that, with provoking regularity, at about four
o'clock in the afternoon a thunder-storm rises and drenches him
to the skin.

One day, after a protracted morning's ride, we stopped to rest
at noon upon the open prairie. No trees were in sight; but close at
hand a little dribbling brook was twisting from side to side
through a hollow; now forming holes of stagnant water, and now

gliding over the mud in a scarcely perceptible current, among a growth of sickly bushes, and great clumps of tall, rank grass. The day was excessively hot and oppressive. The horses and mules were rolling on the prairie to refresh themselves, or feeding among the bushes in the hollow. We had dined; and Deslauriers, puffing at his pipe, knelt on the grass, scrubbing our service of tinplate. Shaw lay in the shade, under the cart, to rest for a while, before the word should be given to 'catch up.' Henry Chatillon, before lying down, was looking about for signs of snakes, the only living things that he feared, and uttering various ejaculations of disgust at finding several suspicious-looking holes close to the cart. I sat leaning against the wheel in a scanty strip of shade, making a pair of hobbles to replace those which my contumacious steed Pontiac had broken the night before. The camp of our friends, a rod or two distant, presented the same scene of lazy tranquillity.

'Hallo!' cried Henry, looking up from his inspection of the snake-holes, 'here comes the old Captain.'

The Captain approached, and stood for a moment contemplating us in silence.

'I say, Parkman,' he began, 'look at Shaw there, asleep under the cart, with the tar dripping off the hub of the wheel on his shoulder.'

At this Shaw got up, with his eyes half opened, and feeling the part indicated, found his hand glued fast to his red flannel shirt.

'He 'll look well, when he gets among the squaws, won't he?' observed the Captain, with a grin.

He then crawled under the cart, and began to tell stories, of which his stock was inexhaustible. Yet every moment he would glance nervously at the horses. At last he jumped up in great excitement. 'See that horse! There—that fellow just walking over the hill! By Jove! he 's off. It 's your big horse, Shaw; no it is n't, it 's Jack's. Jack! Jack! hallo, Jack!' Jack, thus invoked, jumped up and stared vacantly at us.

'Go and catch your horse, if you don't want to lose him,' roared the Captain.

Jack instantly set off at a run through the grass, his broad trousers flapping about his feet. The Captain gazed anxiously till he saw that the horse was caught; then he sat down, with a countenance of thoughtfulness and care.

'I tell you what it is,' he said, 'this will never do at all. We shall lose every horse in the band some day or other, and then a pretty plight we should be in! Now I am convinced that the only way for us is to have every man in the camp stand horse-guard in rotation whenever we stop. Supposing a hundred Pawnees should jump up out of that ravine, all yelling and flapping their buffalo-robes, in the way they do! Why, in two minutes, not a hoof would be in sight.' We reminded the Captain that a hundred Pawnees would probably demolish the horse-guard if he were to resist their depredations.

'At any rate,' pursued the Captain, evading the point, 'our whole system is wrong; I'm convinced of it; it is totally unmilitary. Why, the way we travel, strung out over the prairie for a mile, an enemy might attack the foremost men, and cut them off before the rest could come up.'

'We are not in an enemy's country yet,' said Shaw; 'when we are we'll travel together.'

'Then,' said the Captain, 'we might be attacked in camp. We've no sentinels; we camp in disorder; no precautions at all to guard against surprise. My own convictions are, that we ought to camp in a hollow-square, with the fires in the centre; and have sentinels, and a regular password appointed for every night. Beside, there should be vedettes riding in advance, to find a place for the camp and give warning of an enemy. These are my convictions. I don't want to dictate to any man. I give advice to the best of my judgment, that's all,—and then let people do as they please.'

His plan of sending out vedettes seemed particularly dear to him; and as no one else was disposed to second his views on this point, he took it into his head to ride forward that afternoon himself.

'Come, Parkman,' said he, 'will you go with me?'

We set out together, and rode a mile or two in advance. The Captain, in the course of twenty years' service in the British army, had seen something of life; and being naturally a pleasant fellow, he was a very entertaining companion. He cracked jokes and told stories for an hour or two; until, looking back, we saw the prairie behind us stretching away to the horizon, without a horseman or a wagon in sight.

'Now,' said the Captain, 'I think the vedettes had better stop till the main body comes up.'

I was of the same opinion. There was a thick growth of woods just before us, with a stream running through them. Having crossed this, we found on the other side a level meadow, half en-

circled by the trees; and, fastening our horses to some bushes, we
sat down on the grass, while with an old stump of a tree for a tar-
get, I began to display the superiority of the renowned rifle of the
backwoods over the foreign innovation borne by the Captain. At
length voices could be heard in the distance, behind the trees.

'There they come,' said the Captain; 'let 's go and see how they
get through the creek.'

We mounted and rode to the bank of the stream, where the
trail crossed it. It ran in a deep hollow, full of trees. As we looked
down we saw a confused crowd of horsemen riding through the
water; and among the dingy habiliments of our party glittered
the uniforms of four dragoons.

Shaw came whipping his horse up the bank, in advance of the
rest, with a somewhat indignant countenance. The first word he
spoke was a blessing fervently invoked on the head of R——, who
was riding, with a crest-fallen air, in the rear. Thanks to the
ingenious devices of this gentleman, we had missed the track entirely, and wandered, not towards the Platte, but to the village
of the Iowa Indians. This we learned from the dragoons, who had
lately deserted from Fort Leavenworth. They told us that our
best plan now was to keep to the northward until we should strike
the trail formed by several parties of Oregon emigrants, who had
that season set out from St Joseph, in Missouri.

In extremely bad temper, we encamped on this ill-starred spot,
while the deserters, whose case admitted of no delay, rode rapidly
forward. On the day following, striking the St Joseph trail, we
turned our horses' heads towards Fort Laramie, then about seven
hundred miles to the westward.

5. The 'Big Blue'

The great medley of Oregon and California emigrants at their camps around Independence had heard reports that several additional parties were on the point of setting out from St Joseph farther to the northward. The prevailing impression was that these were Mormons, twenty-three hundred in number; and a great alarm was excited in consequence. The people of Illinois and Missouri, who composed by far the greater part of the emigrants, have never been on the best terms with the 'Latter Day Saints;' and it is notorious throughout the country how much blood has been spilt in their feuds, even far within the limits of the settlements. No one could predict what would be the result when large armed bodies of these fanatics should encounter the most impetuous and reckless of their old enemies on the broad prairie, far beyond the reach of law or military force. The women and children at Independence raised a great outcry; the men themselves were seriously alarmed; and as I learned, they sent to Colonel Kearney, requesting an escort of dragoons as far as the Platte. This was refused; and, as the sequel proved, there was no occasion for it. The St Joseph emigrants were as good Christians and as zealous Mormon-haters as the rest; and the very few families of the 'Saints' who passed out this season by the route of the Platte remained behind until the great tide of emigration had gone by,—standing in quite as much awe of the 'gentiles' as the latter did of them.

We were now upon this St Joseph trail. It was evident, by the traces, that large parties were a few days in advance of us; and as we too supposed them to be Mormons, we had some apprehension of interruption.

The journey was monotonous. One day we rode on for hours, without seeing a tree or a bush: before, behind, and on either side, stretched the vast expanse, rolling in a succession of graceful swells, covered with the unbroken carpet of fresh green grass. Here and there a crow, a raven, or a turkey-buzzard, relieved the uniformity.

'What shall we do to-night for wood and water?' we began to ask of each other; for the sun was within an hour of setting. At length a dark green speck appeared, far off on the right: it was the top of a tree, peering over a swell of the prairie; and, leaving the trail, we made all haste towards it. It proved to be the vanguard of a cluster of bushes and low trees, that surrounded some pools of water in an extensive hollow; so we encamped on the rising ground near it.

Shaw and I were sitting in the tent, when Deslauriers thrust his brown face and old felt hat into the opening, and, dilating his eyes to their utmost extent, announced supper. There were the tin cups and the iron spoons, arranged in order on the grass, and the coffee-pot predominant in the midst. The meal was soon dispatched, but Henry Chatillon still sat cross-legged, dallying with the remnant of his coffee, the beverage in universal use upon the prairie, and an especial favorite with him. He preferred it in its virgin flavor, unimpaired by sugar or cream; and on the present occasion it met his entire approval, being exceedingly strong, or, as he expressed it, 'right black.'

It was a gorgeous sunset; and the ruddy glow of the sky was

reflected from some extensive pools of water among the shadowy copses in the meadow below.

'I must have a bath to-night,' said Shaw. 'How is it, Des-lauriers? Any chance for a swim down there?'

'Ah! I cannot tell; just as you please, Monsieur,' replied Des-lauriers, shrugging his shoulders, perplexed by his ignorance of English, and extremely anxious to conform in all respects to the opinions and wishes of his *bourgeois*.

'Look at his moccasin,' said I. It had evidently been lately immersed in a profound abyss of black mud.

'Come,' said Shaw; 'at any rate we can see for ourselves.'

We set out together; and as we approached the bushes, which were at some distance, we found the ground becoming rather treacherous. We could only get along by stepping upon large clumps of tall rank grass, with fathomless gulfs between, like innumerable little quaking islands in an ocean of mud, where a false step would have involved our boots in a catastrophe like that which had befallen Deslauriers's moccasins. The thing looked desperate; we separated, to search in different directions, Shaw going off to the right, while I kept straight forward. At last I came to the edge of the bushes,—they were young water-willows covered with their caterpillar-like blossoms, but intervening between them and the last grass clump was a black and deep slough, over which, by a vigorous exertion, I contrived to jump. Then I shouldered my way through the willows, trampling them down by main force, till I came to a wide stream of water, three inches deep, languidly creeping along over a bottom of sleek mud. My arrival produced a great commotion. A huge green bull-frog uttered an indignant croak, and jumped off the bank with a loud splash; his webbed feet twinkled above the surface, as he jerked them energetically upward, and I could see him ensconcing himself in the unresisting slime at the bottom, whence several large air-bubbles struggled lazily to the top. Some little spotted frogs followed the patriarch's example; and then three turtles, not larger than a dollar, tumbled themselves off a broad 'lily pad,' where they had been reposing. At the same time a snake, gayly striped with black and yellow, glided out from the bank, and writhed across to the other side; and a small stagnant pool into which my foot had inadvertently pushed a stone was instantly alive with a congregation of black tadpoles.

'Any chance for a bath where you are?' called out Shaw, from a distance.

The answer was not encouraging. I retreated through the willows, and rejoining my companion, we proceeded to push our researches in company. Not far on the right, a rising ground, covered with trees and bushes, seemed to sink down abruptly to the water, and give hope of better success; so towards this we directed our steps. When we reached the place we found it no easy matter to get along between the hill and the water, impeded as we were by a growth of stiff, obstinate young birch-trees, laced together by grape-vines. In the twilight we now and then, to support ourselves, snatched at the touch-me-not stem of some ancient sweetbrier. Shaw, who was in advance, suddenly uttered an emphatic monosyllable; and, looking up, I saw him with one hand grasping a sapling, and one foot immersed in the water, from which he had forgotten to withdraw it, his whole attention being engaged in contemplating the movements of a water-snake, about five feet long, curiously checkered with black and green, who was deliberately swimming across the pool. There being no stick or stone at hand to pelt him with, we looked at him for a time in silent disgust, and then pushed forward. Our perseverance was at last rewarded; for several rods farther on, we emerged upon a little level grassy nook among the brushwood, and by an extraordinary dispensation of fortune, the weeds and floating sticks, which elsewhere covered the pool, seemed to have drawn apart, and left a few yards of clear water just in front of this favored spot. We sounded it with a stick; it was four feet deep: we lifted a specimen in our closed hands; it seemed reasonably transparent, so we decided that the time for action was arrived. But our ablutions were suddenly interrupted by ten thousand punctures, like poisoned needles, and the humming of myriads of overgrown mosquitoes, rising in all directions from their native mud and swarming to the feast. We were fain to beat a retreat with all possible speed.

We made towards the tents, much refreshed by the bath, which the heat of the weather, joined to our prejudices, had rendered very desirable.

'What 's the matter with the Captain? look at him!' said Shaw. The Captain stood alone on the prairie, swinging his hat violently around his head, and lifting first one foot and then the other, without moving from the spot. First he looked down to the ground with an air of supreme abhorrence; then he gazed upward with a perplexed and indignant countenance, as if trying to trace the flight of an unseen enemy. We called to know what was the matter; but he replied only by execrations directed against some unknown object. We approached, when our ears were saluted by a droning sound, as if twenty bee-hives had been overturned at once. The air above was full of large, black insects, in a state of great commotion, and multitudes were flying about just above the tops of the grass-blades.

'Don't be afraid,' called the Captain, observing us recoil. 'The brutes won't sting.'

At this I knocked one down with my hat, and discovered him to be no other than a 'dor-bug;' and, looking closer, we found the ground thickly perforated with their holes.

We took a hasty leave of this flourishing colony, and walking up the rising ground to the tents, found Deslauriers's fire still glowing brightly. We sat down around it, and Shaw began to expatiate on the admirable facilities for bathing that we had discovered, recommending the Captain by all means to go down there before breakfast in the morning. The Captain was in the act of remarking that he could n't have believed it possible, when he suddenly interrupted himself, and clapped his hand to his cheek, exclaiming that 'those infernal humbugs were at him again.' In fact, we began to hear sounds as if bullets were humming over our heads. In a moment something rapped me sharply on the fore-head, then upon the neck, and immediately I felt an indefinite number of sharp, wiry claws in active motion, as if their owner were bent on pushing his explorations farther. I seized him, and dropped him into the fire. Our party speedily broke up, and we adjourned to our respective tents, where, closing the opening fast, we hoped to be exempt from invasion. But all precaution was fruitless. The dor-bugs hummed through the tent, and marched over our faces until daylight; when, opening our blankets, we found several dozen clinging there with the utmost tenacity. The first object that met our eyes in the morning was Deslauriers, who seemed to be apostrophizing his frying-pan, which he held by the handle at arm's length. It appeared that he had left it at night by the fire; and the bottom was now covered with dor-bugs, firmly imbedded. Hundreds of others, curiously parched and shrivelled, lay scattered among the ashes.

The horses and mules were turned loose to feed. We had just taken our seats at breakfast, or rather reclined in the classic mode, when an exclamation from Henry Chatillon, and a shout of alarm from the Captain, gave warning of some casualty, and looking up, we saw the whole band of animals, twenty-three in number, filing off for the settlements, the incorrigible Pontiac at their head, jumping along with hobbled feet, at a gait much more rapid than graceful. Three or four of us ran to cut them off, dashing as best we might through the tall grass, which was glittering with dew-drops. After a race of a mile or more, Shaw caught a horse. Tying the trail-rope by way of bridle round the animal's jaw, and leaping upon his back, he got in advance of the remaining fugitives, while we, soon bringing them together, drove them in a crowd up to the tents, where each man caught and saddled his own. Then were heard lamentations and curses; for half the horses had broke their hobbles, and many were seriously galled by attempting to run in fetters.

It was late that morning before we were on the march; and early in the afternoon we were compelled to encamp, for a thunder-gust came up and suddenly enveloped us in whirling sheets of rain. With much ado we pitched our tents amid the tempest, and all night long the thunder bellowed and growled over our heads. In the morning light peaceful showers succeeded the cataracts of rain that had been drenching us through the canvas of our tents. About noon, when there were some treacherous indications of fair weather, we got in motion again.

Not a breath of air stirred over the free and open prairie; the clouds were like light piles of cotton; and where the blue sky was visible, it wore a hazy and languid aspect. The sun beat down upon us with a sultry, penetrating heat almost insupportable, and as our party crept slowly along over the interminable level, the horses hung their heads as they waded fetlock deep through the mud, and the men slouched into the easiest position upon the saddle. At last, towards evening, the old familiar black heads of thunder-clouds rose fast above the horizon, and the same deep muttering of distant thunder that had become the ordinary accompaniment of our afternoon's journey began to roll hoarsely over the prairie. Only a few minutes elapsed before the whole sky was densely shrouded, and the prairie and some clusters of woods in front assumed a purple hue beneath the inky shadows. Suddenly from the densest fold of the cloud the flash leaped out, quivering again and again down to the edge of the prairie; and at the same instant came the sharp burst and the long rolling peal of the thunder. A cool wind, filled with the smell of rain, just then overtook us, levelling the tall grass by the side of the path.

'Come on; we must ride for it!' shouted Shaw, rushing by at full speed, his led horse snorting at his side. The whole party broke into full gallop, and made for the trees in front. Passing these, we found beyond them a meadow which they half inclosed. We rode pell-mell upon the ground, leaped from horseback, tore off our saddles, and in a moment each man was kneeling at his horse's feet. The hobbles were adjusted, and the animals turned loose; then as the wagons came wheeling rapidly to the spot, we seized upon the tent-poles, and just as the storm broke we were prepared to receive it. It came upon us almost with the darkness of night: the trees, which were close at hand, were completely shrouded by the roaring torrents of rain.

We were sitting in the tent when Deslauriers, with his broad felt hat hanging about his ears, and his shoulders glistening with rain, thrust in his head.

'Voulez vous du souper, tout de suite? I can make fire, sous la charette—I b'lieve so—I try.'

'Never mind supper, man; come in out of the rain.'

Deslauriers accordingly crouched in the entrance, for modesty would not permit him to intrude farther.

Our tent was none of the best defence against such a cataract. The rain could not enter bodily, but it beat through the canvas in a fine drizzle, that wetted us just as effectually. We sat upon our saddles with faces of the utmost surliness, while the water dropped from the visors of our caps and trickled down our cheeks. My india-rubber cloak conducted twenty little rapid streamlets to the ground; and Shaw's blanket coat was saturated like a sponge. But what most concerned us was the sight of several puddles of water rapidly accumulating; one, in particular, that was gathering around the tent-pole, threatened to overspread the whole area within the tent, holding forth but an indifferent promise of a comfortable night's rest. Towards sunset, however, the storm ceased as suddenly as it began. A bright streak of clear red sky appeared above the western verge of the prairie; the horizontal rays of the sinking sun streamed through it, and glittered in a thousand prismatic colors upon the dripping groves and the prostrate grass. The pools in the tent dwindled and sunk into the saturated soil.

But all our hopes were delusive. Scarcely had night set in when the tumult broke forth anew. The thunder here is not like the tame thunder of the Atlantic coast. Bursting with a terrific crash directly above our heads, it roared over the boundless waste of prairie, seeming to roll around the whole circle of the firmament with a peculiar and awful reverberation. The lightning flashed all night, playing with its livid glare upon the neighboring trees, revealing the vast expanse of the plain, and then leaving us shut in as if by a palpable wall of darkness.

It did not disturb us much. Now and then a peal awakened us, and made us conscious of the electric battle that was raging, and of the floods that dashed upon the stanch canvas over our heads. We lay upon india-rubber cloths, placed between our blankets and the soil. For a while they excluded the water to admiration; but when at length it accumulated and began to run over the edges, they served equally well to retain it, so that towards the end of the night we were unconsciously reposing in small pools of rain.

On finally awaking in the morning the prospect was not a cheerful one. The rain no longer poured in torrents; but it pattered with a quiet pertinacity upon the strained and saturated canvas. We disengaged ourselves from our blankets, every fibre of which glistened with little bead-like drops of water, and looked out in the vain hope of discovering some token of fair weather. The clouds, in lead-colored volumes, rested upon the dismal verge of the prairie, or hung sluggishly overhead, while the earth wore an aspect no more attractive than the heavens, exhibiting nothing but pools of water, grass beaten down, and mud well trampled by our mules and horses. Our companions' tent, with an air of forlorn and passive misery, and their wagons in like manner drenched and woe-begone, stood not far off. The Captain was just returning from his morning's inspection of the horses. He stalked through the mist and rain with his plaid around his shoulders, his little pipe, dingy as an antiquarian relic, projecting from beneath his moustache, and his brother Jack at his heels.

At noon the sky was clear, and we set out, trailing through mud and slime six inches deep. That night we were spared the customary infliction of the shower-bath.

On the next afternoon we were moving slowly along, not far from a patch of woods which lay on the right. Jack C—— rode a little in advance,—

'The livelong day he had not spoke;'

when suddenly he faced about, pointed to the woods, and roared
out to his brother,—

'O Bill! here 's a cow.'

The Captain instantly galloped forward, and he and Jack made
a vain attempt to capture the prize; but the cow, with a well-
grounded distrust of their intentions, took refuge among the trees.
R—— joined them, and they soon drove her out. We watched
their evolutions as they galloped around her, trying in vain to
noose her with their trail-ropes, which they had converted into
lariettes for the occasion. At length they resorted to milder
measures, and the cow was driven along with the party. Soon
after the usual thunder-storm came up, the wind blowing with
such fury that the streams of rain flew almost horizontally along
the prairie, roaring like a cataract. The horses turned tail to the
storm, and stood hanging their heads, bearing the infliction with
an air of meekness and resignation; while we drew our heads between our shoulders, and crouched forward, so as to make our
backs serve as a pent-house for the rest of our persons. Meanwhile
the cow taking advantage of the tumult, ran off, to the great dis-
comfiture of the Captain. In defiance of the storm, he pulled his
cap tight over his brows, jerked a huge buffalo-pistol from his
holster, and set out at full speed after her. This was the last we
saw of them for some time, the mist and rain making an impenetrable veil; but at length we heard the Captain's shout, and saw him
looming through the tempest, the picture of a Hibernian cavalier,
with his cocked pistol held aloft for safety's sake, and a countenance of anxiety and excitement. The cow trotted before him,
but exhibited evident signs of an intention to run off again, and
the Captain was roaring to us to head her. But the rain had got
in behind our coat collars, and was travelling over our necks in
numerous little streamlets, and being afraid to move our heads,
for fear of admitting more, we sat stiff and immovable, looking at
the Captain askance, and laughing at his frantic movements. At
last the cow made a sudden plunge and ran off; the Captain
grasped his pistol firmly, spurred his horse, and galloped after,
with evident designs of mischief. In a moment we heard the faint
report, deadened by the rain, and then the conqueror and his
victim reappeared, the latter shot through the body, and quite
helpless. Not long after, the storm moderated, and we advanced
again. The cow walked painfully along under the charge of Jack,
to whom the Captain had committed her, while he himself rode

forward in his old capacity of vedette. We were approaching a long line of trees, that followed a stream stretching across our path far in front, when we beheld the vedette galloping towards us apparently much excited, but with a broad grin on his face.

'Let that cow drop behind!' he shouted to us; 'here's her owners.'

And, in fact, as we approached the line of trees, a large white object like a tent was visible behind them. On approaching, however, we found, instead of the expected Mormon camp, nothing but the lonely prairie, and a large white rock standing by the path. The cow, therefore, resumed her place in our procession. She walked on until we encamped, when R——, approaching with his English double-barrelled rifle took aim at her heart, and discharged into it first one bullet and then the other. She was then butchered on the most approved principles of woodcraft, and furnished a very welcome item to our somewhat limited bill of fare.

In a day or two more we reached the river called the 'Big Blue.' By titles equally elegant, almost all the streams of this region are designated. We had struggled through ditches and little brooks all that morning; but on traversing the dense woods that lined the banks of the Blue, we found that more formidable difficulties waited us, for the stream, swollen by the rains, was wide, deep, and rapid.

No sooner were we on the spot than R—— flung off his clothes, and swam across, or splashed through the shallows, with the end of a rope between his teeth. We all looked on in admiration, wondering what might be the object of this energetic preparation; but soon we heard him shouting: 'Give that rope a turn round that stump. You, Sorel; do you hear? Look sharp, now, Boisverd. Come over to this side, some of you, and help me.' The men to whom these orders were directed paid not the least attention to them, though they were poured out without pause or intermission. Henry Chatillon directed the work, and it proceeded quietly and rapidly. R——'s sharp, brattling voice might have been heard incessantly; and he was leaping about with the utmost activity. His commands were rather amusingly inconsistent; for when he saw that the men would not do as he told them he accommodated himself to circumstances, and with the utmost vehemence ordered them to do precisely that which they were at the time engaged upon, no doubt recollecting the story of Mahomet and the refractory mountain. Shaw smiled; R—— observed it, and, approaching with a countenance of indignation, began to vapor a little, but was instantly reduced to silence.

The raft was at length complete. We piled our goods upon it, with the exception of our guns, which each man chose to retain in his own keeping. Sorel, Boisverd, Wright, and Deslauriers took their stations at the four corners, to hold it together, and swim across with it; and in a moment more all our earthly possessions were floating on the turbid waters of the Big Blue. We sat on the bank, anxiously watching the result, until we saw the raft safe landed in a little cove far down on the opposite bank. The empty wagons were easily passed across; and then, each man mounting a horse, we rode through the stream, the stray animals following of their own accord.

6. The Platte and the Desert

We were now at the end of our solitary journeyings along the St Joseph trail. On the evening of the twenty-third of May we encamped near its junction with the old legitimate trail of the Oregon emigrants. We had ridden long that afternoon, trying in vain to find wood and water, until at length we saw the sunset sky reflected from a pool encircled by bushes and rocks. The water lay in the bottom of a hollow, the smooth prairie gracefully rising in ocean-like swells on every side. We pitched our tents by it; not however before the keen eye of Henry Chatillon had discerned some unusual object upon the faintly defined outline of the distant swell. But in the moist, hazy atmosphere of the evening, nothing could be clearly distinguished. As we lay around the fire after supper, a low and distant sound, strange enough amid the loneliness of the prairie, reached our ears,—peals of laughter, and the faint voices of men and women. For eight days we had not encountered a human being, and this singular warning of their vicinity had an effect extremely impressive.

About dark a sallow-faced fellow descended the hill on horse-back, and splashing through the pool, rode up to the tents. He was enveloped in a huge cloak, and his broad felt hat was weeping about his ears with the drizzling moisture of the evening. Another followed, a stout, square-built, intelligent-looking man, who announced himself as leader of an emigrant party, encamped a mile in advance of us. About twenty wagons, he said, were with him; the rest of his party were on the other side of the Big Blue, waiting for a woman who was in the pains of childbirth, and quarrelling meanwhile among themselves.

These were the first emigrants that we had overtaken, although we had found abundant and melancholy traces of their progress throughout the course of the journey. Sometimes we passed the grave of one who had sickened and died on the way. The earth was usually torn up, and covered thickly with wolf-tracks. Some had escaped this violation. One morning, a piece of plank, standing upright on the summit of a grassy hill, attracted our notice, and riding up to it, we found the following words very roughly traced upon it, apparently with a red-hot iron:—

MARY ELLIS.
DIED MAY 7TH, 1845.
AGED TWO MONTHS

Such tokens were of common occurrence.

We were late in breaking up our camp on the following morning, and scarcely had we ridden a mile when we saw, far in advance of us, drawn against the horizon, a line of objects stretching at regular intervals along the level edge of the prairie. An intervening swell soon hid them from sight, until, ascending it a quarter of an hour after, we saw close before us the emigrant caravan, with its heavy white wagons creeping on in slow procession, and a large drove of cattle following behind. Half a dozen yellow-visaged Missourians, mounted on horseback, were cursing and shouting among them, their lank, angular proportions enveloped in brown homespun, evidently cut and adjusted by the hands of a domestic female tailor. As we approached, they called out to us: 'How are ye, boys? Are ye for Oregon or California?'

As we pushed rapidly by the wagons, children's faces were thrust out from the white coverings to look at us; while the care-worn, thin-featured matron, or the buxom girl, seated in front, suspended the knitting on which most of them were engaged, to stare at us with wondering curiosity. By the side of each wagon stalked the proprietor, urging on his patient oxen, who shouldered heavily along, inch by inch, on their interminable journey. It was easy to see that fear and dissension prevailed among them; some of the men—but these, with one exception, were bachelors,—looked wistfully upon us as we rode lightly and swiftly by, and then impatiently at their own lumbering wagons and heavy-gaited oxen. Others were unwilling to advance at all, until the party they had left behind should have rejoined them. Many were murmuring against the leader they had chosen, and wished to depose him; and this discontent was fomented by some ambitious spirits, who had hopes of succeeding in his place. The women were divided between regrets for the homes they had left and fear of the deserts and savages before them.

We soon left them far behind, and hoped that we had taken a final leave; but our companions' wagon stuck so long in a deep muddy ditch, that before it was extricated the van of the emigrant caravan appeared again descending a ridge close at hand. Wagon after wagon plunged through the mud; and as it was nearly noon, and the place promised shade and water, we saw with satisfaction that they were resolved to encamp. Soon the wagons were wheeled into a circle; the cattle were grazing over the meadow, and the men, with sour, sullen faces, were looking about for wood and water. They seemed to meet but indifferent success. As we left the ground, I saw a tall, slouching fellow, with the nasal accent of 'down east,' contemplating the contents of his tin cup, which he had just filled with water.

'Look here, you,' said he; 'it's chock-full of animals!'

The cup, as he held it out, exhibited in fact an extraordinary variety and profusion of animal and vegetable life.

Riding up the little hill and looking back on the meadow, we could easily see that all was not right in the camp of the emigrants. The men were crowded together, and an angry discussion seemed to be going forward. R—— was missing from his wonted place in the line, and the Captain told us that he had remained behind to get his horse shod by a blacksmith attached to the emigrant party. Something whispered in our ears that mischief was on foot; we kept on, however, and coming soon to a stream of tolerable water, we stopped to rest and dine. Still the absentee lingered behind. At last, at the distance of a mile, he and his horse suddenly appeared, sharply defined against the sky on the summit of a hill; and close behind, a huge white object rose slowly into view.

'What is that blockhead bringing with him now?'

A moment dispelled the mystery. Slowly and solemnly, one behind the other, four long trains of oxen and four emigrant wagons rolled over the crest of the hill and gravely descended, while R—— rode in state in the van. It seems that, during the process of shoeing the horse, the smothered dissensions among the emigrants suddenly broke into open rupture. Some insisted on pushing forward, some on remaining where they were, and some on going back. Kearsley, their captain, threw up his command in disgust. 'And now, boys,' said he, 'if any of you are for going ahead, just you come along with me.'

Four wagons, with ten men, one woman, and one small child, made up the force of the 'go-ahead' faction, and R——, with his usual proclivity toward mischief, invited them to join our party. Fear of the Indians—for I can conceive no other motive—must have induced him to court so burdensome an alliance. At all events the proceeding was a cool one. The men who joined us, it is true, were all that could be desired,—rude indeed in manners, but frank, manly, and intelligent. To tell them we could not travel with them was out of the question. I merely reminded Kearsley that if his oxen could not keep up with our mules he must expect to be left behind, as we could not consent to be farther delayed on the journey; but he immediately replied that his oxen *'should* keep up; and if they could n't, why, he allowed, he 'd find out how to make 'em.'

On the next day, as it chanced, our English companions broke the axle-tree of their wagon, and down came the whole cumbrous machine lumbering into the bed of a brook. Here was a day's work cut out for us. Meanwhile our emigrant associates kept on their way, and so vigorously did they urge forward their powerful oxen that, what with the broken axle-tree and other mishaps, it was full a week before we overtook them; when at length we discovered them, one afternoon, crawling quietly along the sandy brink of the Platte. But meanwhile various incidents occurred to ourselves.

It was probable that at this stage of our journey the Pawnees would attempt to rob us. We began, therefore, to stand guard in turn, dividing the night into three watches, and appointing two men for each. Deslauriers and I held guard together. We did not march with military precision to and fro before the tents; our discipline was by no means so strict. We wrapped ourselves in our blankets and sat down by the fire; and Deslauriers, combining his culinary functions with his duties as sentinel, employed himself in boiling the head of an antelope for our breakfast. Yet we were models of vigilance in comparison with some of the party; for the ordinary practice of the guard was to lay his rifle on the ground, and, enveloping his nose in his blanket, meditate on his mistress, or whatever subject best pleased him. This is all well enough when among Indians who do not habitually proceed further in their hostility than robbing travellers of their horses and mules, though, indeed, a Pawnee's forbearance is always to be trusted; but in certain regions farther to the west, the guard must beware how he exposes his person to the light of the fire, lest some keen-eyed skulking marksman should let fly a bullet or an arrow from the darkness.

Among various tales that circulated around our camp-fire was one told by Boisverd, and not inappropriate here. He was trapping with several companions on the skirts of the Blackfoot country. The man on guard, knowing that it behoved him to put forth his utmost precaution, kept aloof from the fire-light, and sat watching intently on all sides. At length he was aware of a dark, crouching figure, stealing noiselessly into the circle of the light. He hastily cocked his rifle, but the sharp click of the lock caught the ear of the Blackfoot, whose senses were all on the alert. Raising his arrow, already fitted to the string he shot it in the direction of the sound. So sure was his aim that he drove it through the throat of the unfortunate guard, and then, with a loud yell, bounded from the camp.

As I looked at the partner of my watch, puffing and blowing over his fire, it occurred to me that he might not prove the most efficient auxiliary in time of trouble.

'Deslauriers,' said I, 'would you run away if the Pawnees should fire at us?'

'Ah! oui, oui, Monsieur!' he replied very decisively.

At this instant a whimsical variety of voices,—barks, howls, yelps, and whines, all mingled together,—sounded from the prairie, not far off, as if a conclave of wolves of every age and sex were assembled there. Deslauriers looked up from his work with a laugh, and began to imitate this medley of sounds with a ludicrous accuracy. At this they were repeated with redoubled emphasis, the musician being apparently indignant at the successful efforts of a rival. They all proceeded from the throat of one little wolf, not larger than a spaniel, seated by himself at some distance. He was of the species called the prairie-wolf,—a grim-visaged, but harmless little brute, whose worst propensity is creeping among horses and gnawing the ropes of raw hide by which they are picketed around the camp. Other beasts roam the prairies far more formidable in aspect and in character. These are the large white and gray wolves, whose deep howl we heard at intervals from far and near.

At last I fell into a doze, and awaking from it found Deslauriers fast asleep. Scandalized by this breach of discipline, I was about to stimulate his vigilance by stirring him with the stock of my rifle; but compassion prevailing, I determined to let him sleep a while, and then arouse him to administer a suitable reproof for such forgetfulness of duty. Now and then I walked the rounds among the silent horses, to see that all was right. The night was chill, damp, and dark, the dank grass bending under the icy dewdrops. At the distance of a rod or two the tents were invisible, and nothing could be seen but the obscure figures of the horses deeply breathing, and restlessly starting as they slept, or still slowly champing the grass. Far off, beyond the black outline of the prairie, there was a ruddy light, gradually increasing, like the glow of a conflagration; until at length the broad disk of the moon, blood-red, and vastly magnified by the vapors, rose slowly upon the darkness, flecked by one or two little clouds, and as the light poured over the gloomy plain, a fierce and stern howl, close at hand, seemed to greet it as an unwelcome intruder. There was something impressive and awful in the place and the hour; for I and the beasts were all that had consciousness for many a league around.

Some days elapsed, and brought us near the Platte. Two men on horseback approached us one morning, and we watched them with the curiosity and interest that, upon the solitude of the plains, such an encounter always excites. They were evidently whites, from their mode of riding, though, contrary to the usage of that region, neither of them carried a rifle.

'Fools!' remarked Henry Chatillon, 'to ride that way on the prairie; Pawnee find them—then they catch it.'

Pawnee *had* found them, and they had come very near 'catching it;' indeed nothing saved them but the approach of our party. Shaw and I knew one of them,—a man named Turner whom we had seen at Westport. He and his companion belonged to an emigrant party encamped a few miles in advance, and had returned to look for some stray oxen, leaving their rifles, with characteristic rashness or ignorance, behind them. Their neglect had nearly cost them dear; for, just before we came up, half a dozen Indians approached, and seeing them apparently defenceless, one of the rascals seized the bridle of Turner's horse and ordered him to dismount. Turner was wholly unarmed; but the other jerked a pistol out of his pocket, at which the Pawnee recoiled; and just then some of our men appearing in the distance, the whole party whipped their rugged little horses and made off. In no way daunted, Turner foolishly persisted in going forward.

Long after leaving him, and late that afternoon, in the midst of a gloomy and barren prairie, we came suddenly upon the great trail of the Pawnees, leading from their villages on the Platte to their war and hunting grounds to the southward. Here every summer passes the motley concourse: thousands of savages, men, women, and children, horses and mules, laden with their weapons and implements, and an innumerable multitude of unruly wolfish dogs, who have not acquired the civilized accomplishment of barking, but howl like their wild cousins of the prairie.

The permanent winter villages of the Pawnees stand on the lower Platte, but throughout the summer the greater part of the inhabitants are wandering over the plains,—a treacherous, cowardly banditti, who, by a thousand acts of pillage and murder, have deserved chastisement at the hands of government. Last year a Dakota warrior performed a notable exploit at one of these villages. He approached it alone, in the middle of a dark night, and clambering up the outside of one of the lodges, which are in the form of a half-sphere, looked in at the round hole made at the top for the escape of smoke. The dusky light from the embers showed him the forms of the sleeping inmates; and dropping lightly through the opening, he unsheathed his knife, and stirring the fire, coolly selected his victims. One by one he stabbed and scalped them; when a child suddenly awoke and screamed. He rushed from the lodge, yelled a Sioux war-cry, shouted his name in triumph and defiance, and darted out upon the dark prairie, leaving the whole village behind him in a tumult, with the howling and baying of dogs, the screams of women, and the yells of the enraged warriors.

Our friend Kearsley, as we learned on rejoining him, signalized himself by a less bloody achievement. He and his men were good woodsmen, well skilled in the use of the rifle, but found themselves wholly out of their element on the prairie. None of them had ever seen a buffalo; and they had very vague conceptions of his nature and appearance. On the day after they reached the Platte, looking towards a distant swell they beheld a multitude of little black specks in motion upon its surface.

'Take your rifles, boys,' said Kearsley, 'and we 'll have fresh meat for supper.' This inducement was quite sufficient. The ten men left their wagons, and set out in hot haste, some on horseback and some on foot, in pursuit of the supposed buffalo. Meanwhile a high grassy ridge shut the game from view; but mounting it after half an hour's running and riding, they found themselves suddenly confronted by about thirty mounted Pawnees. Amazement and consternation were mutual. Having nothing but their bows and arrows, the Indians thought their hour was come, and the fate that they were conscious of richly deserving about to overtake them. So they began, one and all, to shout forth the most cordial salutations, running up with extreme earnestness to shake hands with the Missourians, who were as much rejoiced as they were to escape the expected conflict.

A low, undulating line of sand-hills bounded the horizon before us. That day we rode ten hours, and it was dusk before we entered the hollows and gorges of these gloomy little hills. At length we gained the summit, and the long-expected valley of the Platte lay before us. We all drew rein, and sat joyfully looking down upon the prospect. It was right welcome,—strange, too, and striking to the imagination; and yet it had not one picturesque or beautiful feature; nor had it any of the features of grandeur, other than its vast extent, its solitude, and its wildness. For league after league, a plain as level as a lake was outspread beneath us; here and there the Platte, divided into a dozen thread-like sluices, was traversing it, and an occasional clump of wood, rising in the midst like a shadowy island, relieved the monotony of the waste. No living thing was moving throughout the vast landscape, except the lizards that darted over the sand and through the rank grass and prickly pears at our feet.

We had passed the more tedious part of the journey; but four hundred miles still intervened between us and Fort Laramie; and to reach that point cost us the travel of three more weeks. During the whole of this time we were passing up the middle of a long, narrow, sandy plain, reaching like an outstretched belt nearly to the Rocky Mountains. Two lines of sandhills, broken often into the wildest and most fantastic forms, flanked the valley at the distance of a mile or two on the right and left; while beyond them lay a barren trackless waste, extending for hundreds of miles to the Arkansas on the one side and the Missouri on the other. Before and behind us the level monotony of the plain was unbroken as far as the eye could reach. Sometimes it glared in the sun, an expanse of hot, bare sand; sometimes it was veiled by long coarse grass. Skulls and whitening bones of buffalo were scattered everywhere; the ground was tracked by myriads of them, and often covered with the circular indentations where the bulls had wallowed in the hot weather. From every gorge and ravine opening from the hills, descended deep, well-worn paths, where the buffalo issue twice a day in regular procession to drink in the Platte. The river itself runs through the midst, a thin sheet of rapid, turbid water, half a mile wide, and scarcely two feet deep. Its low banks, for the most part without a bush or a tree, are of loose sand, with which the stream is so charged that it grates on the teeth in drinking. The naked landscape is, of itself, dreary and monotonous enough; and yet the wild beasts and wild men that frequent the valley of the Platte make it a scene of interest and excitement to the traveller. Of those who have journeyed there, scarcely one, perhaps, fails to look back with fond regret to his horse and his rifle.

Early in the morning after we reached the Platte, a long procession of squalid savages approached our camp. Each was on foot, leading his horse by a rope of bull-hide. His attire consisted merely of a scanty cincture, and an old buffalo-robe, tattered and begrimed by use, which hung over his shoulders. His head was close shaven, except a ridge of hair reaching over the crown from the middle of the forehead, very much like the long bristles on the back of a hyena, and he carried his bow and arrows in his hand, while his meagre little horse was laden with dried buffalo meat, the produce of his hunting. Such were the first specimens that we met—and very indifferent ones they were—of the genuine savages of the plains.

They were the Pawnees whom Kearsley had encountered the day before, and belonged to a large hunting party, known to be ranging the prairie in the vicinity. They strode rapidly by, within a furlong of our tents, not pausing or looking towards us, after the manner of Indians when meditating mischief or conscious of ill desert. I went out to meet them, and had an amicable conference with the chief, presenting him with half a pound of tobacco, at which unmerited bounty he expressed much gratification. These fellows, or some of their companions, had committed a dastardly outrage upon an emigrant party in advance of us. Two men, at a distance from the rest, were seized by them, but, lashing their horses, they broke away and fled. At this the Pawnees raised the yell and shot at them, transfixing the hindmost through the back with several arrows, while his companion galloped away and brought in the news to his party. The panic-stricken emigrants remained for several days in camp, not daring even to go out in quest of the dead body.

Our New England climate is mild and equable compared with that of the Platte. This very morning, for instance, was close and sultry, the sun rising with a faint oppressive heat; when suddenly darkness gathered in the west, and a furious blast of sleet and hail drove full in our faces, icy cold, and urged with such demoniac vehemence that it felt like a storm of needles. It was curious to see the horses; they faced about in extreme displeasure, holding their tails like whipped dogs, and shivering as the angry gusts, howling louder than a concert of wolves, swept over us. Wright's long train of mules came sweeping round before the storm, like a flight of snow-birds driven by a winter tempest. Thus we all remained stationary for some minutes, crouching close to our horses' necks, much too surly to speak, though once the Captain looked up from between the collars of his coat, his face blood-red, and the muscles of his mouth contracted by the cold into a most ludicrous grin of agony. He grumbled something that sounded like a curse, directed, as we believed, against the unhappy hour when he had first thought of leaving home. The thing was too good to last long; and the instant the puffs of wind subsided we pitched our tents, and remained in camp for the rest of a gloomy and lowering day. The emigrants also encamped near at hand. We being first on the ground, had appropriated all the wood within reach; so that our fire alone blazed cheerily. Around it soon gathered a group of uncouth figures, shivering in the drizzling rain. Conspicuous among them were two or three of the half-savage men who spend their reckless lives in trapping among the Rocky Mountains, or in trading for the Fur Company in the Indian villages. They were all of Canadian extraction; their hard, weather-beaten faces and bushy moustaches looked out from beneath the hoods of their white capotes with a bad and brutish expression, as if their owners might be the willing agents of any villainy. And such in fact is the character of many of these men.

On the day following we overtook Kearsley's wagons, and thenceforward for a week or two, we were fellow-travellers. One good effect, at least, resulted from the alliance; it materially diminished the fatigues of standing guard; for the party being now more numerous, there were longer intervals between each man's turn of duty.

7. The Buffalo

Four days on the Platte, and yet no buffalo! Last year's signs of them were provokingly abundant; and wood being extremely scarce, we found an admirable substitute in the *bois de vache*, which burns like peat, producing no unpleasant effects. The wagons one morning had left the camp; Shaw and I were already on horseback, but Henry Chatillon still sat cross-legged by the dead embers of the fire, playing pensively with the lock of his rifle, while his sturdy Wyandot pony stood quietly behind him, looking over his head. At last he got up, patted the neck of the pony (which, from an exaggerated appreciation of his value, he had christened 'Five Hundred Dollar'), and then mounted, with a melancholy air.

'What is it, Henry?'

'Ah, I feel lonesome; I never been here before but I see away

yonder over the buttes, and down there on the prairie, black—
all black with buffalo.'

In the afternoon he and I left the party in search of an antelope,
until, at the distance of a mile or two on the right, the tall white
wagons and the little black specks of horsemen were just visible,
so slowly advancing that they seemed motionless; and far on the
left rose the broken line of scorched, desolate sand-hills. The vast
plain waved with tall rank grass, that swept our horses' bellies;
it swayed to and fro in billows with the light breeze, and far and
near antelope and wolves were moving through it, the hairy backs
of the latter alternately appearing and disappearing, as they
bounded awkwardly along; while the antelope, with the simple
curiosity peculiar to them, would often approach us closely, their
little horns and white throats just visible above the grass tops,
as they gazed eagerly at us with their round black eyes.

I dismounted, and amused myself with firing at the wolves.
Henry attentively scrutinized the surrounding landscape; at
length he gave a shout, and called on me to mount again, pointing
in the direction of the sand-hills. A mile and a half from us tw
black specks slowly traversed the bare, glaring face of one of them,
and disappeared behind the summit. 'Let us go!' cried Henry,
belaboring the sides of 'Five Hundred Dollar;' and I following in
his wake, we galloped rapidly through the rank grass toward the
base of the hills.

From one of their openings descended a deep ravine, widening
as it issued on the prairie. We entered it, and galloping up, in a
moment were surrounded by the bleak sand-hills. Half of their
steep sides were bare; and the rest were scantily clothed with
clumps of grass, and various uncouth plants, conspicuous among
which appeared the reptile-like prickly-pear. They were gashed
with numberless ravines; and as the sky had suddenly darkened,
and a cold, gusty wind arisen, the strange shrubs and the dreary
hills looked doubly wild and desolate. But Henry's face was all
eagerness. He tore off a little hair from the piece of buffalo-robe
under his saddle, and threw it up, to show the course of the wind.
It blew directly before us. The game was therefore to leeward, and
it was necessary to make our best speed to get round them.

We scrambled from this ravine, and galloping away through
the hollows soon found another, winding like a snake among the
hills, and so deep that it completely concealed us. We rode up the
bottom of it, glancing through the bushes at its edge, till Henry

abruptly jerked his rein and slid out of his saddle. Full a quarter
of a mile distant, on the outline of the farthest hill, a long procession of buffalo were walking, in Indian file, with the utmost
gravity and deliberation; then more appeared, clambering from
a hollow not far off, and ascending, one behind the other, the grassy
slope of another hill; then a shaggy head and a pair of short
broken horns issued out of a ravine close at hand, and with a slow,
stately step, one by one, the enormous brutes came into view,
taking their way across the valley, wholly unconscious of an
enemy. In a moment Henry was worming his way, lying flat on
the ground, through grass and prickly-pears, towards his unsuspecting victims. He had with him both my rifle and his own.
He was soon out of sight, and still the buffalo kept issuing into
the valley. For a long time all was silent; I sat holding his horse,
and wondering what he was about, when suddenly in rapid
succession, came the sharp reports of the two rifles, and the whole
line of buffalo, quickening their pace into a clumsy trot, gradually
disappeared over the ridge of the hill. Henry rose to his feet, and
stood looking after them.

'You have missed them,' said I.

'Yes,' said Henry; 'let us go.' He descended into the ravine,
loaded the rifles, and mounted his horse.

We rode up the hill after the buffalo. The herd was out of sight
when we reached the top, but lying on the grass, not far off, was
one quite lifeless, and another violently struggling in the death
agony.

'You see I miss him!' remarked Henry. He had fired from a
distance of more than a hundred and fifty yards, and both balls
had passed through the lungs, the true mark in shooting
buffalo.

The darkness increased, and a driving storm came on. Tying
our horses to the horns of the victims, Henry began the bloody
work of dissection, slashing away with the science of a con-
noisseur, while I vainly tried to imitate him. Old Hendrick recoiled with horror and indignation when I endeavored to tie the
meat to the strings of raw hide, always carried for this purpose,
dangling at the back of the saddle. After some difficulty we over-
came his scruples; and, heavily burdened with the more eligible
portions of the buffalo, we set out on our return. Scarcely had we
emerged from the labyrinth of gorges and ravines, and issued upon
the open prairie, when the prickling sleet came driving, gust

upon gust, directly in our faces. It was strangely dark, though wanting still an hour of sunset. The freezing storm soon penetrated to the skin, but the uneasy trot of our heavy-gaited horses kept us warm enough, as we forced them unwillingly in the teeth of the sleet and rain by the powerful suasion of our Indian whips. The prairie in this place was hard and level. A flourishing colony of prairie-dogs had burrowed into it in every direction, and the little mounds of fresh earth around their holes were about as numerous as the hills in a corn-field; but not a yelp was to be heard; not the nose of a single citizen was visible; all had retired to the depths of their burrows, and we envied them their dry and comfortable habitations. An hour's hard riding showed us our tent dimly looming through the storm, one side puffed out by the force of the wind, and the other collapsed in proportion, while the disconsolate horses stood shivering close around, and the wind kept up a dismal whistling in the boughs of three old half-dead trees above. Shaw, like a patriarch, sat on his saddle in the entrance, with a pipe in his mouth and his arms folded, contemplating with cool satisfaction the piles of meat that we flung on the ground before him. A dark and dreary night succeeded; but the sun rose with a heat so sultry and languid that the Captain excused himself on that account from waylaying an old buffalo bull, who with stupid gravity was walking over the prairie to drink at the river. So much for the climate of the Platte.

But it was not the weather alone that had produced this sudden abatement of the sportsman-like zeal which the Captain had always professed. He had been out on the afternoon before, together with several members of his party; but their hunting was attended with no other result than the loss of one of their best horses, severely injured by Sorel, in vainly chasing a wounded bull. The Captain, whose ideas of hard riding were all derived from transatlantic sources, expressed the utmost amazement at the feats of Sorel, who went leaping ravines, and dashing at full speed up and down the sides of precipitous hills, lashing his horse with the recklessness of a Rocky Mountain rider. Unfortunately for the poor animal, he was the property of R——, against whom Sorel entertained an unbounded aversion. The Captain himself, it seemed, had also attempted to 'run' a buffalo, but though a good and practised horseman, he had soon given over the attempt, being astonished and utterly disgusted at the nature of the ground he was required to ride over.

'Here's old Papin and Frederic, down from Fort Laramie,' shouted Henry, as we returned from a reconnoitring tour on the next morning. We had for some days expected this encounter. Papin was the *bourgeois*, or 'boss,' of Fort Laramie. He had come down the river with the buffalo-robes and the beaver, the produce of the last winter's trading. I had among our baggage a letter which I wished to commit to his hands; so requesting Henry to detain the boats if he could until my return, I set out after the wagons. They were about four miles in advance. In half an hour I overtook them, got the letter, trotted back upon the trail, and looking carefully, as I rode, saw a patch of broken storm-blasted trees, and moving near them, some little black specks like men and horses. Arriving at the place, I found a strange assembly. The boats, eleven in number, deep-laden with the skins, hugged close to the shore, to escape being borne down by the swift current. The rowers, swarthy, ignoble Mexicans, turned up their brutish faces to look, as I reached the bank. Papin sat in the middle of one of the boats, upon the canvas covering that protected the cargo. He was a stout, robust fellow, with a little gray eye that had a peculiarly sly twinkle. 'Frederic,' also, stretched his tall, raw-boned proportions close by the *bourgeois*, and 'mountain men' completed the group: some lounging in the boats, some strolling on shore; some attired in gayly painted buffalo robes, like Indian dandies; some with hair saturated with red paint, and plastered with glue to their temples; and one bedaubed with vermilion upon the forehead and each cheek. They were a mongrel race; yet the French blood seemed to predominate; in a few, indeed, might be seen the black, snaky eye of the Indian half-breed, and one and all, they seemed to aim at assimilating themselves to their red associates.

I shook hands with the *bourgeois*, and delivered the letter; then the boats swung round into the stream and floated away. They had reason for haste, for already the voyage from Fort Laramie had occupied a full month, and the river was growing daily more shallow. Fifty times a day the boats had been aground; indeed, those who navigate the Platte invariably spend half their time upon sand-bars. Two of these boats, the property of private traders, afterwards separating from the rest, got hopelessly involved in the shallows not very far from the Pawnee villages, and were soon surrounded by a swarm of the inhabitants. They carried off everything that they thought valuable, including most of the robes; and amused themselves by tying up the men left on guard, and soundly whipping them with sticks.

We encamped that night upon the bank of the river. Among the emigrants was an overgrown boy, some eighteen years old, with a head as round and about as large as a pumpkin, and fever-and-ague fits had dyed his face to a corresponding color. He wore an old white hat, tied under his chin with a handkerchief; his body was short and stout, but his legs were of disproportioned and appalling length. I observed him at sunset, breasting the hill with gigantic strides, and standing against the sky on the summit, like a colossal pair of tongs. In a moment after we heard him screaming frantically behind the ridge, and nothing doubting that he was in the clutches of Indians or grizzly bears, some of the party caught up their rifles and ran to the rescue. His outcries, however, were but an ebullition of joyous excitement; he had chased two wolf pups to their burrow, and was on his knees, grubbing away like a dog at the mouth of the hole to get at them.

Before morning he caused more serious disquiet in the camp. It was his turn to hold the middle-guard; but no sooner was he called up than he coolly arranged a pair of saddle-bags under a wagon, laid his head upon them, closed his eyes, opened his mouth, and fell asleep. The guard on our side of the camp, thinking it no part of his duty to look after the cattle of the emigrants, contented himself with watching our own horses and mules; the wolves, he said, were unusually noisy; still no mischief was foreboded, but when the sun rose not a hoof or horn was in sight. The cattle were gone. While Tom was quietly slumbering, the wolves had driven them away.

Then we reaped the fruits of R——'s precious plan of travelling in company with emigrants. To leave them in their distress was not to be thought of, and we felt bound to wait until the cattle could be searched for, and if possible, recovered. But the reader may be curious to know what punishment awaited the faithless Tom. By the wholesome law of the prairie, he who falls asleep on guard is condemned to walk all day, leading his horse by the bridle; and we found much fault with our companions for not enforcing such a sentence on the offender. Nevertheless, had he been of our own party, I have no doubt that he would in like manner have escaped scot-free. But the emigrants went farther than mere forbearance; they decreed that since Tom couldn't stand guard without falling asleep, he should n't stand guard at all, and henceforward his slumbers were unbroken. Establishing such a premium on drowsiness could have no very beneficial effect upon the vigilance of our sentinels; for it is far from agreeable, after riding from sunrise to sunset, to feel your slumbers interrupted by the butt of a rifle nudging your side, and a sleepy voice growling in your ear that you must get up, to shiver and freeze for three weary hours at midnight.

'Buffalo! buffalo!' It was but a grim old bull, roaming the prairie by himself in misanthropic seclusion; but there might be more behind the hills. Dreading the monotony and languor of the camp, Shaw and I saddled our horses, buckled our holsters in their places, and set out with Henry Chatillon in search of the game. Henry, not intending to take part in the chase, but merely conducting us, carried his rifle with him while we left ours behind as incumbrances. We rode for some five or six miles, and saw no living thing but wolves, snakes, and prairie-dogs.

'This won't do at all,' said Shaw.

'What won't do?'

'There 's no wood about here to make a litter for the wounded man; I have an idea that one of us will need something of the sort before the day is over.'

There was some foundation for such an idea, for the ground was none of the best for a race, and grew worse continually as we proceeded; indeed, it soon became desperately bad, consisting of abrupt hills and deep hollows, cut by frequent ravines not easy to pass. At length, a mile in advance, we saw a band of bulls. Some were scattered grazing over a green declivity, while the rest were crowded together in the wide hollow below. Making a circuit, to keep out of sight, we rode towards them, until we ascended a hill within a furlong of them, beyond which nothing intervened that could possibly screen us from their view. We dismounted behind the ridge, just out of sight, drew our saddle-girths, examined our pistols, and mounting again, rode over the hill, and descended at a canter towards them, bending close to our horses' necks. Instantly they took the alarm; those on the hill descended, those below gathered into a mass, and the whole got into motion, shouldering each other along at a clumsy gallop. We followed, spurring our horses to full speed; and as the herd rushed, crowding and trampling in terror through an opening in the hills, we were close at their heels, half suffocated by the clouds of dust. But as we drew near, their alarm and speed increased; our horses, being new to the work, showed signs of the utmost fear, bounding violently aside as we approached, and refusing to enter among the herd. The buffalo now broke into several small bodies, scampering over the hills in different directions, and I lost sight of Shaw; neither of us knew where the other had gone. Old Pontiac ran like a frantic elephant up hill and down hill, his ponderous hoofs striking the prairie like sledge-hammers. He showed a curious mixture of eagerness and terror, straining to overtake the panic-stricken herd, but constantly recoiling in dismay as we drew near. The fugitives, indeed, offered no very attractive spectacle, with their shaggy manes and the tattered remnants of their last winter's hair covering their backs in irregular shreds and patches, and flying off in the wind as they ran. At length I urged my horse close behind a bull, and after trying in vain, by blows and spurring to bring him alongside, I fired from this disadvantageous position. At the report Pontiac swerved so much that I was again thrown a little behind the game. The bullet, entering too much in the rear, failed to disable the bull; for a buffalo requires to be shot at particular points, or he will certainly escape. The herd ran up a hill, and I followed in pursuit. As Pontiac rushed headlong down on the other side, I saw Shaw and Henry descending the hollow on the right, at a leisurely gallop; and in front, the buffalo were just disappearing behind the crest of the next hill, their short tails erect, and their hoofs twinkling through a cloud of dust.

At that moment I heard Shaw and Henry shouting to me; but the muscles of a stronger arm than mine could not have checked at once the furious course of Pontiac, whose mouth was as insensible as leather. Added to this, I rode him that morning with a snaffle, having the day before, for the benefit of my other horse, unbuckled from my bridle the curb which I commonly used. A stronger and hardier brute never trod the prairie; but the novel sight of the buffalo filled him with terror, and when at full speed he was almost incontrollable. Gaining the top of the ridge, I saw nothing of the buffalo; they had all vanished amid the intricacies of the hills and hollows. Reloading my pistols in the best way I could, I galloped on until I saw them again scuttling along at the base of the hill, their panic somewhat abated. Down went old Pontiac among them, scattering them to the right and left; and then we had another long chase. About a dozen bulls were before us, scouring over the hills, rushing down the declivities with tremendous weight and impetuosity, and then laboring with a weary gallop upward. Still Pontiac, in spite of spurring and beating, would not close with them. One bull at length fell a little behind the rest, and by dint of much effort, I urged my horse within six or eight yards of his side. His back was darkened with sweat; he was panting heavily, while his tongue lolled out a foot from his jaws. Gradually I came up abreast of him, urging Pontiac with leg and rein nearer to his side, when suddenly he did what buffalo in such circumstances will always do: he slackened his gallop, and turning towards us, with an aspect of mingled rage and distress, lowered his huge, shaggy head for a charge. Pontiac, with a snort, leaped aside in terror, nearly throwing me to the ground, as I was wholly unprepared for such an evolution. I raised my pistol in a passion to strike him on the head, but thinking better of it, fired the bullet after the bull, who had resumed his flight; then drew rein and determined to rejoin my companions. It was high time. The breath blew hard from Pontiac's nostrils, and the sweat rolled in big drops down his sides; I myself felt as if drenched in warm water. Pledging myself to take my revenge at a future opportunity, I looked about for some indications to show me where I was, and what course I ought to pursue; I might as well have looked for landmarks in the midst of the ocean. How many miles I had run, or in what direction, I had no idea; and around me the prairie was rolling in steep swells and pitches, without a single distinctive feature to guide me. I had a little compass hung at my neck; and ignorant that the Platte at this point diverged considerably from its easterly course, I thought that by keeping to the northward I should certainly reach it. So I turned and rode about two hours in that direction. The prairie changed as I advanced, softening away into easier undulations, but nothing like the Platte appeared, nor any sign of a human being: the same wild, endless expanse lay around me still; and to all appearance I was as far from my object as ever. I began now to think myself in danger of being lost, and, reining in my horse, summoned the scanty share of woodcraft that I possessed (if that term be applicable on the prairie) to extricate me. It occurred to me that the buffalo might prove my best guides. I soon found one of the paths made by them in their passage to the river: it ran nearly at right angles to my course; but turning my horse's head in the direction it indicated, his freer gait and erected ears assured me that I was right.

But in the mean time my ride had been by no means a solitary
one. The face of the country was dotted far and wide with
countless hundreds of buffalo. They trooped along in files and
columns, bulls, cows, and calves, on the green faces of the declivities in front. They scrambled away over the hills to the right
and left; and far off, the pale blue swells in the extreme distance
were dotted with innumerable specks. Sometimes I surprised
shaggy old bulls grazing alone, or sleeping behind the ridges I
ascended. They would leap up at my approach, stare stupidly at
me through their tangled manes, and then gallop heavily away.
The antelope were very numerous; and as they are always bold
when in the neighborhood of buffalo, they would approach to look
at me, gaze intently with their great round eyes, then suddenly
leap aside, and stretch lightly away over the prairie, swift as a
race-horse. Squalid, ruffian-like wolves sneaked through the
hollows and sandy ravines. Several times I passed through villages
of prairie-dogs, who sat, each at the mouth of his burrow, holding
his paws before him in a supplicating attitude, and yelping away
most vehemently, whisking his little tail with every squeaking cry
he uttered. Prairie-dogs are not fastidious in their choice of companions; various long, checkered snakes were sunning themselves in the midst of the village, and demure little gray owls, with
a large white ring round each eye, were perched side by side with
the rightful inhabitants. The prairie teemed with life. Again and
again I looked toward the crowded hill-sides, and was sure I
saw horsemen; and riding near, with a mixture of hope and dread,
for Indians were abroad, I found them transformed into a group
of buffalo. There was nothing in human shape amid all this vast
congregation of brute forms.

When I turned down the buffalo path, the prairie seemed
changed; only a wolf or two glided by at intervals, like conscious
felons, never looking to the right or left. Being now free from
anxiety, I was at leisure to observe minutely the objects around
me; and here, for the first time, I noticed insects wholly different
from any of the varieties found farther eastward. Gaudy butter-
flies fluttered about my horse's head; strangely formed beetles,
glittering with metallic lustre, were crawling upon plants that I
had never seen before; multitudes of lizards, too, were darting
like lightning over the sand.

I had run to a great distance from the river. It cost me a long
ride on the buffalo path before I saw, from the ridge of a sand-hill,

the pale surface of the Platte glistening in the midst of its desert
valley, and the faint outline of the hills beyond waving along the
sky. From where I stood, not a tree nor a bush nor a living thing
was visible throughout the whole extent of the sun-scorched
landscape. In half an hour I came upon the trail, not far from the
river; and seeing that the party had not yet passed, I turned
eastward to meet them, old Pontiac's long swinging trot again
assuring me that I was right in doing so. Having been slightly ill
on leaving camp in the morning, six or seven hours of rough
riding had fatigued me extremely. I soon stopped, therefore,
flung my saddle on the ground, and with my head resting on it,
and my horse's trail-rope tied loosely to my arm, lay waiting the
arrival of the party, speculating meanwhile on the extent of the
injuries Pontiac had received.

At length the white wagon-coverings rose from the verge of the
plain. By a singular coincidence, almost at the same moment two
horsemen appeared coming down from the hills. They were Shaw
and Henry, who had searched for me awhile in the morning, but
well knowing the futility of the attempt in such a broken country,
had placed themselves on the top of the highest hill they could
find, and picketing their horses near them, as a signal to me, had
lain down and fallen asleep. The stray cattle had been recovered,
as the emigrants told us, about noon. Before sunset we pushed
forward eight miles farther.

'JUNE 7, 1846. Four men are missing: R——, Sorel, and two
emigrants. They set out this morning after buffalo, and have
not yet made their appearance; whether killed or lost, we
cannot tell.'

I find the above in my note-book, and well remember the
council held on the occasion. Our fire was the scene of it; for the
superiority of Henry Chatillon's experience and skill made him
the resort of the whole camp upon every question of difficulty.
He was moulding bullets at the fire, when the Captain drew near,
with a perturbed and care-worn expression of countenance, faithfully reflected on the heavy features of Jack, who followed close
behind. Then the emigrants came straggling from their wagons
towards the common centre. Various suggestions were made to
account for the absence of the four men, and one or two of the
emigrants declared that, when out after cattle, they had seen
Indians dogging them, and crawling like wolves along the ridges

of the hills. At this the Captain slowly shook his head with double gravity, and solemnly remarked,—

'It 's a serious thing to be travelling through this cursed wilderness;' an opinion in which Jack immediately expressed a thorough coincidence. Henry would not commit himself by declaring any positive opinion.

'Maybe he only followed the buffalo too far; maybe Indian kill him; maybe he got lost; I cannot tell.'

With this the auditors were obliged to rest content; the emigrants, not in the least alarmed, though curious to know what had become of their comrades, walked back to their wagons, and the Captain betook himself pensively to his tent. Shaw and I followed his example.

8. Taking French Leave

On the eighth of June, at eleven o'clock, we reached the South
Fork of the Platte, at the usual fording-place. For league upon
league the desert uniformity of the prospect was almost unbroken;
the hills were dotted with little tufts of shrivelled grass, but
betwixt these the white sand was glaring in the sun; and the
channel of the river, almost on a level with the plain, was but
one great sand-bed, about half a mile wide. It was covered with
water, but so scantily that the bottom was scarcely hidden; for,
wide as it is, the average depth of the Platte does not at this
point exceed a foot and a half. Stopping near its bank, we gathered
bois de vache, and made a meal of buffalo-meat. Far off, on the
other side, was a green meadow, where we could see the white
tents and wagons of an emigrant camp; and just opposite to us

we could discern a group of men and animals at the water's edge.
Four or five horsemen soon entered the river, and in ten minutes
had waded across and clambered up the loose sand-bank. They
were ill-looking fellows, thin and swarthy, with care-worn, anxious
faces, and lips rigidly compressed. They had good cause for
anxiety; it was three days since they first encamped here, and on
the night of their arrival they had lost a hundred and twenty-
three of their best cattle, driven off by the wolves, through the
neglect of the man on guard. This discouraging and alarming
calamity was not the first that had overtaken them. Since leaving
the settlements they had met with nothing but misfortune. Some
of their party had died; one man had been killed by the Pawnees;
and about a week before, they had been plundered by the Dakota
of all their best horses, the wretched animals on which our visitors
were mounted being the only ones that were left. They had
encamped, they told us, near sunset, by the side of the Platte,
and their oxen were scattered over the meadow, while the horses
were feeding a little farther off. Suddenly the ridges of the hills
were alive with a swarm of mounted Indians, at least six hundred
in number, who came pouring with a yell down towards the camp,
rushing up within a few rods, to the great terror of the emigrants;
when suddenly wheeling, they swept around the band of horses,
and in five minutes disappeared with their prey through the
openings of the hills.

As these emigrants were telling their story, we saw four other
men approaching. They proved to be R—— and his companions,
who had encountered no mischance of any kind, but had only
wandered too far in pursuit of the game. They said they had seen
no Indians, but only 'millions of buffalo;' and both R—— and
Sorel had meat dangling behind their saddles.

The emigrants recrossed the river, and we prepared to follow.
First the heavy ox-wagons plunged down the bank and dragged
slowly over the sand-beds; sometimes the hoofs of the oxen were
scarcely wet by the thin sheet of water; and the next moment the
river would be boiling against their sides, and eddying around the
wheels. Inch by inch they receded from the shore, dwindling every
moment, until at length they seemed to be floating far out in the
middle of the river. A more critical experiment awaited us; for
our little mule-cart was ill-fitted for the passage of so swift a
stream. We watched it with anxiety, till it seemed a motionless
white speck in the midst of the waters; and it was motionless, for

it had stuck fast in a quicksand. The mules were losing their footing, the wheels were sinking deeper and deeper, and the water began to rise through the bottom and drench the goods within. All of us who had remained on the hither bank galloped to the rescue; the men jumped into the water, adding their strength to that of the mules, until by much effort the cart was extricated, and conveyed in safety across.

As we gained the other bank a rough group of men surrounded us. They were not robust, nor large of frame, yet they had an aspect of hardy endurance. Finding at home no scope for their energies, they had betaken themselves to the prairie; and in them seemed to be revived, with redoubled force, that fierce spirit which impelled their ancestors, scarcely more lawless than themselves, from the German forests, to inundate Europe, and overwhelm the Roman empire. A fortnight afterwards this unfortunate party passed Fort Laramie, while we were there. Not one of their missing oxen had been recovered, though they had remained encamped a week in search of them; and they had been compelled to abandon a great part of their baggage and provisions, and yoke cows and heifers to their wagons to carry them forward upon their journey, the most toilsome and hazardous part of which lay still before them.

It is worth noticing that on the Platte one may sometimes see the shattered wrecks of ancient claw-footed tables, well waxed and rubbed, or massive bureaus of carved oak. These, some of them no doubt the relics of ancestral prosperity in the colonial time, must have encountered strange vicissitudes. Brought, perhaps, originally from England; then, with the declining fortunes of their owners, borne across the Alleghanies to the wilderness of Ohio or Kentucky; then to Illinois or Missouri; and now at last fondly stowed away in the family wagon for the interminable journey to Oregon. But the stern privations of the way are little anticipated. The cherished relic is soon flung out to scorch and crack upon the hot prairie.

We resumed our journey; but we had gone scarcely a mile, when R—— called out from the rear,—

'We 'll 'camp here.'

'Why do you want to 'camp? Look at the sun. It is not three o'clock yet.'

'We 'll 'camp here!'

This was the only reply vouchsafed. Deslauriers was in advance with his cart. Seeing the mule-wagon wheeling from the track, he began to turn his own team in the same direction.

'Go on, Deslauriers;' and the little cart advanced again. As we rode on, we soon heard the wagon of our confederates creaking and jolting behind us, and the driver, Wright, discharging a furious volley of oaths against his mules; no doubt venting upon them the wrath which he dared not direct against a more appropriate object.

Something of this sort had frequently occurred. Our English companion was by no means partial to us, and we thought we discovered in his conduct an intention to thwart and annoy us, especially by retarding the movements of the party, which he knew that we were anxious to quicken. Therefore he would insist on encamping at all unseasonable hours, saying that fifteen miles was a sufficient day's journey. Finding our wishes disregarded, we took the direction of affairs into our own hands. Keeping always in advance, to the inexpressible indignation of R——, we encamped at what time and place we thought proper, not much caring whether the rest chose to follow or not. They always did so, however, pitching their tent near ours, with sullen and wrathful countenances.

Travelling together on these terms did not suit our tastes, and for some time we had meditated a separation. We resolved to leave camp early in the morning, and push forward as rapidly as possible for Fort Laramie, which we hoped to reach, by hard travelling, in four or five days. The Captain soon trotted up between us, and we explained our intentions.

'A very extraordinary proceeding, upon my word!' he remarked. The most prominent impression in his mind evidently was that we were deserting his party, in what he regarded as a very dangerous stage of the journey. We ventured to suggest that we were only four in number, while his party still included sixteen men; and as we were to go forward and they were to follow, a full proportion of the perils he apprehended would fall upon us. But the austerity of the Captain's features would not relax. 'A very extraordinary proceeding, gentlemen!' and repeating this, he rode off to confer with his principal.

Before sunrise on the next morning our tent was down, we harnessed our best horses to the cart, and left the camp. But first we shook hands with our friends the emigrants, who sincerely wished us a safe journey, though some others of the party

might easily have been consoled had we encountered an Indian
war-party on the way. The Captain and his brother were standing
on the top of a hill, wrapped in their plaids, like spirits of the
mist, keeping an anxious eye on the band of horses below. We
waved adieu to them as we rode off the ground. The Captain
replied with a salutation of the utmost dignity, which Jack tried
to imitate, though not with perfect success.

In five minutes we had gained the foot of the hills, but here we
came to a stop. Hendrick was in the shafts, and being the incarna-
tion of perverse and brutish obstinacy, he utterly refused to move.
Deslauriers lashed and swore till he was tired, but Hendrick stood
like a rock, grumbling to himself and looking askance at his enemy,
until he saw a favorable opportunity to take his revenge, when he
struck out under the shaft with such cool malignity of intention
that Deslauriers only escaped the blow by a sudden skip into the
air, such as no one but a Frenchman could achieve. Shaw and he
then joined forces, and lashed on both sides at once. The brute
stood still for a while, till he could bear it no longer, when he began
to kick and plunge till he threatened the utter demolition of the
cart and harness. We glanced back at the camp, which was in full
sight. Our companions, inspired by emulation, were levelling their
tents and driving in their cattle and horses.

'Take the horse out,' said I.

I took the saddle from Pontiac and put it upon Hendrick; the
former was harnessed to the cart in an instant. '*Avance donc!*'
cried Deslauriers. Pontiac strode up the hill, twitching the little
cart after him as if it were a feather's weight; and though, as
we gained the top we saw the wagons of our deserted comrades
just getting into motion, we had little fear that they could
overtake us.

Leaving the trail, we struck directly across the country, and
took the shortest cut to reach the main stream of the Platte.
A deep ravine suddenly intercepted us. We followed its sides until
we found them less abrupt, and then plunged through in the best
way we could. Passing behind the sandy ravines called 'Ash
Hollow,' we stopped for a short nooning at the side of a pool of
rain-water; but soon resumed our journey, and some hours
before sunset descended the ravines and gorges opening down-
ward upon the Platte west of Ash Hollow. Our horses waded to
the fetlock in sand; the sun scorched like fire, and the air swarmed
with sand-flies and mosquitoes.

At last we gained the Platte. Following it for about five miles
we saw, just as the sun was sinking, a great meadow, dotted with
hundreds of cattle, and beyond them an encampment of emigrants. A party of them came out to meet us, looking upon us at
first with cold and suspicious faces. Seeing four men, different in
appearance and equipment from themselves, emerging from the
hills, they had taken us for the van of the much-dreaded Mormons, whom they were very apprehensive of encountering. We
made known our true character, and then they greeted us cordially. They expressed much surprise that so small a party should
venture to traverse that region, though in fact such attempts are
often made by trappers and Indian traders. We rode with them
to their camp. The wagons, some fifty in number, with here and
there a tent intervening, were arranged as usual in a circle; the
best horses were picketed in the area within, and the whole
circumference was glowing with the dusky light of fires, displaying
the forms of the women and children who were crowded around
them. This patriarchal scene was curious and striking enough;
but we made our escape from the place with all possible dispatch,
being tormented by the intrusive questioning of the men who
thronged about us. Yankee curiosity was nothing to theirs. They
demanded our names, whence we came, whither we were going,
and what was our business. The last query was particularly
embarrassing; since travelling in that country, or indeed
anywhere, from any other motive than gain, was an idea
of which they took no cognizance. Yet they were fine-looking
fellows, with an air of frankness, generosity, and even courtesy,
having come from one of the least barbarous of the frontier
counties.

We passed about a mile beyond them, and encamped. Being
too few in number to stand guard without excessive fatigue, we
extinguished our fire, lest it should attract the notice of wandering
Indians; and, picketing our horses close around us, slept undisturbed till morning. For three days we travelled without
interruption, and on the evening of the third encamped by the
well-known spring on Scott's Bluff.

Henry Chatillon and I rode out in the morning, and, descending
the western side of the Bluff, were crossing the plain beyond.
Something that seemed to me a file of buffalo came into view,
descending the hills several miles before us. But Henry reined in
his horse, and peering across the prairie with a better and more

practised eye, soon discovered its real nature. 'Indians!' he said. 'Old Smoke's lodges, I b'lieve. Come; let us go! Wah! get up, now, "Five Hundred Dollar." ' And laying on the lash with good will, he galloped forward, and I rode by his side. Not long after, a black speck became visible on the prairie full two miles off. It grew larger and larger; it assumed the form of a man and horse; and soon we could discern a naked Indian, careering at full gallop towards us. When within a furlong he wheeled his horse in a wide circle, and made him describe various mystic figures upon the prairie; Henry immediately compelled 'Five Hundred Dollar' to execute similar evolutions. 'It *is* Old Smoke's village,' said he, interpreting these signals; 'did n't I say so?'

As the Indian approached we stopped to wait for him, when suddenly he vanished, sinking, as it were, into the earth. He had come upon one of the deep ravines that everywhere intersect these prairies. In an instant the rough head of his horse stretched upward from the edge, and rider and steed came scrambling out, and bounded up to us; a sudden jerk of the rein brought the wild, panting horse to a full stop. Then followed the needful formality of shaking hands. I forget our visitor's name. He was a young fellow, of no note in his nation; yet in his person and equipments he was a good specimen of a Dakota warrior in his ordinary travelling dress. Like most of his people he was nearly six feet high; lithely and gracefully, yet strongly proportioned; and with a skin singularly clear and delicate. He wore no paint; his head was bare; and his long hair was gathered in a clump behind, to the top of which was attached transversely, both by way of ornament and of talisman, the mystic whistle, made of the wing-bone of the war-eagle, and endowed with various magic virtues. From the back of his head descended a line of glittering brass plates, tapering from the size of a doubloon to that of a half-dime, a cumbrous ornament, in high vogue among the Dakota, and for which they pay the traders a most extravagant price. His chest and arms were naked; the buffalo-robe, worn over them when at rest, had fallen about his waist, and was confined there by a belt. This, with the gay moccasins on his feet, completed his attire. For arms he carried a quiver of dog-skin at his back, and a rude but powerful bow in his hand. His horse had no bridle; a cord of hair, lashed around his jaw, served in place of one. The saddle was made of wood covered with raw hide, and both pommel and cantle rose perpendicularly full eighteen inches, so that the warrior was wedged firmly in his seat, whence nothing could dislodge him but the bursting of the girths.

Advancing with our new companion, we found more of his people, seated in a circle on the top of a hill; while a rude procession came straggling down the neighboring hollow, men, women and children, with horses dragging the lodge-poles behind them. All that morning, as we moved forward, tall savages were stalking silently about us. At noon we reached Horse Creek. The main body of the Indians had arrived before us. On the farther bank stood a large and strong man, nearly naked, holding a white horse by a long cord, and eying us as we approached. This was the chief, whom Henry called 'Old Smoke.' Just behind him, his youngest and favorite squaw sat astride a fine mule, covered with caparisons of whitened skins, garnished with blue and white beads, and fringed with little ornaments of metal that tinkled with every movement of the animal. The girl had a light clear complexion, enlivened by a spot of vermilion on each cheek; she smiled, not to say grinned, upon us, showing two gleaming rows of white teeth. In her hand she carried the tall lance of her unchivalrous lord, fluttering with feathers; his round white shield hung at the side of her mule; and his pipe was slung at her back. Her dress was a tunic of deer-skin, made beautifully white by means of a species of clay found on the prairie, ornamented with beads, arranged in figures more gay than tasteful, and with long fringes at all the seams. Not far from the chief stood a group of stately figures, their white buffalo-robes thrown over their shoulders, gazing coldly upon us; and in the rear for several acres, the ground was covered with a temporary encampment. Warriors, women, and children swarmed like bees; hundreds of dogs, of all sizes and colors, ran restlessly about; and, close at hand, the wide shallow stream was alive with boys, girls, and squaws, splashing, screaming, and laughing in the water. At the same time a long train of emigrants with their heavy wagons was crossing the creek, and dragging on in slow procession by the encampment of the people whom they and their descendants, in the space of a century, are to sweep from the face of the earth.

The encampment itself was merely a temporary bivouac during the heat of the day. None of the lodges were pitched; but their heavy leather coverings, and the long poles used to support them, were scattered everywhere, among weapons, domestic utensils, and the rude harness of mules and horses. The squaws of each lazy warrior had made him a shelter from the sun, by stretching a few buffalo-robes, or the corner of a lodge-covering, upon poles; and here he sat in the shade, with a favorite young squaw, perhaps, at his side, glittering with all imaginable trinkets. Before him stood the insignia of his rank as a warrior, his white shield of bull-hide, his medicine-bag, his bow and quiver, his lance and his pipe, raised aloft on a tripod of poles. Except the dogs, the most active and noisy tenants of the camp were the old women, ugly as Macbeth's witches, with hair streaming loose in the wind, and nothing but the tattered fragments of an old buffalo-robe to hide their shrivelled limbs. The day of their favoritism passed two generations ago; now, the heaviest labors of the camp devolved upon them; they must harness the horses, pitch the lodges, dress the buffalo-robes, and bring in meat for the hunters. With the cracked voices of these hags, the clamor of dogs, the shouting and laughing of children and girls, and the listless tranquillity of the warriors, the whole scene had an effect too lively and picturesque to be forgotten.

We stopped not far from the Indian camp, and having invited some of the chiefs and warriors to dinner, placed before them a repast of biscuit and coffee. Squatted in a half-circle on the ground, they soon disposed of it. As we rode forward on the afternoon journey, several of our late guests accompanied us. Among the rest was a bloated savage, of more than three hundred pounds' weight, christened, *le Cochon* in consideration of his preposterous dimensions, and certain corresponding traits of his character. 'The Hog' bestrode a little white pony, scarcely able to bear up under the enormous burden, though, by way of keeping up the necessary stimulus, the rider kept both feet in constant motion, playing alternately against his ribs. The old man was not a chief; he never had ambition enough to become one; he was not a warrior nor a hunter, for he was too fat and lazy; but he was the richest man in the village. Riches among the Dakota consist in horses, and of these 'The Hog' had accumulated more than thirty. He had already ten times as many as he wanted, yet still his appetite for horses was insatiable. Trotting up to me, he shook me by the hand and gave me to understand that he was my devoted friend; then he began a series of signs and gesticulation, his oily countenance radiant with smiles, and his little eyes peeping out with a cunning twinkle from between the masses of flesh that almost obscured them. Knowing nothing at that time of the sign-

language of the Indians, I could only guess at his meaning. So I
called on Henry to explain it.

'The Hog,' it seems, was anxious to conclude a matrimonial
bargain, and barter one of his daughters for my horse. These
overtures I chose to reject; at which 'The Hog,' still laughing with
undiminished good humor, gathered his robe about his shoulders,
and rode away.

Where we encamped that night, an arm of the Platte ran
between high bluffs; it was turbid and swift as heretofore, but
trees were growing on its crumbling banks, and there was a nook
of grass between the water and the hill. Just before entering
this place, we saw the emigrants encamping two or three miles
distant on the right; while the whole Indian rabble were pouring
down the neighboring hill in hope of the same sort of entertainment which they had experienced from us. In the savage landscape before our camp, nothing but the rushing of the Platte
broke the silence. Through the ragged boughs of the trees, dilapidated and half dead, we saw the sun setting in crimson behind the
peaks of the Black Hills; the restless bosom of the river was suf-
fused with red; our white tent was tinged with it, and the sterile
bluffs, up to the rocks that crowned them, partook of the same
fiery hue. It soon passed away; no light remained but that from
our fire, blazing high among the dusky trees and bushes, while we
lay around it wrapped in our blankets, smoking and conversing
through half the night.

We crossed a sun-scorched plain on the next morning; the line
of old cotton-wood trees that fringed the bank of the Platte
forming its extreme verge. Nestled close beneath them, we could
discern in the distance something like a building. As we came
nearer, it assumed form and dimensions, and proved to be a rough
structure of logs. It was a little trading fort, belonging to two
private traders; and originally intended, like all the forts of the
country, to form a hollow square, with rooms for lodging and
storage opening upon the area within. Only two sides of it had
been completed; the place was now as ill-fitted for the purposes
of defence as any of those little log-houses which upon our constantly shifting frontier have been so often successfully held
against overwhelming odds of Indians. Two lodges were pitched
close to the fort; the sun beat scorching upon the logs; no living
thing was stirring except one old squaw, who thrust her round
head from the opening of the nearest lodge, and three or four stout

young puppies, who were peeping with looks of eager inquiry from
under the covering. In a moment a door opened, and a little,
swarthy, black-eyed Frenchman came out. His dress was rather
singular; his black curling hair was parted in the middle of his head,
and fell below his shoulders; he wore a tight frock of smoked deer-
skin, gayly ornamented with figures worked in dyed porcupine-
quills. His moccasins and leggings were also gaudily adorned
in the same manner; and the latter had in addition a line of long
fringes, reaching down the seams. The small frame of Richard, for
by this name Henry made him known to us, was in the highest
degree athletic and vigorous. There was no superfluity, and indeed
there seldom is among the white men of this country, but every
limb was compact and hard; every sinew had its full tone and
elasticity, and the whole man wore an air of mingled hardihood
and buoyancy.

Richard committed our horses to a Navaho slave, a mean-
looking fellow, taken prisoner on the Mexican frontier; and,
relieving us of our rifles with ready politeness, led the way into
the principal apartment of his establishment. This was a room ten
feet square. The walls and floor were of black mud, and the roof
of rough timber; there was a huge fireplace made of four flat rocks,
picked up on the prairie. An Indian bow and otter-skin quiver,
several gaudy articles of Rocky Mountain finery, an Indian
medicine-bag, and a pipe and tobacco-pouch garnished the walls,
and rifles rested in a corner. There was no furniture except a sort
of rough settle, covered with buffalo-robes, upon which lolled a
tall half-breed with his hair glued in masses upon each temple,
and saturated with vermilion. Two or three more 'mountain
men' sat cross-legged on the floor. Their attire was not unlike
that of Richard himself; but the most striking figure of the group
was a naked Indian boy of sixteen, with a handsome face, and
light, active proportions, who sat in an easy posture in the corner
near the door. Not one of his limbs moved the breadth of a hair;
his eye was fixed immovably, not on any person present, but, as it
appeared, on the projecting corner of the fireplace opposite to
him.

On the prairie the custom of smoking with friends is seldom
omitted whether among Indians or whites. The pipe, therefore,
was taken from the wall, and its red bowl crammed with the
tobacco and *shongsasha*, mixed in suitable proportions. Then it
passed round the circle, each man inhaling a few whiffs and

handing it to his neighbor. Having spent half an hour here we took our leave; first inviting our new friends to drink a cup of coffee with us at our camp a mile farther up the river.

By this time we had grown rather shabby; our clothes had burst into rags and tatters; and, what was worse, we had little means of renovation. Fort Laramie was but seven miles before us. Being averse to appearing in such a plight among any society that could boast an approximation to the civilized, we stopped by the river to make our toilet in the best way we could. We hung up small looking-glasses against the trees and shaved, an operation neglected for six weeks; we performed our ablutions in the Platte, though the utility of such a proceeding was questionable, the water looking exactly like a cup of chocolate, and the banks consisting of the softest and richest yellow mud, so that we were obliged, as a preliminary, to build a causeway of branches and twigs. Having also put on radiant moccasins, procured from a squaw of Richard's establishment, and made what other improvements our narrow circumstances allowed, we took our seats on the grass with a feeling of greatly increased respectability, to await the arrival of our guests. They came; the banquet was concluded, and the pipe smoked. Bidding them adieu, we turned our horses' heads towards the fort.

An hour elapsed. The barren hills closed across our front, and we could see no farther; until, having surmounted them, a rapid stream appeared at the foot of the descent, running into the Platte; beyond was a green meadow, dotted with bushes, and in the midst of these, at the point where the two rivers joined, were the low clay walls of a fort. This was not Fort Laramie, but another post, of less recent date, which having sunk before its successful competitor, was now deserted and ruinous. A moment after, the hills seeming to draw apart as we advanced, disclosed Fort Laramie itself, its high bastions and perpendicular walls of clay crowning an eminence on the left beyond the stream, while behind stretched a line of arid and desolate ridges, and behind these again, towering seven thousand feet aloft, rose the grim Black Hills.

We tried to ford Laramie Creek at a point nearly opposite the fort, but the stream, swollen with rains, was too rapid. We passed up along its bank to find a better crossing-place. Men gathered on the wall to look at us. 'There's Bordeaux!' called Henry, his face brightening as he recognized his acquaintance;

'him there with the spy-glass; and there's old Vaskiss, and Tucker, and May; and, by George! there's Simoneau.' This Simoneau was Henry's fast friend, and the only man in the country who could rival him in hunting.

We soon found a ford. Henry led the way, the pony approaching the bank with a countenance of cool indifference, bracing his feet and sliding into the stream with the most unmoved composure. We followed; the water boiled against our saddles, but our horses bore us easily through. The unfortunate little mules were near going down with the current, cart and all; and we watched them with some solicitude scrambling over the loose round stones at the bottom, and bracing stoutly against the stream. All landed safely at last; we crossed a little plain, descended a hollow, and riding up a steep bank, found ourselves before the gateway of Fort Laramie, under the impending block-house erected above it to defend the entrance.

9. Scenes at Fort Laramie

Looking back, after the expiration of a year, upon Fort Laramie and its inmates, they seem less like a reality than like some fanciful picture of the olden time; so different was the scene from any which this tamer side of the world can present. Tall Indians, enveloped in their white buffalo-robes, were striding across the area or reclining at full length on the low roofs of the buildings which enclosed it. Numerous squaws, gayly bedizened, sat grouped in front of the rooms they occupied; their mongrel offspring, restless and vociferous, rambled in every direction through the fort; and the trappers, traders, and *engagés* of the establishment were busy at their labor or their amusements.

We were met at the gate, but by no means cordially welcomed. Indeed we seemed objects of some distrust and suspicion, until

Henry Chatillon explained that we were not traders, and we, in confirmation, handed to the *bourgeois* a letter of introduction from his principals. He took it, turned it upside down, and tried hard to read it; but his literary attainments not being adequate to the task, he applied for relief to the clerk, a sleek, smiling Frenchman, named Monthalon. The letter read, Bordeaux (the *bourgeois*) seemed gradually to awaken to a sense of what was expected of him. Though not deficient in hospitable intentions, he was wholly unaccustomed to act as master of ceremonies. Discarding all formalities of reception, he did not honor us with a single word, but walked swiftly across the area, while we followed in some admiration to a railing and a flight of steps opposite the entrance. He signed to us that we had better fasten our horses to the railing; then he walked up the steps, tramped along a rude balcony, and, kicking open a door, displayed a large room, rather more elaborately furnished than a barn. For furniture it had a rough bedstead, but no bed, two chairs, a chest of drawers, a tin pail to hold water, and a board to cut tobacco upon. A brass crucifix hung on the wall, and close at hand a recent scalp, with hair full a yard long, was suspended from a nail. I shall again have occasion to mention this dismal trophy, its history being connected with that of our subsequent proceedings.

This apartment, the best in Fort Laramie, was that usually occupied by the legitimate *bourgeois*, Papin, in whose absence the command devolved upon Bordeaux. The latter, a stout, bluff little fellow, much inflated by a sense of his new authority, began to roar for buffalo-robes. These being brought and spread upon the floor formed our beds,—much better ones than we had of late been accustomed to. Our arrangements made, we stepped out to the balcony to take a more leisurely survey of the long looked-for haven at which we had arrived at last. Beneath us was the square area surrounded by little rooms, or rather cells, which opened upon it. These were devoted to various purposes, but served chiefly for the accommodation of the men employed at the fort, or of the equally numerous squaws whom they were allowed to maintain in it. Opposite to us rose the block-house above the gateway; it was adorned with the figure of a horse at full speed, daubed upon the boards with red paint, and exhibiting a degree of skill which might rival that displayed by the Indians in executing similar designs upon their robes and lodges. A busy scene was enacting in the area. The wagons of Vaskiss, an old trader, were about to set out for a remote post in the mountains, and the Canadians were going through their preparations with all possible bustle, while here and there an Indian stood looking on with imperturbable gravity.

Fort Laramie is one of the posts established by the 'American Fur Company,' which well-nigh monopolizes the Indian trade of this region. Here its officials rule with an absolute sway; the arm of the United States has little force; for when we were there, the extreme outposts of her troops were about seven hundred miles to the eastward. The little fort is built of bricks dried in the sun, and externally is of an oblong form, with bastions of clay, in the form of ordinary block-houses, at two of the corners. The walls are about fifteen feet high, and surmounted by a slender palisade. The roofs of the apartments within, which are built close against the walls, serve the purpose of a banquette. Within, the fort is divided by a partition: on one side is the square area, surrounded by the store-rooms, offices, and apartments of the inmates; on the other is the *corral*, a narrow place, encompassed by the high clay walls, where at night, or in presence of dangerous Indians, the horses and mules of the fort are crowded for safe keeping. The main entrance has two gates, with an arched passage intervening. A little square window, high above the ground, opens laterally from an adjoining chamber into this passage; so that when the inner gate is closed and barred, a person without may still hold communication with those within, through this narrow aperture. This obviates the necessity of admitting suspicious Indians, for purposes of trading, into the body of the fort; for when danger is apprehended, the inner gate is shut fast, and all traffic is carried on by means of the window. This precaution, though necessary at some of the Company's posts, is seldom resorted to at Fort Laramie; where, though men are frequently killed in the neighborhood, no apprehensions are felt of any general designs of hostility from the Indians.

We did not long enjoy our new quarters undisturbed. The door was silently pushed open, and two eyeballs and a visage as black as night looked in upon us; then a red arm and shoulder intruded themselves, and a tall Indian, gliding in, shook us by the hand, grunted his salutation, and sat down on the floor. Others followed, with faces of the natural hue, and letting fall their heavy robes from their shoulders, took their seats, quite at ease, in a semi-circle before us. The pipe was now to be lighted and passed from one to another; and this was the only entertainment that at present they expected from us. These visitors were fathers, brothers, or other relatives of the squaws in the fort, where they were permitted to remain, loitering about in perfect idleness. All those who smoked with us were men of standing and repute. Two or three others dropped in also; young fellows who neither by their years nor their exploits were entitled to rank with the old men and warriors, and who, abashed in the presence of their superiors, stood aloof, never withdrawing their eyes from us. Their cheeks were adorned with vermilion, their ears with pendants of shell, and their necks with beads. Never yet having signalized themselves as hunters, or performed the honorable exploit of killing a man, they were held in slight esteem, and were diffident and bashful in proportion. Certain formidable inconveniences attended this influx of visitors. They were bent on inspecting everything in the room; our equipments and our dress alike underwent their scrutiny, for though the contrary has been asserted, few beings have more curiosity than Indians in regard to subjects within their ordinary range of thought. As to other matters, indeed, they seem utterly indifferent. They will not trouble themselves to inquire into what they cannot comprehend, but are quite contented to place their hands over their mouths in token of wonder, and exclaim that it is 'great medicine.' With this comprehensive solution, an Indian never is at a loss. He never launches into speculation and conjecture; his reason moves in its beaten track. His soul is dormant; and no exertions of the missionaries, Jesuit or Puritan, of the old world or of the new, have as yet availed to arouse it.

As we were looking, at sunset, from the wall, upon the desolate plains that surround the fort, we observed a cluster of strange objects like scaffolds, rising in the distance against the red western sky. They bore aloft some singular-looking burdens; and at their foot glimmered something white, like bones. This was the place of sepulture of some Dakota chiefs, whose remains their people are fond of placing in the vicinity of the fort, in the hope that they may thus be protected from violation at the hands of their enemies. Yet it has happened more than once, and quite recently, that war parties of the Crow Indians, ranging through the country, have thrown the bodies from the scaffolds, and broken them to pieces, amid the yells of the Dakota, who remained pent up in the fort, too few to defend the honored relics from insult. The white objects upon the ground were buffalo skulls, arranged in the mystic circle commonly seen at Indian places of sepulture upon the prairie.

We soon discovered, in the twilight, a band of fifty or sixty horses approaching the fort. These were the animals belonging to the establishment; who, having been sent out to feed, under the care of armed guards, in the meadows below, were now being driven into the *corral* for the night. A gate opened into this in-closure; by the side of it stood one of the guards, an old Canadian, with gray bushy eyebrows, and a dragoon pistol stuck into his belt; while his comrade, mounted on horseback, his rifle laid across the saddle in front, and his long hair blowing before his swarthy face, rode at the rear of the disorderly troop, urging them up the ascent. In a moment the narrow *corral* was thronged with the half-wild horses, kicking, biting, and crowding restlessly together.

The discordant jingling of a bell, rung by a Canadian in the area, summoned us to supper. The repast was served on a rough table in one of the lower apartments of the fort, and consisted of cakes of bread and dried buffalo meat, an excellent thing for strengthening the teeth. At this meal were seated the *bourgeois* and superior dignitaries of the establishment, among whom Henry Chatillon was worthily included. No sooner was it finished than the table was spread a second time (the luxury of bread being now, however, omitted), for the benefit of certain hunters and trappers of an inferior standing; while the ordinary Canadian *engagés* were regaled on dried meat in one of their lodging rooms. By way of illustrating the domestic economy of Fort Laramie, it may not be amiss to introduce in this place a story current among the men when we were there.

There was an old man named Pierre, whose duty it was to bring the meat from the store-room for the men. Old Pierre, in the kind-ness of his heart, used to select the fattest and the best pieces for his companions. This did not long escape the keen-eyed *bourgeois*, who was greatly disturbed at such improvidence, and cast about for some means to stop it. At last he hit on a plan that exactly suited him. At the side of the meat-room, and separated from it by a clay partition, was another apartment, used for the storage of furs. It had no communication with the fort, except through a square hole in the partition; and of course it was perfectly dark. One evening the *bourgeois*, watching for a moment when no one observed him, dodged into the meat-room, clambered through the hole, and ensconced himself among the furs and buffalo-robes. Soon after, old Pierre came in with his lantern, and muttering to himself, began to pull over the bales of meat and select the best pieces, as usual. But suddenly a hollow and sepulchral voice proceeded from the inner room: 'Pierre, Pierre! Let that fat meat alone. Take nothing but lean.' Pierre dropped his lantern, and bolted out into the fort, screaming, in an agony of terror, that the devil was in the store-room; but tripping on the threshold, he pitched over the gravel, and lay senseless, stunned by the fall. The Canadians ran out to the rescue. Some lifted the unlucky Pierre; and others, making an extempore crucifix of two sticks, were proceeding to attack the devil in his stronghold, when the *bourgeois*, with a crestfallen countenance, appeared at the door. To add to his mortification, he was obliged to explain the whole stratagem to Pierre, in order to bring him to his senses.

We were sitting, on the following morning, in the passage-way between the gates, conversing with the traders Vaskiss and May. These two men, together with our sleek friend, the clerk Monthalon, were, I believe, the only persons then in the fort who could read and write. May was telling a curious story about the traveller Catlin, when an ugly, diminutive Indian, wretchedly mounted, came up at a gallop, and rode by us into the fort. On being questioned, he said that Smoke's village was close at hand. Accordingly only a few minutes elapsed before the hills beyond the river were covered with a disorderly swarm of savages, on horseback and on foot. May finished his story; and by that time the whole array had descended to Laramie Creek, and begun to cross it in a mass. I walked down to the bank. The stream is wide, and was then between three and four feet deep, with a swift current. For several rods the water was alive with dogs, horses, and Indians. The long poles used in pitching the lodges are carried by the horses, fastened by the heavier end, two or three on each side, to a rude sort of pack-saddle, while the other end drags on the ground. About a foot behind the horse, a kind of large basket or pannier is suspended between the poles, and firmly lashed in its place. On the back of the horse are piled various articles of luggage; the basket also is well filled with domestic utensils, or, quite as often, with a litter of puppies, a brood of small children, or a superannuated old man. Numbers of these curious vehicles, *traineaux*, or, as the Canadians called them, *travois*, were now splashing together through the stream. Among them swam countless dogs, often burdened with miniature *traineaux*; and dashing forward on horseback through the throng came the warriors, the slender figure of some lynx-eyed boy clinging fast behind them. The women sat perched on the pack-saddles, adding not a little to the load of the already over-burdened horses. The confusion was prodigious. The dogs yelled and howled in chorus; the puppies in the *travois* set up a dismal whine as the water invaded their comfortable retreat; the little black-eyed children, from one year of age upward, clung fast with both hands to the edge of their basket, and looked over in alarm at the water rushing so near them, sputtering and making wry mouths as it splashed against their faces. Some of the dogs, encumbered by their load, were carried down by the current, yelping piteously; and the old squaws would rush into the water, seize their favorites by the neck, and drag them out. As each horse gained the bank, he scrambled up as he could. Stray horses and colts came among the rest, often breaking away at full speed through the crowd, followed by the old hags, screaming after their fashion on all occasions of excitement. Buxom young squaws, blooming in all the charms of vermilion, stood here and there on the bank, holding aloft their master's lance, as a signal to collect the scattered portions of his household. In a few moments the crowd melted away; each family with its horses and equipage, filing off to the plain at the rear of the fort; and here, in the space of half an hour, arose sixty or seventy of their tapering lodges. Their horses were feeding by hundreds over the surrounding prairie, and their dogs were roaming everywhere. The fort was full of warriors, and the children were whooping and yelling incessantly under the walls.

These new-comers were scarcely arrived, when Bordeaux ran across the fort, shouting to his squaw to bring him his spy-glass. The obedient Marie, the very model of a squaw, produced the instrument, and Bordeaux hurried with it to the wall. Pointing it eastward, he exclaimed, with an oath, that the families were coming. But a few moments elapsed before the heavy caravan of the emigrant wagons could be seen, steadily advancing from the hills. They gained the river, and, without turning or pausing, plunged in, passed through, and slowly ascending the opposing bank, kept directly on their way by the fort and the Indian village, until, gaining a spot a quarter of a mile distant, they wheeled into a circle. For some time our tranquillity was undisturbed. The emigrants were preparing their encampment; but no sooner was this accomplished than Fort Laramie was taken by storm. A crowd of broad-brimmed hats, thin visages, and staring eyes, appeared suddenly at the gate. Tall, awkward men, in brown homespun, women, with cadaverous faces and long lank figures, came thronging in together, and, as if inspired by the very demon of curiosity, ransacked every nook and corner of the fort. Dismayed at this invasion we withdrew in all speed to our chamber, vainly hoping that it might prove a sanctuary. The emigrants prosecuted their investigations with untiring vigor. They penetrated the rooms, or rather dens, inhabited by the astonished squaws. Resolved to search every mystery to the bottom, they explored the apartments of the men, and even that of Marie and the *bourgeois*. At last a numerous deputation appeared at our door, but found no encouragement to remain.

Having at length satisfied their curiosity, they next proceeded to business. The men occupied themselves in procuring supplies for their onward journey,—either buying them, or giving in exchange superfluous articles of their own.

The emigrants felt a violent prejudice against the French Indians, as they called the trappers and traders. They thought, and with some reason, that these men bore them no good-will. Many of them were firmly persuaded that the French were instigating the Indians to attack and cut them off. On visiting the encampment we were at once struck with the extraordinary perplexity and indecision that prevailed among them. They seemed like men totally out of their element,—bewildered and amazed, like a troop of schoolboys lost in the woods. It was impossible to be long among them without being conscious of the bold spirit with which most of them were animated. But the *forest* is the home of the backwoodsman. On the remote prairie he is totally at a loss. He differs as much from the genuine 'mountain-man' as a Canadian voyageur, paddling his canoe on the rapids of the Ottawa, differs from an American sailor among the storms of Cape Horn. Still my companion and I were somewhat at a loss to account for this perturbed state of mind. It could not be cowardice; these men were of the same stock with the volunteers of Monterey and Buena Vista. Yet, for the most part, they were the rudest and most ignorant of the frontier population; they knew absolutely nothing of the country and its inhabitants; they had already experienced much misfortune, and apprehended more; they had

seen nothing of mankind, and had never put their own resources to the test.

A full share of suspicion fell upon us. Being strangers, we were
looked upon as enemies. Having occasion for a supply of lead and
a few other necessary articles, we used to go over to the emigrant
camps to obtain them. After some hesitation, some dubious
glances, and fumbling of the hands in the pockets, the terms
would be agreed upon, the price tendered, and the emigrant would
go off to bring the article in question. After waiting until our
patience gave out, we would go in search of him, and find him
seated on the tongue of his wagon.

'Well, stranger,' he would observe, as he saw us approach, 'I
reckon I won't trade.'

Some friend of his had followed him from the scene of the
bargain, and whispered in his ear that clearly we meant to cheat
him, and he had better have nothing to do with us.

This timorous mood of the emigrants was doubly unfortunate,
as it exposed them to real danger. Assume, in the presence of
Indians, a bold bearing, self-confident yet vigilant, and you will
find them tolerably safe neighbors. But your safety depends on the
respect and fear you are able to inspire. If you betray timidity or
indecision, you convert them from that moment into insidious and
dangerous enemies. The Dakota saw clearly enough the perturba-
tion of the emigrants, and instantly availed themselves of it. They
became extremely insolent and exacting in their demands. It has
become an established custom with them to go to the camp of
every party, as it arrives in succession at the fort, and demand a
feast. Smoke's village had come with this express design, having
made several days' journey with no other object than that of
enjoying a cup of coffee and two or three biscuit. So the 'feast' was
demanded, and the emigrants dared not refuse it.

One evening about sunset the village was deserted. We met
old men, warriors, squaws, and children in gay attire, trooping off
to the encampment with faces of anticipation; and, arriving here,
they seated themselves in a semi-circle. Smoke occupied the
centre, with his warriors on either hand; the young men and boys
came next, and the squaws and children formed the horns of the
crescent. The biscuit and coffee were promptly despatched, the
emigrants staring open-mouthed at their savage guests. With
each emigrant party that arrived at Fort Laramie this scene was
renewed; and every day the Indians grew more rapacious and

presumptuous. One evening they broke in pieces, out of mere
wantonness, the cups from which they had been feasted; and this
so exasperated the emigrants that many of them seized their
rifles and could scarcely be restrained from firing on the insolent
mob of Indians. Before we left the country this dangerous spirit
on the part of the Dakota had mounted to a yet higher pitch.
They began openly to threaten the emigrants with destruction, and actually fired upon one or two parties of them. A military
force and military law are urgently called for in that perilous
region; and unless troops are speedily stationed at Fort Laramie,
or elsewhere in the neighborhood, both emigrants and other
travellers will be exposed to most imminent risks.

The Ogillallah, the Brulé, and the other western bands of the
Dakota or Sioux, are thorough savages, unchanged by any
contact with civilization. Not one of them can speak a European
tongue, or has ever visited an American settlement. Until within
a year or two, when the emigrants began to pass through their
country on the way to Oregon, they had seen no whites, except the
few employed about the Fur Company's posts. They thought them
a wise people, inferior only to themselves, living in leather lodges,
like their own, and subsisting on buffalo. But when the swarm of
Meneaska, with their oxen and wagons, began to invade them,
their astonishment was unbounded. They could scarcely believe
that the earth contained such a multitude of white men. Their
wonder is now giving way to indignation; and the result, unless
vigilantly guarded against, may be lamentable in the extreme.

But to glance at the interior of a lodge. Shaw and I used often
to visit them. Indeed we spent most of our evenings in the Indian
village, Shaw's assumption of the medical character giving us a
fair pretext. As a sample of the rest I will describe one of these
visits. The sun had just set, and the horses were driven into the
corral. The Prairie Cock, a noted beau, came in at the gate with
a bevy of young girls, with whom he began a dance in the area,
leading them round and round in a circle, while he jerked up
from his chest a succession of monotonous sounds, to which
they kept time in a rueful chant. Outside the gate boys and young
men were idly frolicking; and close by, looking grimly upon them,
stood a warrior in his robe, with his face painted jet-black, in
token that he had lately taken a Pawnee scalp. Passing these, the
tall dark lodges rose between us and the red western sky. We
repaired at once to the lodge of Old Smoke himself. It was by no

means better than the others; indeed, it was rather shabby; for
in this democratic community the chief never assumes superior
state. Smoke sat cross-legged on a buffalo-robe, and his grunt of
salutation as we entered was unusually cordial, out of respect,
no doubt, to Shaw's medical character. Seated around the lodge
were several squaws, and an abundance of children. The com-
plaint of Shaw's patients was, for the most part, a severe inflammation of the eyes, occasioned by exposure to the sun, a species of
disorder which he treated with some success. He had brought
with him a homoeopathic medicine-chest, and was, I presume, the
first who introduced that harmless system of treatment among the
Ogillallah. No sooner had a robe been spread at the head of the
lodge for our accommodation, and we had seated ourselves upon
it, than a patient made her appearance,—the chief's daughter
herself, who, to do her justice, was the best-looking girl in the
village. Being on excellent terms with the physician, she placed
herself readily under his hands, and submitted with a good grace
to his applications, laughing in his face during the whole process,
for a squaw hardly knows how to smile. This case despatched,
another of a different kind succeeded. A hideous, emaciated
old woman sat in the darkest corner of the lodge, rocking to
and fro with pain, and hiding her eyes from the light by pressing
the palms of both hands against her face. At Smoke's command
she came forward, very unwillingly, and exhibited a pair of
eyes that had nearly disappeared from excess of inflammation.
No sooner had the doctor fastened his grip upon her, than she
set up a dismal moaning, and writhed so in his grasp that he lost
all patience; but being resolved to carry his point, he succeeded
at last in applying his favorite remedies.

'It is strange,' he said when the operation was finished, 'that
I forgot to bring any Spanish flies with me; we must have something here to answer for a counter-irritant.'

So, in the absence of better, he seized upon a red-hot brand
from the fire, and clapped it against the temple of the old squaw,
who set up an unearthly howl, at which the rest of the family
broke into a laugh.

During these medical operations Smoke's eldest squaw entered
the lodge, with a mallet in her hand, the stone head of which,
precisely like those sometimes ploughed up in the fields of New
England, was made fast to the handle by a covering of raw hide.
I had observed some time before a litter of well-grown black

puppies, comfortably nestled among some buffalo-robes at one side; but this new-comer speedily disturbed their enjoyment; for seizing one of them by the hind paw, she dragged him out and carrying him to the entrance of the lodge, hammered him on the head till she killed him. Aware to what this preparation tended, I looked through a hole in the back of the lodge to see the next steps of the process. The squaw, holding the puppy by the legs, was swinging him to and fro through the blaze of a fire, until the hair was singed off. This done, she unsheathed her knife and cut him into small pieces, which she dropped into a kettle to boil. In a few moments a large wooden dish was set before us filled with this delicate preparation. A dog-feast is the greatest compliment a Dakota can offer to his guest; and, knowing that to refuse eating would be an affront, we attacked the little dog, and devoured him before the eyes of his unconscious parent. Smoke in the mean time was preparing his great pipe. It was lighted when we had finished our repast, and we passed it from one to another till the bowl was empty. This done, we took our leave without further ceremony, knocked at the gate of the fort, and after making ourselves known, were admitted.

10. The War Parties

The summer of 1846 was a season of warlike excitement among all
the western bands of the Dakota. In 1845 they encountered great
reverses. Many war-parties had been sent out; some of them had
been cut off, and others had returned broken and disheartened; so
that the whole nation was in mourning. Among the rest, ten
warriors had gone to the Snake country, led by the son of a
prominent Ogillallah chief, called the Whirlwind. In passing over
Laramie Plains they encountered a superior number of their
enemies, were surrounded, and killed to a man. Having performed
this exploit, the Snakes became alarmed, dreading the resentment
of the Dakota, and they hastened therefore to signify their
wish for peace by sending the scalp of the slain partisan, with

a small parcel of tobacco attached, to his tribesmen and relations. They had employed old Vaskiss, the trader, as their
messenger, and the scalp was the same that hung in our room at
the fort. But the Whirlwind proved inexorable. Though his
character hardly corresponds with his name, he is nevertheless
an Indian, and hates the Snakes with his whole soul. Long before
the scalp arrived he had made his preparations for revenge. He
sent messengers with presents and tobacco to all the Dakota
within three hundred miles, proposing a grand combination to
chastise the Snakes, and naming a place and time of rendezvous.
The plan was readily adopted, and at this moment many villages,
probably embracing in the whole five or six thousand souls,
were slowly creeping over the prairies and tending toward the
common centre at 'La Bonté's camp' on the Platte. Here their
warlike rites were to be celebrated with more than ordinary
solemnity, and a thousand warriors, as it was said, were to set out
for the enemy's country. The characteristic result of this preparation will appear in the sequel.

I was greatly rejoiced to hear of it. I had come into the country
chiefly with a view to observing the Indian character. To accomplish my purpose it was necessary to live in the midst of them, and
become, as it were, one of them. I proposed to join a village, and
make myself an inmate of one of their lodges; and henceforward
this narrative, so far as I am concerned, will be chiefly a record of
the progress of this design, and the unexpected impediments that
opposed it.

We resolved on no account to miss the rendezvous at 'La
Bonté's camp.' Our plan was to leave Deslauriers at the fort, in
charge of our equipage and the better part of our horses, while we
took with us nothing but our weapons and the worst animals we
had. In all probability, jealousies and quarrels would arise among
so many hordes of fierce, impulsive savages, congregated together
under no common head, and many of them strangers from
remote prairies and mountains. We were bound in common
prudence to be cautious how we excited any feeling of cupidity.
This was our plan; but unhappily we were not destined to visit
'La Bonté's camp' in this manner, for one morning a young Indian
came to the fort and brought us evil tidings. The new-comer was
an arrant dandy. His ugly face was painted with vermilion; on his
head fluttered the tail of a prairie-cock (a large species of pheasant,
not found, as I have heard, eastward of the Rocky Mountains);

in his ears were hung pendants of shell, and a flaming red blanket
was wrapped around him. He carried a dragoon-sword in his hand,
solely for display, since the knife, the arrow, and the rifle are the
arbiters of every prairie fight; but as no one in this country goes
abroad unarmed, the dandy carried a bow and arrows in an otter-
skin quiver at his back. In this guise, and bestriding his yellow
horse with an air of extreme dignity, 'The Horse,' for that was his
name, rode in at the gate, turning neither to the right nor the
left, but casting glances askance at the groups of squaws who,
with their mongrel progeny, were sitting in the sun before their
doors. The evil tidings brought by 'The Horse' were of the following import: The squaw of Henry Chatillon, a woman with whom
he had been connected for years by the strongest ties which in
that country exist between the sexes, was dangerously ill. She and
her children were in the village of The Whirlwind, at the distance
of a few days' journey. Henry was anxious to see the woman
before she died, and provide for the safety and support of his
children, of whom he was extremely fond. To have refused him
this would have been inhumanity. We abandoned our plan of
joining Smoke's village and proceeding with it to the rendezvous, and determined to meet The Whirlwind, and go in his
company.

I had been slightly ill for several weeks, but on the third night
after reaching Fort Laramie a violent pain awoke me, and I
found myself attacked by the same disorder that occasioned such
heavy losses to the army on the Rio Grande. In a day and a half
I was reduced to extreme weakness, so that I could not walk without pain and effort. Having no medical adviser, nor any choice of
diet, I resolved to throw myself upon Providence for recovery,
using, without regard to the disorder, any portion of strength
that might remain to me. So on the twentieth of June we set out
from Fort Laramie to meet The Whirlwind's village. Though
aided by the high-bowed 'mountain-saddle,' I could scarcely keep
my seat on horseback. Before we left the fort we hired another
man, a long-haired Canadian, named Raymond, with a face like
an owl's, contrasting oddly enough with Deslauriers's mercurial
countenance. This was not the only reinforcement to our party.
A vagrant Indian trader, named Reynal, joined us, together with
his squaw Margot, and her two nephews, our dandy friend, 'The
Horse,' and his youngest brother, 'The Hail Storm.' Thus accompanied we betook ourselves to the prairie, leaving the beaten

trail, and passing over the desolate hills that flank the valley of
Laramie Creek. In all, Indians and whites, we counted eight men
and one woman.

Reynal, the trader, the image of sleek and selfish complacency,
carried 'The Horse's' dragoon-sword in his hand, delighting apparently in this useless parade; for, from spending half his life
among Indians, he had caught not only their habits but their
ideas. Margot, a female animal of more than two hundred pounds'
weight, was crouched in the basket of a *travois*, such as I have
before described; besides her ponderous bulk, various domestic
utensils were attached to the vehicle, and she led by a trail-rope
a packhorse, which carried the covering of Reynal's lodge. Deslauriers walked briskly by the side of the cart, and Raymond came
behind, swearing at the spare horses which it was his business to
drive. The restless young Indians, their quivers at their backs and
their bows in their hands, galloped over the hills, often starting a
wolf or an antelope from the thick growth of wild-sage bushes.
Shaw and I were in keeping with the rest of the rude cavalcade,
having, in the failure of other clothing, adopted the bucksin
attire of the trappers. Henry Chatillon rode in advance of the
whole. Thus we passed hill after hill and hollow after hollow, a
country arid, broken, and so parched by the sun that none of the
plants familiar to our more favored soil would flourish upon it,
though there were multitudes of strange medicinal herbs, more
especially the wild sage, which covered every declivity, while cacti
were hanging like reptiles at the edges of every ravine. At length
we ascended a high hill, our horses treading upon pebbles of flint,
agate, and rough jasper, until, gaining the top, we looked down on
the wild bottoms of Laramie Creek, which far below us wound like
a writhing snake from side to side of the narrow interval, amid
a growth of shattered cotton-wood and ash trees. Lines of tall
cliffs, white as chalk, shut in this green strip of woods and meadow-
land, into which we descended and encamped for the night. In
the morning we passed a wide grassy plain by the river; there
was a grove in front, and beneath its shadows the ruins of an old
trading fort of logs. The grove bloomed with myriads of wild
roses, with their sweet perfume fraught with recollections of
home. As we emerged from the tress, a rattlesnake, as large as a
man's arm, and more than four feet long, lay coiled on a rock,
fiercely rattling and hissing at us; a gray hare, twice as large as
those of New England, leaped up from the tall ferns; curlew flew

screaming over our heads, and a host of little prairie-dogs sat
yelping at us at the mouths of their burrows on the dry plain
beyond. Suddenly an antelope leaped up from the wild-sage
bushes, gazed eagerly at us, and then, erecting his white tail,
stretched away like a greyhound. The two Indian boys found a
white wolf, as large as a calf, in a hollow, and giving a sharp
yell, they galloped after him; but the wolf leaped into the stream
and swam across. Then came the crack of a rifle, the bullet
whistling harmlessly over his head, as he scrambled up the steep
declivity, rattling down stones and earth into the water below.
Advancing a little, we beheld, on the farther bank of the stream,
a spectacle not common even in that region; for, emerging from
among the trees, a herd of some two hundred elk came out upon
the meadow, their antlers clattering as they walked forward in a
dense throng. Seeing us, they broke into a run, rushing across the
opening and disappearing among the trees and scattered groves.
On our left was a barren prairie, stretching to the horizon; on our
right, a deep gulf, with Laramie Creek at the bottom. We found
ourselves at length at the edge of a steep descent,—a narrow valley,
with long rank grass and scattered trees, stretching before us for a
mile or more along the course of the stream. Reaching the farther
end, we stopped and encamped. A huge old cotton-wood tree
spread its branches horizontally over our tent. Laramie Creek,
circling before our camp, half inclosed us; it swept along the
bottom of a line of tall white cliffs that looked down on us from
the farther bank. There were dense copses on our right; the cliffs,
too, were half hidden by bushes, though behind us a few cotton-
wood trees, dotting the green prairie, alone impeded the view, and
friend or enemy could be discerned in that direction at a mile's
distance. Here we resolved to remain and await the arrival of
The Whirlwind, who would certainly pass this way in his progress
towards La Bonté's camp. To go in search of him was not ex-
pedient, both on account of the broken and impracticable nature
of the country, and the uncertainty of his position and movements;
besides, our horses were almost worn out, and I was in no condition to travel. We had good grass, good water, tolerable fish
from the stream, and plenty of small game, such as antelope and
deer, though no buffalo. There was one little drawback to our
satisfaction,—a certain extensive tract of bushes and dried grass,
just behind us, which it was by no means advisable to enter, since
it sheltered a numerous brood of rattlesnakes. Henry Chatillon

again despatched 'The Horse' to the village, with a message to his squaw that she and her relatives should leave the rest and push on as rapidly as possible to our camp.

Our daily routine soon became as regular as that of a well-ordered household. The weather-beaten old tree was in the centre; our rifles generally rested against its vast trunk, and our saddles were flung on the ground around it; its distorted roots were so twisted as to form one or two convenient arm-chairs, where we could sit in the shade and read or smoke; but meal-times became, on the whole, the most interesting hours of the day and a bountiful provision was made for them. An antelope or a deer usually swung from a bough, and haunches were suspended against the trunk. That camp is daguerrotyped on my memory,—the old tree, the white tent, with Shaw sleeping in the shadow of it, and Reynal's miserable lodge close by the bank of the stream. It was a wretched oven-shaped structure, made of begrimed and tattered buffalo-hides stretched over a frame of poles; one side was open, and at the side of the opening hung the powder-horn and bullet-pouch of the owner, together with his long red pipe, and a rich quiver of otter-skin, with a bow and arrows; for Reynal, an Indian in most things but color, chose to hunt buffalo with these primitive weapons. In the darkness of this cavern-like habitation might be discerned Madame Margot, her overgrown bulk stowed away among her domestic implements, furs, robes, blankets, and painted cases of raw hide, in which dried meat is kept. Here she sat from sunrise to sunset, an impersonation of gluttony and laziness, while her affectionate proprietor was smoking, or begging pretty gifts from us, or telling lies concerning his own achievements, or perchance engaged in the more profitable occupation of cooking some preparation of prairie delicacies. Reynal was an adept at this work; he and Deslauriers have joined forces, and are hard at work together over the fire, while Raymond spreads, by way of table-cloth, a buffalo-hide carefully whitened with pipe-clay, on the grass before the tent. Here he arranges the teacups and plates; and then creeping on all fours, like a dog, thrusts his head in at the opening of the tent. For a moment we see his round, owlish eyes rolling wildly, as if the idea he came to communicate had suddenly escaped him; then collecting his scattered thoughts, as if by an effort, he informs us that supper is ready, and instantly withdraws.

When sunset came, and at that hour the wild and desolate

scene would assume a new aspect, the horses were driven in. They had been grazing all day in the neighboring meadow, but now they were picketed close about the camp. As the prairie darkened we sat and conversed around the fire, until, becoming drowsy, we spread our saddles on the ground, wrapped our blankets around us, and lay down. We never placed a guard, having by this time become too indolent; but Henry Chatillon folded his loaded rifle in the same blanket with himself, observing that he always took it to bed with him when he 'camped in that place. Henry was too bold a man to use such a precaution without good cause. We had a hint now and then that our situation was none of the safest; several Crow war-parties were known to be in the vicinity, and one of them, that passed here some time before, had peeled the bark from a neighboring tree, and engraved upon the white wood certain hieroglyphics to signify that they had invaded the territories of their enemies, the Dakota, and set them at defiance. One morning a thick mist covered the whole country. Shaw and Henry went out to ride, and soon came back with a startling piece of intelligence; they had found within rifle-shot of our camp the recent trail of about thirty horsemen. They could not be whites, and they could not be Dakota, since we knew no such parties to be in the neighborhood; therefore they must be Crows. Thanks to that friendly mist, we had escaped a hard battle; they would inevitably have attacked us and our Indian companions had they seen our camp. Whatever doubts we might have entertained were removed a day or two after by two or three Dakota, who came to us with an account of having hidden in a ravine on that very morning, from whence they saw and counted the Crows; they said that they followed them, carefully keeping out of sight, as they passed up Chugwater; that here the Crows discovered five dead bodies of Dakota, placed according to custom in trees, and flinging them to the ground, held their guns against them and blew them to atoms.

If our camp was not altogether safe, still it was comfortable enough; at least it was so to Shaw, for I was tormented with illness and vexed by the delay in the accomplishment of my designs. When a respite in my disorder gave me some returning strength, I rode out well armed upon the prairie, or bathed with Shaw in the stream, or waged a petty warfare with the inhabitants of a neighboring prairie-dog village. Around our fire at night we employed ourselves in inveighing against the fickleness and inconstancy of

Indians, and execrating The Whirlwind and all his crew. At last the thing grew insufferable.

'To-morrow morning,' said I, 'I will start for the fort, and see if I can hear any news there.' Late that evening, when the fire had sunk low and all the camp were asleep, a loud cry sounded from the darkness. Henry leaped up, recognized the voice, replied to it, and our dandy friend, 'The Horse,' rode in among us, just returned from his mission to the village. He coolly picketed his mare without saying a word, sat down by the fire, and began to eat; but his imperturbable philosophy was too much for our patience. Where was the village?—about fifty miles south of us; it was moving slowly, and would not arrive in less than a week. And where was Henry's squaw?—coming as fast as she could, with Mahto-Tatonka and the rest of her brothers, but she would never reach us, for she was dying, and asking every moment for Henry. Henry's manly face became clouded and downcast; he said that if we were willing he would go in the morning to find her, at which Shaw offered to accompany him.

We saddled our horses at sunrise. Reynal protested vehemently against being left alone, with nobody but the two Canadians and the young Indians, when enemies were in the neighborhood. Disregarding his complaints, we left him, and, coming to the mouth of Chugwater, separated, Shaw and Henry turning to the right, up the bank of the stream, while I made for the fort.

Taking leave for a while of my friend and the unfortunate squaw, I will relate by way of episode what I saw and did at Fort Laramie. It was not more than eighteen miles distant, and I reached it in three hours. A shrivelled little figure, wrapped from head to foot in a dingy white Canadian capote, stood in the gateway, holding by a cord of bull-hide a shaggy wild-horse, which he had lately caught. His sharp prominent features, and his keen, snake-like eyes, looked out from beneath the shadowy hood of the capote, which was drawn over his head like the cowl of a Capuchin friar. His face was like an old piece of leather, and his mouth spread from ear to ear. Extending his long, wiry hand, he welcomed me with something more cordial than the ordinary cold salute of an Indian, for we were excellent friends. We had made an exchange of horses to our mutual advantage; and Paul, thinking himself well treated, had declared everywhere that the white man had a good heart. He was a Dakota from the Missouri, a reputed son of the half-breed interpreter, Pierre Dorion, so often mentioned in

Irving's 'Astoria.' He said that he was going to Richard's trading-house to sell his horse to some emigrants who were encamped there, and asked me to go with him. We forded the stream together, Paul dragging his wild charge behind him. As we passed over the sandy plains beyond, he grew communicative. Paul was a cosmopolitan in his way; he had been to the settlements of the whites, and visited in peace and war most of the tribes within the range of a thousand miles. He spoke a jargon of French and another of English, yet nevertheless he was a thorough Indian; and as he told of the bloody deeds of his own people against their enemies, his little eyes would glitter with a fierce lustre. He told how the Dakota exterminated a village of the Hohays on the Upper Missouri, slaughtering men, women, and children; and how, in overwhelming force, they cut off sixteen of the brave Delawares, who fought like wolves to the last, amid the throng of their enemies. He told me also another story, which I did not believe until I had heard it confirmed from so many independent sources that my skepticism was almost overcome.

Six years ago, a fellow named Jim Beckworth, a mongrel of French, American, and negro blood, was trading for the Fur Company, in a large village of the Crows. Jim Beckworth was last summer at St Louis. He is a ruffian of the worst stamp; bloody and treacherous, without honor or honesty; such at least is the character he bears upon the prairie. Yet in his case the standard rules of character fail, for though he will stab a man in his sleep, he will also perform desperate acts of daring; such, for instance, as the following: While he was in the Crow village, a Blackfoot war-party, between thirty and forty in number, came stealing through the country, killing stragglers and carrying off horses. The Crow warriors got upon their tail and pressed them so closely that they could not escape; at which the Blackfeet, throwing up a semi-circular breastwork of logs at the foot of a precipice, coolly awaited their approach. The logs and sticks, piled four or five feet high, protected them in front. The Crows might have swept over the breastwork and exterminated their enemies; but though outnumbering them tenfold, they did not dream of storming the little fortification. Such a proceeding would be altogether repugnant to their notions of warfare. Whooping and yelling, and jumping from side to side like devils incarnate, they showered bullets and arrows upon the logs; not a Blackfoot was hurt, but several Crows, in spite of their leaping and dodging, were shot down. In this childish manner the fight went on for an hour or two. Now and then a Crow warrior in an ecstasy of valor and vainglory would scream out his war-song, boast himself the bravest and greatest of mankind, grasp his hatchet, rush up, strike it upon the breastwork, and then as he retreated to his companions, fall dead under a shower of arrows; yet no combined attack was made. The Blackfeet remained secure in their intrenchment. At last Jim Beckworth lost patience.

'You are all fools and old women,' he said to the Crows; 'come with me, if any of you are brave enough, and I will show you how to fight.'

He threw off his trapper's frock of buckskin and stripped himself naked, like the Indians themselves. He left his rifle on the ground, took in his hand a small light hatchet, and ran over the prairie to the right, concealed by a hollow from the eyes of the Blackfeet. Then climbing up the rocks, he gained the top of the precipice behind them. Forty or fifty young Crow warriors followed him. By the cries and whoops that rose from below he knew that the Blackfeet were just beneath him; and running forward he leaped down the rock into the midst of them. As he fell he caught one by the long loose hair, and dragging him down tomahawked him; then grasping another by the belt at his waist, he struck him also a stunning blow, and gaining his feet, shouted the Crow war-cry. He swung his hatchet so fiercely around him that the astonished Blackfeet bore back and gave him room. He might, had he chosen, have leaped over the breastwork and escaped; but this was not necessary, for with devilish yells the Crow warriors came dropping in quick succession over the rock among their enemies. The main body of the Crows, too, answered the cry from the front, and rushed up simultaneously. The convulsive struggle within the breastwork was frightful; for an instant the Blackfeet fought and yelled like pent-up tigers; but the butchery was soon complete, and the mangled bodies lay piled together under the precipice. Not a Blackfoot made his escape.

As Paul finished his story we came in sight of Richard's Fort, a disorderly crowd of men around it, and an emigrant camp a little in front.

'Now, Paul,' said I, 'where are your Minneconjou lodges?'

'Not come yet,' said Paul; 'maybe come to-morrow.'

Two large villages of a band of Dakota had come three hundred miles from the Missouri, to join in the war, and they were expected to reach Richard's that morning. There was as yet no sign of their approach; so pushing through a noisy, drunken crowd, I entered an apartment of logs and mud, the largest in the fort; it was full of men of various races and complexions, all more or less drunk. A company of California emigrants, it seemed, had made the discovery at this late day that they had encumbered themselves with too many supplies for their journey. A part, therefore, they had thrown away, or sold at great loss to the traders; but had determined to get rid of their very copious stock of Missouri whiskey, by drinking it on the spot. Here were maudlin squaws stretched on piles of buffalo-robes; squalid Mexicans, armed with bows and arrows; Indians sedately drunk; long-haired Canadians and trappers, and American backwoodsmen in brown homespun, the well-beloved pistol and bowie-knife displayed openly at their sides. In the middle of the room a tall, lank man, with a dingy broadcloth coat, was haranguing the company in the style of the stump orator. With one hand he sawed the air, and with the other clutched firmly a brown whiskey-jug, which he applied every moment to his lips, forgetting that he had drained the contents long ago. Richard formally introduced me to this personage, who was no less a man than Colonel R——, once the leader of the party. Instantly the Colonel, seizing me, in the absence of buttons, by the leather fringes of my frock, began to define his position. His men, he said, had mutinied and deposed him; but still he exercised over them the influence of a superior mind; in all but the name he was yet their chief. As the Colonel spoke I looked round on the wild assemblage, and could not help thinking that he was but ill-fitted to conduct such men across the deserts to California. Conspicuous among the rest stood three tall young men, grandsons of Daniel Boone. They had clearly inherited the adventurous character of that prince of pioneers; but I saw no signs of the quiet and tranquil spirit that so remarkably distinguished him.

Fearful was the fate that, months after, overtook some of the members of that party. General Kearney, on his late return from California, brought back their story. They were interrupted by the deep snows among the mountains, and, maddened by cold and hunger, fed upon each other's flesh!

I got tired of the confusion. 'Come, Paul,' said I, 'we will be off.' Paul sat in the sun, under the wall of the fort. He jumped up, mounted, and we rode towards Fort Laramie. When we reached it, a man came out of the gate with a pack at his back and a rifle on his shoulder; others were gathering about him, shaking him by the hand, as if taking leave. I thought it a strange thing that a man should set out alone and on foot for the prairie. I soon got an explanation. Perrault—this, if I recollect right, was the Canadian's name—had quarrelled with the *bourgeois*, and the fort was too hot to hold him. Bordeaux, inflated with his transient authority, had abused him, and received a blow in return. The men then sprang at each other, and grappled in the middle of the fort. Bordeaux was down in an instant, at the mercy of the incensed Canadian; had not an old Indian, the brother of his squaw, seized hold of his antagonist, it would have fared ill with him. Perrault broke loose from the old Indian, and both the white men ran to their rooms for their guns; but when Bordeaux, looking from his door, saw the Canadian, gun in hand, standing in the area and calling on him to come out and fight, his heart failed him; he chose to remain where he was. In vain the old Indian, scandalized by his brother-in-law's cowardice, called upon him to go to the prairie and fight it out in the white man's manner; and Bordeaux's own squaw, equally incensed, screamed to her lord and master that he was a dog and an old woman. It all availed nothing. Bordeaux's prudence got the better of his valor, and he would not stir. Perrault stood showering opprobrious epithets at the recreant *bourgeois*, till, growing tired of this, he made up a pack of dried meat, and slinging it at his back, set out alone for Fort Pierre, on the Missouri, a distance of three hundred miles, over a desert country, full of hostile Indians.

I remained in the fort that night. In the morning, as I was coming out from breakfast, talking with a trader named McCluskey, I saw a strange Indian leaning against the side of the gate. He was a tall, strong man, with heavy features.

'Who is he?' I asked.

'That's The Whirlwind,' said McCluskey. 'He is the fellow that made all this stir about the war. It's always the way with the Sioux; they never stop cutting each other's throats,—it's all they are fit for,—instead of sitting in their lodges, and getting robes to trade with us in the winter. If this war goes on, we'll make a poor trade of it next season, I reckon.'

And this was the opinion of all the traders, who were vehemently opposed to the war, from the injury that it must occasion to their interests. The Whirlwind left his village the day before to make a visit to the fort. His warlike ardor had abated not a little since

he first conceived the design of avenging his son's death. The long
and complicated preparations for the expedition were too much
for his fickle disposition. That morning Bordeaux fastened upon
him, made him presents, and told him that if he went to war he
would destroy his horses and kill no buffalo to trade with the
white men; in short, that he was a fool to think of such a thing, and
had better make up his mind to sit quietly in his lodge and smoke
his pipe, like a wise man. The Whirlwind's purpose was evidently
shaken; he had become tired, like a child, of his favorite plan.
Bordeaux exultingly predicted that he would not go to war. My
philanthropy was no match for my curiosity, and I was vexed at
the possibility that after all I might lose the rare opportunity of
seeing the ceremonies of war. The Whirlwind, however, had
merely thrown the firebrand; the conflagration was become
general. All the western bands of the Dakota were bent on war;
and, as I heard from McCluskey, six large villages were already
gathered on a little stream, forty miles distant, and were daily
calling to the Great Spirit to aid them in their enterprise. McCluskey had just left them, and represented them as on their way to
La Bonté's camp, which they would reach in a week, *unless they
should learn that there were no buffalo there.* I did not like this
condition, for buffalo this season were rare in the neighborhood.
There were also the two Minneconjou villages that I mentioned
before; but about noon an Indian came from Richard's Fort
with the news that they were quarrelling, breaking up, and dispersing. So much for the whiskey of the emigrants! Finding themselves unable to drink the whole, they had sold the residue to these
Indians, and it needed no prophet to foretell the result; a spark
dropped into a powder-magazine would not have produced a
quicker effect. Instantly the old jealousies and rivalries and
smothered feuds that exist in an Indian village broke out into
furious quarrels. They forgot the warlike enterprise that had
already brought them three hundred miles. They seemed like
ungoverned children inflamed with the fiercest passions of men.
Several of them were stabbed in the drunken tumult; and in the
morning they scattered and moved back towards the Missouri in
small parties. I feared that, after all, the long-projected meeting
and the ceremonies that were to attend it might never take place,
and I should lose so admirable an opportunity of seeing the Indian
under his most fearful and characteristic aspect; however, in
foregoing this, I should avoid a very fair probability of being

plundered and stripped, and it might be, stabbed or shot into the bargain. Consoling myself with this reflection, I prepared to carry the news, such as it was, to the camp.

I caught my horse, and to my vexation found that he had lost a shoe and broken his hoof against the rocks. Horses are shod at Fort Laramie at the moderate rate of three dollars a foot; so I tied Hendrick to a beam in the *corral*, and summoned Roubidou the blacksmith. Roubidou, with the hoof between his knees, was at work with hammer and file, and I was inspecting the process, when a strange voice addressed me.

'Two more gone under! Well, there 's more of us left yet. Here 's Gingras and me off to the mountains to-morrow. Our turn will come next, I suppose. It 's a hard life, anyhow!'

I looked up and saw a man, not much more than five feet high, but of very square and strong proportions. In appearance he was particularly dingy; for his old buckskin frock was black and polished with time and grease, and his belt, knife, pouch, and powder-horn appeared to have seen the roughest service. The first joint of each foot was entirely gone, having been frozen off several winters before, and his moccasins were curtailed in proportion. His whole appearance and equipment bespoke the 'free trapper.' He had a round, ruddy face, animated with a spirit of carelessness and gayety not at all in accordance with the words he had just spoken.

' "Two more gone," ' said I; 'what do you mean by that?'

'Oh, the Arapahoes have just killed two of us in the mountains. Old Bull-Tail has come to tell us. They stabbed one behind his back, and shot the other with his own rifle. That 's the way we live here! I mean to give up trapping after this year. My squaw says she wants a pacing horse and some red ribbons; I 'll make enough beaver to get them for her, and then I 'm done! I 'll go below and live on a farm.'

'Your bones will dry on the prairie, Rouleau!' said another trapper, who was standing by,—a strong, brutal-looking fellow, with a face as surly as a bull-dog's.

Rouleau only laughed, and began to hum a tune, and shuffle a dance on his stumps of feet.

'You 'll see us, before long, passing up your way,' said the other man.

'Well,' said I, 'stop and take a cup of coffee with us;' and, as it was late in the afternoon, I prepared to leave the fort at once.

As I rode out, a train of emigrant wagons was passing across the stream. 'Whar are ye goin', stranger?' Thus I was saluted by two or three voices at once.

'About eighteen miles up the creek.'

'It 's mighty late to be going that far! Make haste, ye 'd better, and keep a bright look-out for Indians!'

I thought the advice too good to be neglected. Fording the stream, I passed at a round trot over the plains beyond. But 'the more haste, the worse speed.' I proved the truth of the proverb by the time I reached the hills three miles from the fort. The trail was faintly marked, and, riding forward with more rapidity than caution, I lost sight of it. I kept on in a direct line, guided by Laramie Creek, which I could see at intervals darkly glistening in the evening sun, at the bottom of the woody gulf on my right. Half an hour before sunset I came upon its banks. There was something exciting in the wild solitude of the place. An antelope sprang suddenly from the sage-bushes before me. As he leaped gracefully not thirty yards before my horse, I fired, and instantly he spun round and fell. Quite sure of him, I walked my horse towards him, leisurely reloading my rifle, when to my surprise he sprang up and trotted rapidly away on three legs into the dark recesses of the hills, whither I had no time to follow. Ten minutes after, I was passing along the bottom of a deep valley, and, chancing to look behind me, I saw in the dim light that something was following. Supposing it to be a wolf, I slid from my seat and sat down behind my horse to shoot it; but as it came up, I saw by its motions that it was another antelope. It approached within a hundred yards, arched its neck, and gazed intently. I levelled at the white spot on its breast, and was about to fire when it started off, ran first to one side and then to the other, like a vessel tacking against the wind, and at last stretched away at full speed. Then it stopped again, looked curiously behind it, and trotted up as before; but not so boldly, for it soon paused and stood gazing at me. I fired; it leaped upward and fell upon its tracks. Measuring the distance, I found it two hundred and four paces. When I stood by his side, the antelope turned his expiring eye upward. It was like a beautiful woman's, dark and bright. 'Fortunate that I am in a hurry,' thought I; 'I might be troubled with remorse if I had time for it.'

Cutting the animal up, not in the most skilful manner, I hung the meat at the back of my saddle, and rode on again. The hills

(I could not remember one of them) closed around me. 'It is too
late,' thought I, 'to go forward. I will stay here to-night, and look
for the path in the morning.' As a last effort, however, I ascended
a high hill, from which, to my great satisfaction, I could see Laramie Creek stretching before me, twisting from side to side amid
ragged patches of timber; and far off, close beneath the shadows
of the trees, the ruins of the old trading-fort were visible. I
reached them at twilight. It was far from pleasant, in that uncertain light, to be pushing through the dense trees and bushes of the
grove beyond. I listened anxiously for the foot-fall of man or beast.
Nothing was stirring but one harmless brown bird, chirping among
the branches. I was glad when I gained the open prairie once
more, where I could see if anything approached. When I came to
the mouth of Chugwater, it was totally dark. Slackening the reins,
I let my horse take his own course. He trotted on with unerring
instinct, and by nine o'clock was scrambling down the steep
descent into the meadows where we were encamped. While I
was looking in vain for the light of the fire, Hendrick, with keener
perceptions, gave a loud neigh, which was immediately answered
by another neigh from the distance. In a moment I was hailed
from the darkness by the voice of Reynal, who had come out,
rifle in hand, to see who was approaching.

He, with his squaw, the two Canadians and the Indian boys,
were the sole inmates of the camp, Shaw and Henry Chatillon
being still absent. At noon of the following day they came back,
their horses looking none the better for the journey. Henry seemed
dejected. The woman was dead, and his children must henceforward be exposed, without a protector, to the hardships and
vicissitudes of Indian life. Even in the midst of his grief he had
not forgotten his attachment to his *bourgeois,* for he had procured
among his Indian relatives two beautifully ornamented buffalo-
robes, which he spread on the ground as a present to us.

Shaw lighted his pipe, and told me in a few words the history of
his journey. When I went to the fort they left me as I mentioned,
at the mouth of Chugwater. They followed the course of the little
stream all day, traversing a desolate and barren country. Several
times they came upon the fresh traces of a large war-party, the
same, no doubt, from whom we had so narrowly escaped an
attack. At an hour before sunset, without encountering a human
being by the way, they came upon the lodges of the squaw and
her brothers, who, in compliance with Henry's message, had left

the Indian village in order to join us at our camp. The lodges were
already pitched, five in number, by the side of the stream. The
woman lay in one of them, reduced to a mere skeleton. For some
time she had been unable to move or speak. Indeed, nothing had
kept her alive but the hope of seeing Henry, to whom she was
strongly and faithfully attached. No sooner did he enter the lodge
than she revived, and she talked with him the greater part of the
night. Early in the morning she was lifted into a *travois*, and the
whole party set out towards our camp. There were but five
warriors; the rest were women and children. They were all in
great alarm at the proximity of the Crow war-party, who would
certainly have killed them without mercy had they met. They
had advanced only a mile or two when they discerned a horseman,
far off, on the edge of the horizon. They all stopped, gathering
together in the greatest anxiety, from which they did not recover
until long after the horseman disappeared; then they set out again.
Henry was riding with Shaw a few rods in advance of the Indians,
when Mahto-Tatonka, a younger brother of the woman, hastily
called after them. Turning back, they found all the Indians
crowded around the *travois* in which the woman was lying. They
reached her just in time to hear the death-rattle in her throat. In
a moment she lay dead in the basket of the vehicle. A complete
stillness succeeded; then the Indians raised in concert their cries
of lamentation over the corpse, and among them Shaw clearly
distinguished those strange sounds resembling the word 'Hallelu-
yah,' which, together with some other accidental coincidences,
has given rise to the absurd notion that the Indians are descended
from the ten lost tribes of Israel.

The Indian usage required that Henry, as well as the other
relatives of the woman, should make valuable presents, to be
placed by the side of the body at its last resting-place. Leaving
the Indians, he and Shaw set out for the camp, and reached it, as
we have seen, by hard pushing, at about noon. Having obtained
the necessary articles, they immediately returned. It was very
late and quite dark when they again reached the lodges. They were
all placed in a deep hollow among dreary hills. Four of them were
just visible through the gloom, but the fifth and largest was illumined by the blaze of a fire within, glowing through the half-
transparent covering of raw hides. There was a perfect stillness as
they approached. The lodges seemed without a tenant. Not a
living thing was stirring; there was something awful in the

scene. They rode up to the entrance of the lodge, and there was no sound but the tramp of their horses. A squaw came out and took charge of the animals, without speaking a word. Entering, they found the lodge crowded with Indians; a fire was burning in the middle, and the mourners encircled it in a triple row. Room was made for the new-comers at the head of the lodge, a robe spread for them to sit upon, and a pipe lighted and handed to them in perfect silence. Thus they passed the greater part of the night. At times the fire would subside into a heap of embers, until the dark figures seated around it were scarcely visible; then a squaw would drop upon it a piece of buffalo-fat, and a bright flame instantly springing up would reveal the crowd of wild faces, motionless as bronze. The silence continued unbroken. It was a relief to Shaw when daylight returned and he could escape from this house of mourning. He and Henry prepared to return homeward; first, however, they placed the presents they had brought near the body of the squaw, which, gaudily attired, remained in a sitting posture in one of the lodges. A fine horse was picketed not far off, destined to be killed that morning for the service of her spirit; for the woman was lame, and could not travel on foot over the dismal prairies to the villages of the dead. Food, too, was provided, and household implements, for her use upon this last journey.

Henry left her to the care of her relatives, and came immediately with Shaw to the camp. It was some time before he entirely recovered from his dejection.

11. Scenes at the Camp

Reynal heard guns fired one day at the distance of a mile or two from the camp. He grew nervous instantly. Visions of Crow war-parties began to haunt his imagination; and when we returned (for we were all absent) he renewed his complaints about being left alone with the Canadians and the squaw. The day after, the cause of the alarm appeared. Four trappers, called Morin, Sara-phin, Rouleau, and Gingras, came to our camp and joined us. They it was who fired the guns, and disturbed the dreams of our confederate Reynal. They soon encamped by our side. Their rifles, dingy and battered with hard service, rested with ours against the old tree; their strong rude saddles, their buffalo-robes, their traps, and a few rough and simple articles of their travel-ling equipment were piled near our tent. Their mountain-horses were turned out to graze in the meadow among our own; and the men themselves, no less rough and hardy, used to lie half the day in the shade of our tree, lolling on the grass, lazily smoking, and telling stories of their adventures; and I defy the annals of chivalry to furnish the record of a life more wild and perilous than that of a Rocky Mountain trapper.

With this efficient reinforcement the agitation of Reynal's nerves subsided. We began to conceive a sort of attachment to our old camping ground; yet it was time to change our quarters, since remaining too long on one spot must lead to unpleasant results, not to be borne unless in case of dire necessity. The grass no longer presented a smooth surface of turf; it was trampled into mud and clay. So we removed to another old tree, larger yet, that grew by the side of the river a furlong distant. Its trunk was full six feet in diameter; on one side it was marked by a party of Indians with various inexplicable hieroglyphics, commemorating some warlike enterprise, and aloft among the branches were the remains of a scaffold, where dead bodies had once been deposited, after the Indian manner.

'There comes Bull-Bear,' said Henry Chatillon, as we sat on the grass at dinner. Looking up, we saw several horsemen coming over the neighboring hill, and in a moment four stately young men rode up and dismounted. One of them was Bull-Bear, or Mahto-Tatonka, a compound name which he inherited from his father, the principal chief in the Ogillallah band. One of his brothers and two other young men accompanied him. We shook hands with the visitors, and when we had finished our meal— for this is the approved manner of entertaining Indians, even the best of them—we handed to each a tin cup of coffee and a biscuit, at which they ejaculated from the bottom of their throats, 'How! how!' a monosyllable by which a Dakota contrives to express half the emotions of which he is capable. Then we lighted the pipe, and passed it to them as they squatted on the ground.

'Where is the village?'

'There,' said Mahto-Tatonka, pointing southward; 'it will come in two days.'

'Will they go to the war?'

'Yes.'

No man is a philanthropist on the prairie. We welcomed this news cordially, and congratulated ourselves that Bordeaux's interested efforts to divert The Whirlwind from his congenial

vocation of bloodshed had failed of success, and that no further
obstacles would interpose between us and our plan of repairing to
the rendezvous at La Bonté's camp.

For that and several succeeding days Mahto-Tatonka and his
friends remained our guests. They devoured the relics of our
meals; they filled the pipe for us, and also helped us to smoke it.
Sometimes they stretched themselves side by side in the shade,
indulging in raillery and equivocal jokes, ill becoming the dignity
of brave and aspiring warriors, such as two of them in reality
were.

Two days dragged away, and on the morning of the third we
hoped confidently to see the Indian village. It did not come; so
we rode out to look for it. In place of the eight hundred Indians
we expected, we met one solitary savage riding towards us over
the prairie, who told us that the Indians had changed their plan,
and would not come within three days. Taking along with us this
messenger of evil tidings, we retraced our footsteps to the camp,
amusing ourselves by the way with execrating Indian inconstancy.
When we came in sight of our little white tent under the big tree,
we saw that it no longer stood alone. A huge old lodge was erected
by its side, discolored by rain and storms, rotten with age, with
the uncouth figures of horses and men and outstretched hands
that were painted upon it well-nigh obliterated. The long poles
which supported this squalid habitation thrust themselves rakishly
out from its pointed top, and over its entrance were suspended
a 'medicine-pipe' and various other implements of the magic
art. While we were yet at a distance we observed a greatly
increased population, of various colors and dimensions, swarming
about our quiet encampment. Morin, the trapper, having been
absent for a day or two, had returned, it seemed, bringing all his
family with him. He had taken to himself a wife, for whom he had
paid the established price of one horse. This looks cheap at first
sight, but in truth the purchase of a squaw is a transaction which
no man should enter into without mature deliberation, since it
involves not only the payment of the price, but the burden of
feeding and supporting a rapacious horde of the bride's relatives,
who hold themselves entitled to feed upon the indiscreet white
man. They gather about him like leeches, and drain him of all
he has.

Morin had not made a distinguished match. His bride's relatives occupied but a contemptible position in Ogillallah society;

for among these democrats of the prairie, as among others more civilized, there are virtual distinctions of rank and place. Morin's partner was not the most beautiful of her sex, and he had the bad taste to array her in an old calico gown, bought from an emigrant woman, instead of the neat tunic of whitened deer-skin usually worn by the squaws. The moving spirit of the establishment was an old hag of eighty. Human imagination never conceived hob-goblin or witch more ugly than she. You could count all her ribs through the wrinkles of her leathery skin. Her withered face more resembled an old skull than the countenance of a living being, even to the hollow, darkened sockets, at the bottom of which glittered her little black eyes. Her arms had dwindled into nothing but whip-cord and wire. Her hair, half black, half gray, hung in total neglect nearly to the ground, and her sole garment consisted of the remnant of a discarded buffalo-robe tied round her waist with a string of hide. Yet the old squaw's meagre anatomy was wonderfully strong. She pitched the lodge, packed the horses, and did the hardest labor of the camp. From morning till night she bustled about the lodge, screaming like a screech-owl when any-thing displeased her. Her brother, a 'medicine-man,' or magician, was as gaunt and sinewy as herself. His mouth spread from ear to ear, and his appetite, as we had occasion to learn, was ravenous in proportion. The other inmates of the lodge were a young bride and bridegroom, the latter one of those idle, good-for-nothing fellows who infest an Indian village as well as more civilized com-munities. He was fit neither for hunting nor war, as one might see from the stolid, unmeaning expression of his face. The happy pair had just entered upon the honeymoon. They would stretch a buffalo-robe upon poles to protect them from the sun, and spread-ing under it a couch of furs, would sit affectionately side by side for half the day, though I could not discover that any conver-sation passed between them. Probably they had nothing to say; for an Indian's supply of topics for conversation is far from being copious. There were half a dozen children, too, playing and whooping about the camp, shooting birds with little bows and arrows, or making miniature lodges of sticks, as children of a different complexion build houses of blocks.

A day passed, and Indians began rapidly to come in. Parties of two, three, or more would ride up and silently seat themselves on the grass. The fourth day came at last, when about noon horsemen appeared in view on the top of the neighboring ridge.

Behind followed a wild procession, hurrying in disorder down the hill and over the plain below; horses, mules, and dogs, heavily-burdened *travois*, mounted warriors, squaws walking amid the throng, and a host of children. For a full half-hour they continued to pour down; and keeping directly to the bend of the stream, within a furlong of us, they soon assembled there, a dark and confused throng, until, as if by magic, a hundred and fifty tall lodges sprang up. The lonely plain was transformed into the site of a swarming encampment. Countless horses were soon grazing over the meadows around us, and the prairie was animated by restless figures careering on horseback, or sedately stalking in their long white robes. The Whirlwind was come at last. One question yet remained to be answered: 'Will he go to the war in order that we, with so respectable an escort, may pass over to the somewhat perilous rendezvous at La Bonté's camp?'

This still remained in doubt. Characteristic indecision perplexed their councils. Indians cannot act in large bodies. Though their object be of the highest importance, they cannot combine to attain it by a series of connected efforts. King Philip, Pontiac, and Tecumseh, all felt this to their cost. The Ogillallah once had a war-chief who could control them; but he was dead, and now they were left to the sway of their own unsteady impulses.

As this Indian village and its inhabitants will hold a prominent place in the rest of the story, perhaps it may not be amiss to glance for an instant at the savage people of which they form a part. The Dakota, or Sioux, range over a vast territory, from the river St Peter to the Rocky Mountains. They are divided into independent bands, united under no central government, and acknowledging no common head. The same language, usages, and superstitions form the sole bond between them. They do not unite even in their wars. The bands of the east fight the Ojibwas on the Upper Lakes; those of the west make incessant war upon the Snake Indians in the Rocky Mountains. As the whole people is divided into bands, so each band is divided into villages. Each village has a chief, who is honored and obeyed only so far as his personal qualities may command respect and fear. Sometimes he is a mere nominal chief; sometimes his authority is little short of absolute, and his fame and influence reach beyond his own village, so that the whole band to which he belongs is ready to acknowledge him as their head. This was, a few years since, the case with the Ogillallah. Courage, address, and enterprise may

raise any warrior to the highest honor, especially if he be the son
of a former chief, or a member of a numerous family, to support
him and avenge his quarrels; but when he has reached the dignity
of chief, and the old men and warriors, by a peculiar ceremony,
have formally installed him, let it not be imagined that he assumes
any of the outward signs of rank and honor. He knows too well
on how frail a tenure he holds his station. He must conciliate his
uncertain subjects. Many a man in the village lives better, owns
more squaws and more horses, and goes better clad than he. Like
the Teutonic chiefs of old, he ingratiates himself with his young
men by making them presents, thereby often impoverishing
himself. If he fails to gain their favor they will set his authority
at naught, and may desert him at any moment; for the usages of
his people have provided no means of enforcing his authority.
Very seldom does it happen, at least among these western bands,
that a chief attains to much power, unless he is the head of a
numerous family. Frequently the village is principally made up of
his relatives and descendants, and the wandering community
assumes much of the patriarchal character.

The western Dakota have no fixed habitations. Hunting and
fighting, they wander incessantly, through summer and winter.
Some follow the herds of buffalo over the waste of prairie; others
traverse the Black Hills, thronging, on horseback and on foot,
through the dark gulfs and sombre gorges, and emerging at last
upon the 'Parks,'—those beautiful but most perilous hunting
grounds. The buffalo supplies them with the necessaries of life;
with habitations, food, clothing, beds, and fuel, strings for their
bows, glue, thread, cordage, trail-ropes for their horses, coverings
for their saddles, vessels to hold water, boats to cross streams,
and the means of purchasing all that they want from the traders.
When the buffalo are extinct, they too must dwindle away.

War is the breath of their nostrils. Against most of the neighboring tribes they cherish a rancorous hatred, transmitted from
father to son, and inflamed by constant aggression and retaliation.
Many times a year, in every village, the Great Spirit is called upon,
fasts are made, the war-parade is celebrated, and the warriors
go out by handfuls at a time against the enemy. This fierce spirit
awakens their most eager aspirations, and calls forth their
greatest energies. It is chiefly this that saves them from lethargy
and utter abasement. Without its powerful stimulus they would be
like the unwarlike tribes beyond the mountains, scattered among

the caves and rocks like beasts, and living on roots and reptiles. These latter have little of humanity except the form; but the proud and ambitious Dakota warrior can sometimes boast heroic virtues. It is seldom that distinction and influence are attained among them by any other course than that of arms. Their superstition, however, sometimes gives great power to those among them who pretend to the character of magicians; and their orators, such as they are, have their share of honor.

But to return. Look into our tent, or enter, if you can bear the stifling smoke and the close air. There, wedged close together, you will see a circle of stout warriors, passing the pipe around, joking, telling stories, and making themselves merry after their fashion. We were also infested by little copper-colored naked boys and snake-eyed girls. They would come up to us muttering certain words, which being interpreted conveyed the concise invitation, 'Come and eat.' Then we would rise, cursing the pertinacity of Dakota hospitality, which allowed scarcely an hour of rest between sun and sun, and to which we were bound to do honor, unless we would offend our entertainers. This necessity was particularly burdensome to me, as I was scarcely able to walk from the effects of illness, and was poorly qualified to dispose of twenty meals a day. So bounteous an entertainment looks like an outgushing of good-will; but, doubtless, half at least of our kind hosts, had they met us alone and unarmed on the prairie, would have robbed us of our horses, and perhaps have bestowed an arrow upon us besides.

One morning we were summoned to the lodge of an old man, the Nestor of his tribe. We found him half sitting, half reclining, on a pile of buffalo-robes; his long hair, jet-black, though he had seen some eighty winters, hung on either side of his thin features. His gaunt but symmetrical frame did not more clearly exhibit the wreck of bygone strength, than did his dark, wasted features, still prominent and commanding, bear the stamp of mental energies. Opposite the patriarch was his nephew, the young aspirant Mahto-Tatonka; and besides these, there were one or two women in the lodge.

The old man's story is peculiar, and illustrative of a superstition that prevails in full force among many of the Indian tribes. He was one of a powerful family, renowned for warlike exploits. When a very young man he submitted to the singular rite to which most of the tribe subject themselves before entering upon life. He painted his face black; then seeking out a cavern in a sequestered part of the Black Hills, he lay for several days, fasting, and praying to the spirits. In the dreams and visions produced by his weakened and excited state he fancied, like all Indians, that he saw supernatural revelations. Again and again the form of an antelope appeared before him. The antelope is the graceful peace-spirit of the Ogillallah; but seldom is it that such a gentle visitor presents itself during the initiatory fasts of their young men. The terrible grizzly bear, the divinity of war, usually appears, to fire them with martial ardor and thirst for renown. At length the antelope spoke. It told the young dreamer that he was not to follow the path of war; that a life of peace and tranquillity was marked out for him; that thenceforward he was to guide the people by his counsels and protect them from the evils of their own feuds and dissensions. Others were to gain renown by fighting the enemy; but greatness of a different kind was in store for him.

The visions beheld during the period of this fast usually determine the whole course of the dreamer's life. From that time, Le Borgne, which was the only name by which we knew him, abandoned all thoughts of war, and devoted himself to the labors of peace. He told his vision to the people. They honored his commission and respected him in his novel capacity.

A far different man was his brother, Mahto-Tatonka, who had left his name, his features, and many of his qualities, to his son. He was the father of Henry Chatillon's squaw, a circumstance which proved of some advantage to us, as it secured the friendship of a family perhaps the most noted and influential in the whole Ogillallah band. Mahto-Tatonka, in his way, was a hero. No chief could vie with him in warlike renown, or in power over his people. He had a fearless spirit, and an impetuous and inflexible resolution. His will was law. He was politic and sagacious, and with true Indian craft, always befriended the whites, knowing that he might thus reap great advantages for himself and his adherents. When he had resolved on any course of conduct, he would pay to the warriors the compliment of calling them together to deliberate upon it, and when their debates were over, quietly state his own opinion, which no one ever disputed. It fared hard with those who incurred his displeasure. He would strike them or stab them on the spot; and this act, which if attempted by any other chief would have cost him his life, the awe inspired by his name enabled him to repeat again and again with impunity. In a community where, from immemorial time, no man has acknowledged any law but his own will, Mahto-Tatonka raised himself to power little short of despotic. His career came at last to an end. He had a host of enemies patiently biding their time; and our old friend Smoke in particular, together with all his kinsmen, hated him cordially. Smoke sat one day in his lodge, in the midst of his own village, when Mahto-Tatonka entered it alone, and approaching the dwelling of his enemy, challenged him in a loud voice to come out and fight. Smoke would not move. At this, Mahto-Tatonka proclaimed him a coward and an old woman, and striding to the entrance of the lodge, stabbed the chief's best horse, which was picketed there. Smoke was daunted, and even this insult failed to bring him out. Mahto-Tatonka moved haughtily away; all made way for him; but his hour of reckoning was near.

One hot day, five or six years ago, numerous lodges of Smoke's kinsmen were gathered about some of the Fur Company's men, who were trading in various articles with them, whiskey among the rest. Mahto-Tatonka was also there with a few of his people. As he lay in his own lodge, a fray arose between his adherents and the kinsmen of his enemy. The war-whoop was raised, bullets and arrows began to fly, and the camp was in confusion. The chief sprang up, and rushing in a fury from the lodge shouted to the combatants on both sides to cease. Instantly—for the attack was preconcerted—came the reports of two or three guns, and the twanging of a dozen bows, and the savage hero, mortally wounded, pitched forward headlong to the ground. Rouleau was present, and told me the particulars. The tumult became general, and was not quelled until several had fallen on both sides. When we were in the country the feud between the two families was still rankling.

Thus died Mahto-Tatonka; but he left behind him a goodly army of descendants, to perpetuate his renown and avenge his fate. Besides daughters, he had thirty sons, a number which need not stagger the credulity of those acquainted with Indian usages and practices. We saw many of them, all marked by the same dark complexion, and the same peculiar cast of features. Of these, our visitor, young Mahto-Tatonka, was the eldest, and some reported him as likely to succeed to his father's honors. Though he appeared not more than twenty-one years old, he had oftener struck the enemy, and stolen more horses and more squaws, than any other young man in the village. Horse-stealing is well known as an avenue to distinction on the prairies, and the other kind of depredation is esteemed equally meritorious. Not that the act can confer fame from its own intrinsic merits. Any one can steal a squaw, and if he chooses afterwards to make an adequate present to her rightful proprietor, the easy husband for the most part rests content, his vengeance falls asleep, and all danger from that quarter is averted. Yet this is regarded as a pitiful and mean-spirited transaction. The danger is averted, but the glory of the achievement also is lost. Mahto-Tatonka proceeded after a more dashing fashion. Out of several dozen squaws whom he had stolen he could boast that he had never paid for one, but snapping his fingers in the face of the injured husband, had defied the extremity of his indignation, and no one yet had dared to lay the finger of violence upon him. He was following close in the footsteps of his father. The young men and the young squaws, each in their way, admired him. The former would always follow him to war, and he was esteemed to have an unrivalled charm in the eyes of the latter. Perhaps his impunity may excite some wonder. An arrow shot from a ravine, or a stab given in the dark require no great valor, and are especially suited to the Indian genius; but Mahto-Tatonka had a strong protection. It was not alone his courage and audacious will that enabled him to career so dashingly among his compeers. His enemies did not forget that he was one of thirty warlike brethren, all growing up to manhood. Should they wreak their anger upon him many keen eyes would be ever upon them and many fierce hearts thirst for their blood. The avenger would dog their footsteps everywhere. To kill Mahto-Tatonka would be an act of suicide.

Though he found such favor in the eyes of the fair, he was no dandy. He was indifferent to the gaudy trappings and ornaments of his companions, and was content to rest his chances of success upon his own warlike merits. He never arrayed himself in gaudy blanket and glittering necklaces, but left his statue-like form, limbed like an Apollo of bronze, to win its way to favor. His voice was singularly deep and strong, and sounded from his chest like the deep notes of an organ. Yet after all, he was but an Indian. See him as he lies there in the sun before our tent, kicking his heels in the air and cracking jokes with his brother. Does he look like a hero? See him now in the hour of his glory, when at sunset the whole village empties itself to behold him; for to-morrow their favorite young partisan goes out against the enemy. His head-dress is adorned with a crest of the war-eagle's feathers, rising in a waving ridge above his brow, and sweeping far behind him. His round white shield hangs at his breast, with feathers radiating from the centre like a star. His quiver is at his back; his tall lance in his hand, the iron point flashing against the declining sun, while the long scalplocks of his enemies flutter from the shaft. Thus, gorgeous as a champion in panoply, he rides round and round within the great circle of lodges, balancing with a graceful buoyancy to the free movements of his war-horse, while with a sedate brow he sings his song to the Great Spirit. Young rival warriors look askance at him; vermilion-cheeked girls gaze in admiration; boys whoop and scream in a thrill of delight; and old women yell forth his name and proclaim his praises from lodge to lodge.

Mahto-Tatonka was the best of all our Indian friends. Hour after hour, and day after day, when swarms of savages of every age, sex, and degree beset our camp, he would lie in our tent, his lynx-eye ever open to guard our property from pillage.

The Whirlwind invited us one day to his lodge. The feast was finished and the pipe began to circulate. It was a remarkably large and fine one, and I expressed admiration of it.

'If the Meneaska likes the pipe,' asked The Whirlwind, 'why does he not keep it?'

Such a pipe among the Ogillallah is valued at the price of a horse. The gift seemed worthy of a chieftain and a warrior; but The Whirlwind's generosity rose to no such pitch. He gave me the pipe, confidently expecting that I in return would make him a present of equal or superior value. This is the implied condition of every gift among the Indians, and should it not be complied with, the present is usually reclaimed. So I arranged upon a gaudy calico handkerchief an assortment of vermilion, tobacco, knives, and gunpowder, and summoning the chief to camp, assured him of my friendship, and begged his acceptance of a slight token of it. Ejaculating 'How! how!' he folded up the offerings and withdrew to his lodge.

Late one afternoon a party of Indians on horseback came suddenly in sight from behind some clumps of bushes that lined the bank of the stream, leading with them a mule, on whose back was a wretched negro, sustained in his seat by the high pommel and cantle of the Indian saddle. His cheeks were shrunken in the hollow of his jaws; his eyes were unnaturally dilated, and his lips shrivelled and drawn back from his teeth like those of a corpse. When they brought him before our tent, and lifted him from the saddle, he could not walk or stand, but crawled a short distance, and with a look of utter misery sat down on the grass. All the children and women came pouring out of the lodges, and with screams and cries made a circle about him, while he sat supporting himself with his hands, and looking from side to side with a vacant stare. The wretch was starving to death. For thirty-three days he had wandered alone on the prairie, without weapon of any kind; without shoes, moccasins, or any other clothing than an old jacket and trousers; without intelligence to guide his course, or any knowledge of the productions of the prairie. All this time he had subsisted on crickets and lizards, wild onions, and three eggs which he found in the nest of a prairie-dove. He had not seen a human being. Bewildered in the boundless, hopeless desert that stretched around him, he had walked on in despair, till he could walk no longer, and then crawled on his knees, till the bone was laid bare. He chose the night for travelling, lying down by day to sleep in the glaring sun, always dreaming as he said, of the broth and corncake he used to eat under his old master's shed in Missouri. Every man in the camp, both white and red, was astonished at his escape not only from starvation, but from the grizzly bears, which abound in that neighborhood, and the wolves which howled around him every night.

Reynal recognized him the moment the Indians brought him in. He had run away from his master about a year before and joined the party of Richard, who was then leaving the frontier for the mountains. He had lived with Richard until, at the end of May, he with Reynal and several other men went out in search of some stray horses, when he was separated from the rest in a storm, and had never been heard of to this time. Knowing his inexperience and helplessness, no one dreamed that he could still be living. The Indians had found him lying exhausted on the ground.

As he sat there, with the Indians gazing silently on him, his haggard face and glazed eye were disgusting to look upon. Deslauriers made him a bowl of gruel, but he suffered it to remain untasted before him. At length he languidly raised the spoon to his lips; again he did so, and again; and then his appetite seemed suddenly inflamed into madness, for he seized the bowl, swallowed all its contents in a few seconds, and eagerly demanded meat. This we refused, telling him to wait until morning; but he begged so eagerly that we gave him a small piece, which he devoured, tearing it like a dog. He said he must have more. We told him that his life was in danger if he ate so immoderately at first. He assented, and said he knew he was a fool to do so, but he must have meat. This we absolutely refused, to the great indignation of the sense less squaws, who, when we were not watching him, would slyly bring dried meat and *pommes blanches,* and place them on the ground by his side. Still this was not enough for him. When it grew dark he contrived to creep away between the legs of the horses and crawl over to the Indian camp. Here he fed to his heart's content, and was brought back again in the morning, when Gingras, the trapper, put him on horseback and carried him to the fort. He managed to survive the effects of his greediness. Though slightly deranged when we left this part of the country, he was otherwise in tolerable health, and expressed his firm con-viction that nothing could ever kill him.

When the sun was yet an hour high it was a gay scene in the village. The warriors stalked sedately among the lodges, or along the margin of the stream, or walked out to visit the bands of horses that were feeding over the prairie. Half the population deserted the close and heated lodges and betook themselves to the water; and here you might see boys and girls, and young squaws, splashing, swimming, and diving, beneath the afternoon sun, with merry screams and laughter. But when the sun was resting above the broken peaks, and the purple mountains threw their shadows for miles over the prairie; when our old tree basked peacefully in the horizontal rays, and the swelling plains and scattered groves were softened into a tranquil beauty,—then the scene around our tent was worthy of a Salvator. Savage figures, with quivers at their backs, and guns, lances, or tomahawks in their hands, sat on horseback, motionless as statues, their arms crossed on their breasts and their eyes fixed in a steady, un-wavering gaze upon us. Others stood erect, wrapped from head to foot in their long white robes of buffalo-hide. Others sat together on the grass, holding their shaggy horses by a rope, with their dark busts exposed to view as they suffered their robes to fall from their shoulders. Others again stood carelessly among the throng, with nothing to conceal the matchless symmetry of their forms. There was one in particular, a ferocious fellow, named The Mad Wolf, who, with the bow in his hand and the quiver at his back, might have seemed, but for his face, the Pythian Apollo himself. Such a figure rose before the imagination of West, when

on first seeing the Belvedere in the Vatican, he exclaimed, 'By
God, a Mohawk!'

When the prairie grew dark the horses were driven in and
secured near the camp, and the crowd began to melt away. Fires
gleamed around, duskily revealing the rough trappers and the
graceful Indians. One of the families near us was always gathered
about a bright fire that lighted up the interior of their lodge.
Withered, witch-like hags flitted around the blaze; and here for
hour after hour sat a circle of children and young girls, laughing
and talking, their round, merry faces glowing in the ruddy light.
We could hear the monotonous notes of the drum from the Indian
camp, with the chant of the war-song, deadened in the distance,
and the long chorus of quavering yells, where the war-dance was
going on in the largest lodge. For several nights, too, we heard
wild and mournful cries, rising and dying away like the melancholy voice of a wolf. They came from the sisters and other
female relatives of Mahto-Tatonka, who were gashing their limbs
with knives, and bewailing the death of Henry Chatillon's squaw.
The hour would grow late before all went to rest in our camp. Then,
while the embers of the fires glowed dimly, the men lay stretched
in their blankets on the ground, and nothing could be heard but
the restless motions of the crowded horses.

I recall these scenes with a mixed feeling of pleasure and pain.
At this time I was so reduced by illness that I could seldom walk
without reeling like a drunken man; and when I rose from my
seat upon the ground the landscape suddenly grew dim before
my eyes, the trees and lodges seemed to sway to and fro, and the
prairie to rise and fall like the swells of the ocean. Such a state of
things is not enviable anywhere. In a country where a man's life
may at any moment depend on the strength of his arm, or it may
be on the activity of his legs, it is more particularly inconvenient.
Nor is sleeping on damp ground, with an occasional drenching from
a shower, very beneficial in such cases. I sometimes suffered the
extremity of exhaustion, and was in a tolerably fair way of
atoning for my love of the prairie, by resting there forever.

I tried repose and a very sparing diet. For a long time, with
exemplary patience, I lounged about the camp, or at the utmost
staggered over to the Indian village, and walked faint and dizzy
among the lodges. It would not do; and I bethought me of starvation. During five days I sustained life on one small biscuit a day.
At the end of that time I was weaker than before, but the dis-

order seemed shaken in its stronghold, and very gradually I began to resume a less rigid diet.

I used to lie languid and dreamy before our tent, musing on the past and the future, and when most overcome with lassitude, my eyes turned always towards the distant Black Hills. There is a spirit of energy in mountains, and they impart it to all who approach them. At that time I did not know how many dark superstitions and gloomy legends are associated with the Black Hills in the minds of the Indians, but I felt an eager desire to penetrate their hidden recesses, and explore the chasms and precipices, black torrents, and silent forests that I fancied were concealed there.

12. Ill-luck

A Canadian came from Fort Laramie, and brought a curious piece of intelligence. A trapper, fresh from the mountains, had become enamoured of a Missouri damsel belonging to a family who with other emigrants had been for some days encamped in the neighborhood of the fort. If bravery be the most potent charm to win the favor of the fair, then no wooer could be more irresistible than a Rocky Mountain trapper. In the present instance, the suit was not urged in vain. The lovers concerted a scheme, which they proceeded to carry into effect with all possible despatch. The emigrant party left the fort, and on the next night but one encamped as usual, and placed a guard. A little after midnight the enamoured trapper drew near, mounted on a strong horse, and leading another by the bridle. Fastening both animals to a tree, he stealthily moved towards the wagons, as if he were approaching a band of

buffalo. Eluding the vigilance of the guard, who were probably
half asleep, he met his mistress by appointment at the outskirts
of the camp, mounted her on his spare horse, and made off with
her through the darkness. The sequel of the adventure did not
reach our ears, and we never learned how the imprudent fair one
liked an Indian lodge for a dwelling, and a reckless trapper for a
bridegroom.

At length The Whirlwind and his warriors determined to move.
They had resolved, after all their preparations, not to go to the
rendezvous at La Bonté's camp, but to pass through the Black
Hills and spend a few weeks in hunting the buffalo on the other
side, until they had killed enough to furnish them with a stock
of provisions and with hides to make their lodges for the next
season. This done, they were to send out a small independent war-
party against the enemy. Their final determination placed us in
some embarrassment. Should we go to La Bonté's camp, it was
not impossible that the other villages would prove as vacillating
as The Whirlwind's, and that no assembly whatever would take
place. Our old companion Reynal had conceived a liking for us,
or rather for our biscuit and coffee, and for the occasional small
presents which we made him. He was very anxious that we should
go with the village, which he himself intended to follow. He was
certain that no Indians would meet at the rendezvous, and said,
moreover, that it would be easy to convey our cart and baggage
through the Black Hills. He knew, however, nothing of the matter.
Neither he nor any white man with us had ever seen the difficult
and obscure defiles through which the Indians intended to make
their way. I passed them afterwards, and had much ado to force
my distressed horse along the narrow ravines, and through chasms
where daylight could scarcely penetrate. Our cart might as
easily have been driven over the summit of Pike's Peak. But of
this we were ignorant; and in view of the difficulties and uncer-
tainties of an attempt to visit the rendezvous, we recalled the
old proverb about 'a bird in the hand,' and decided to follow the
village.

Both camps, the Indians' and our own, broke up on the morning
of the first of July. I was so weak that the aid of a spoonful of
whiskey, swallowed at short intervals, alone enabled me to sit my
horse through the short journey of that day. For half a mile
before us and half a mile behind, the prairie was covered far and
wide with the moving throng of savages. The barren, broken plain

stretched away to the right and left, and far in front rose the precipitous ridge of the Black Hills. We pushed forward to the head
of the scattered column, passing burdened *traineaux*, heavily
laden pack-horses, gaunt old women on foot, gay young squaws on
horseback, restless children running among the crowd, old men
striding along in their white buffalo-robes, and groups of young
warriors mounted on their best horses. Henry Chatillon, looking
backward over the distant prairie, exclaimed suddenly that a
horseman was coming; and in truth we could just discern a
small black speck slowly moving over the face of a distant
swell, like a fly creeping on a wall. It rapidly grew larger as it
approached.

'White man, I b'lieve,' said Henry; 'look how he ride. Indian
never ride that way. Yes; he got rifle on the saddle before him.'

The horseman disappeared in a hollow of the prairie, but we soon
saw him again, and as he came riding at a gallop towards us
through the crowd of Indians, his long hair streaming in the wind
behind him, we recognized the ruddy face and old buckskin
frock of Gingras the trapper. He was just arrived from Fort
Laramie, and said he had a message for us. A trader named Bisonette, one of Henry's friends, had lately come from the settlements,
and intended to go with a party of men to La Bonté's camp,
where, as Gingras assured us, ten or twelve villages of Indians
would certainly assemble. Bisonette desired that we would cross
over and meet him there, and promised that his men should
protect our horses and baggage while we went among the Indians.
Shaw and I stopped our horses, held a council, and in an evil hour
resolved to go.

For the rest of that day our course and that of the Indians was
the same. In less than an hour we came to where the high barren
prairie terminated, sinking down abruptly in steep descent;
and standing on the verge we saw below us a great meadow.
Laramie Creek bounded it on the left sweeping along in the shadow
of the heights, and passing with its shallow and rapid current
just beneath us. We sat on horseback, waiting and looking on,
while the whole savage array went pouring by, hurrying down the
declivity and spreading over the meadow below. In a few moments
the plain was swarming with the moving multitude, some just
visible, like specks in the distance, others still hastening by and
fording the stream in bustle and confusion. On the edge of the
heights sat a group of the elder warriors, gravely smoking

and looking with unmoved faces on the wild and striking spectacle.

Up went the lodges in a circle on the margin of the stream. For the sake of quiet we pitched our tent among some trees half a mile distant. In the afternoon we were in the village. The day was a glorious one, and the whole camp seemed lively and animated in sympathy. Groups of children and young girls were laughing gayly outside the lodges. The shields, the lances, and the bows were removed from the tall tripods on which they usually hung, before the dwellings of their owners. The warriors were mounting their horses, and one by one riding away over the prairie toward the neighboring hills.

Shaw and I sat on the grass near the lodge of Reynal. An old woman, with true Indian hospitality, brought a bowl of boiled venison and placed it before us. We amused ourselves with watching a few young squaws who were playing together and chasing each other in and out of one of the lodges. Suddenly the wild yell of the war-whoop came pealing from the hills. A crowd of horsemen appeared, rushing down their sides, and riding at full speed towards the village, each warrior's long hair flying behind him in the wind like a ship's streamer. As they approached, the confused throng assumed a regular order, and entering two by two, they circled round the area at full gallop, each warrior singing his war-song as he rode. Some of their dresses were superb. They wore crests of feathers, and close tunics of antelope skins, fringed with the scalplocks of their enemies; many of their shields, too, fluttered with the war-eagle's feathers. All had bows and arrows at their backs; some carried long lances, and a few were armed with guns. The White Shield, their partisan, rode in gorgeous attire at their head, mounted on a black-and-white horse. Mahto-Tatonka and his brothers took no part in this parade, for they were in mourning for their sister, and were all sitting in their lodges, their bodies bedaubed from head to foot with white clay, and a lock of hair cut from the forehead of each.

The warriors rode three times round the village; and as each noted champion passed, the old women would scream out his name to honor his bravery and excite the emulation of the younger warriors. Little urchins, not two years old, followed the warlike pageant with glittering eyes, and gazed with eager admiration at the heroes of their tribe.

The procession rode out of the village as it had entered it, and in half an hour all the warriors had returned again, dropping quietly in, singly or in parties of two or three.

The parade over, we were entertained with an episode of Indian domestic life. A vicious-looking squaw, beside herself with rage, was berating her spouse, who, with a look of total unconcern, sat cross-legged in the middle of his lodge, smoking his pipe in silence. At length, maddened by his coolness, she made a rush at the lodge, seized the poles which supported it, and tugged at them, one after the other, till she brought down the whole structure, poles, hides, and all, clattering on his head, burying him in the wreck of his habitation. He pushed aside the hides with his hand, and presently his head emerged, like a turtle's from its shell. Still he sat smoking sedately as before, a wicked glitter in his eyes alone betraying the pent-up storm within. The squaw, scolding all the while, proceeded to saddle her horse, bestride him, and canter out of the camp, intending, as it seemed, to return to her father's lodge, wherever that might be. The warrior, who had not deigned even to look at her, now coolly rose, disengaged himself from the ruins, tied a cord of hair by way of bridle round the jaw of his buffalo-horse, broke a stout cudgel, about four feet long from the butt-end of a lodge pole, mounted, and galloped majestically over the prairie to discipline his offending helpmeet.

As the sun rose next morning we looked across the meadow, and could see the lodges levelled and the Indians gathering together in preparation to leave the camp. Their course lay to the westward. We turned towards the north with our three men, the four trappers following us, with the Indian family of Morin. We travelled until night, and encamped among some trees by the side of a little brook, where during the whole of the next day we lay waiting for Bisonette; but no Bisonette appeared. Here two of our trapper friends left us, and set out for the Rocky Mountains. On the second morning, despairing of Bisonette's arrival, we resumed our journey, traversing a forlorn and dreary monotony of sun-scorched plains, where no living thing appeared save here and there an antelope flying before us like the wind. When noon came we saw an unwonted and welcome sight,—a fine growth of trees, marking the course of a little stream called Horseshoe Creek. They stood wide asunder, spreading a thick canopy of leaves above a surface of rich, tall grass. The stream ran swiftly, as clear as crystal, through the bosom of the wood, sparkling over its bed of white sand, and darkening again as it entered a deep cavern of foliage. I was thoroughly exhausted, and flung myself on the ground, scarcely able to move.

In the morning, as glorious a sun rose upon us as ever animated that wilderness. We advanced, and soon were surrounded by tall bare hills, overspread from top to bottom with prickly pears and other cacti, that seemed like clinging reptiles. A plain, flat and hard, with scarcely the vestige of grass, lay before us, and a line of tall, misshapen trees bounded the onward view. There was no sight or sound of man or beast, or any living thing, although behind those trees was the long-looked-for place of rendezvous, where we hoped to have found the Indians congregated by thousands. We looked and listened anxiously. We pushed forward with our best speed, and forced our horses through the trees. There were copses of some extent beyond, with a scanty stream creeping among them; and as we pressed through the yielding branches, deer sprang up to the right and left. At length we caught a glimpse of the prairie beyond, emerged upon it, and saw, not a plain covered with encampments and swarming with life, but a vast unbroken desert stretching away before us league upon league, without bush or tree, or any living thing. We drew rein and gave to the winds our sentiments concerning the whole aboriginal race of America. Our journey was worse than vain. For myself, I was vexed beyond measure; as I well knew that a slight aggravation of my disorder would render this false step irrevocable, and make it impossible to accomplish effectually the object which had led me an arduous journey of between three and four thousand miles.

And where were the Indians? They were mustered in great numbers at a spot about twenty miles distant, where at that very moment they were dancing their war-dances. The scarcity of buffalo in the vicinity of La Bonté's camp, which would render their supply of provisions scanty and precarious, had probably prevented them from assembling there; but of all this we knew nothing until some weeks after.

Shaw lashed his horse and galloped forward. I, though much more vexed than he, was not strong enough to adopt this convenient vent to my feelings; so I followed at a quiet pace. We rode up to a solitary old tree, which seemed the only place fit for encampment. Half its branches were dead, and the rest were so scantily furnished with leaves that they cast but a meagre and wretched shade. We threw down our saddles in the strip of shadow cast by the old twisted trunk, and sat down upon them. In silent indignation we remained smoking for an hour or more, shifting our saddles with the shifting shadow, for the sun was intolerably hot.

13. Hunting Indians

At last we had reached La Bonté's camp, towards which our eyes had turned so long. Of all weary hours, those that passed between noon and sunset of that day may bear away the palm of exquisite discomfort. I lay under the tree reflecting on what course to pursue, watching the shadows which seemed never to move, and the sun which seemed fixed in the sky, and hoping every moment to see the men and horses of Bisonette emerging from the woods. Shaw and Henry had ridden out on a scouting expedition, and did not return till the sun was setting. There was nothing very cheering in their faces or in the news they brought.

'We have been ten miles from here,' said Shaw. 'We climbed the highest butte we could find, and could not see a buffalo or an Indian; nothing but prairie for twenty miles around us.' Henry's

horse was disabled by clambering up and down the sides of
ravines, and Shaw's was greatly fatigued.

After supper that evening, as we sat round the fire, I proposed
to Shaw to wait one day longer, in hopes of Bisonette's arrival,
and if he should not come, to send Deslauriers with the cart and
baggage back to Fort Laramie, while we ourselves followed
The Whirlwind's village, and attempted to overtake it as it
passed the mountains. Shaw, not having the same motive for
hunting Indians that I had, was averse to the plan; I therefore
resolved to go alone. This design I adopted very unwillingly, for I
knew that in the present state of my health the attempt would
be painful and hazardous. I hoped that Bisonette would appear
in the course of the following day, and bring us some information
by which to direct our course, thus enabling me to accomplish
my purpose by means less objectionable.

The rifle of Henry Chatillon was necessary for the subsistence
of the party in my absence; so I called Raymond, and ordered
him to prepare to set out with me. Raymond rolled his eyes
vacantly about, but at length, having succeeded in grappling with
the idea, he withdrew to his bed under the cart. He was a heavy-
moulded fellow, with a broad face expressing impenetrable
stupidity and entire self-confidence. As for his good qualities, he
had a sort of stubborn fidelity, an insensibility to danger, and a
kind of instinct or sagacity, which sometimes led him right where
better heads than his were at a loss. Besides this, he knew very
well how to handle a rifle and picket a horse.

Through the following day the sun glared down upon us with a
pitiless, penetrating heat. The distant blue prairie seemed quivering under it. The lodge of our Indian associates parched in the
burning rays, and our rifles as they leaned against the tree were
too hot for the touch. There was a dead silence through our camp,
broken only by the hum of gnats and mosquitoes. The men,
resting their foreheads on their arms, were sleeping under the
cart. The Indians kept close within their lodge, except the newly
married pair, who were seated together under an awning of
buffalo-robes, and the old conjurer, who, with his hard, emaciated
face and gaunt ribs, was perched aloft like a turkey-buzzard,
among the dead branches of an old tree, constantly on the lookout
for enemies. We dined, and then Shaw saddled his horse.

'I will ride back,' said he, 'to Horseshoe Creek, and see if Bisonette is there.'

'I would go with you,' I answered, 'but I must reserve all the strength I have.'

The afternoon dragged away at last. I occupied myself in cleaning my rifle and pistols, and making other preparations for the journey. It was late before I wrapped myself in my blanket, and lay down for the night, with my head on my saddle. Shaw had not returned, but this gave us no uneasiness, for we supposed that he had fallen in with Bisonette and was spending the night with him. For a day or two past I had gained in strength and health, but about midnight an attack of pain awoke me, and for some hours I could not sleep. The moon was quivering on the broad breast of the Platte; nothing could be heard except those low, inexplicable sounds, like whisperings and footsteps, which no one who has spent the night alone amid deserts and forests will be at a loss to understand. As I was falling asleep a familiar voice, shouting from the distance, awoke me again. A rapid step approached the camp, and Shaw, on foot, with his gun in his hand, hastily entered.

'Where's your horse?' said I, raising myself on my elbow.

'Lost!' said Shaw. 'Where's Deslauriers?'

'There,' I replied, pointing to a confused mass of blankets and buffalo-robes.

Shaw touched them with the butt of his gun, and up sprang our faithful Canadian.

'Come, Deslauriers; stir up the fire and get me something to eat.'

'Where's Bisonette?' asked I.

'The Lord knows; there's nobody at Horseshoe Creek.'

Shaw had gone back to the spot where we had encamped two days before, and finding nothing there but the ashes of our fires, he had tied his horse to the tree while he bathed in the stream. Something startled his horse, which broke loose, and for two hours Shaw tried in vain to catch him. Sunset approached, and it was twelve miles to camp. So he abandoned the attempt, and set out on foot to join us. The greater part of his solitary and perilous walk was in darkness. His moccasins were worn to tatters, and his feet severely lacerated. He sat down to eat, however, the usual equanimity of his temper not at all disturbed by his misfortune; and my last recollection before falling asleep was of Shaw, seated cross-legged before the fire, smoking his pipe.

When I awoke again there was a fresh, damp smell in the air, a gray twilight involved the prairie, and above its eastern verge was a streak of cold, red sky. I called to the men, and in a moment a fire was blazing brightly in the dim morning light, and breakfast was getting ready. We sat down together on the grass, to the last civilized meal which Raymond and I were destined to enjoy for some time.

'Now bring in the horses.'

My little mare Pauline was soon standing by the fire. She was a fleet, hardy, and gentle animal, christened after Paul Dorion, from whom I had procured her in exchange for Pontiac. She did not look as if equipped for a morning pleasure-ride. In front of the black, high-bowed mountain-saddle were fastened holsters, with heavy pistols. A pair of saddle-bags, a blanket tightly rolled, a small parcel of Indian presents tied up in buffalo-skin, a leather bag of flour, and a smaller one of tea, were all secured behind, and a long trail-rope was wound round her neck. Raymond had a strong black mule, equipped in a similar manner. We crammed our powder-horns to the throat, and mounted.

'I will meet you at Fort Laramie on the first of August,' said I to Shaw.

'That is,' he replied, 'if we don't meet before that. I think I shall follow you in a day or two.'

This in fact he attempted, and would have succeeded if he had not encountered obstacles against which his resolute spirit was of no avail. Two days after I left him he sent Deslauriers to the fort with the cart and baggage, and set out for the mountains with Henry Chatillon; but a violent thunder-storm had deluged the prairie, and obliterated not only our trail but that of the Indians themselves. They encamped at the base of the mountains, at a loss in what direction to go. In the morning Shaw found himself poisoned by the plant popularly known in New England as 'poison ivy,' in such a manner that it was impossible for him to travel. So they turned back reluctantly toward Fort Laramie. Shaw lay seriously ill for a week, and remained at the fort till I rejoined him some time after.

To return to my own story. Raymond and I shook hands with our friends, rode out upon the prairie, and clambering the sandy hollows channelled in the sides of the hills, gained the high plains above. If a curse had been pronounced upon the land, it could not have worn an aspect more forlorn. There were abrupt broken hills, deep hollows, and wide plains; but all alike glared with an insupportable whiteness under the burning sun. The country, as if parched by the heat, was cracked into innumerable fissures and ravines, that not a little impeded our progress. Their steep sides were white and raw, and along the bottom we several times discovered the broad tracks of the grizzly bear, nowhere more abundant than in this region. The ridges of the hills were hard as rock, and strewn with pebbles of flint and coarse red jasper; looking from them, there was nothing to relieve the desert uniformity, save here and there a pine-tree clinging at the edge of a ravine, and stretching its rough, shaggy arms into the scorching air. Its resinous odors recalled the pine-clad mountains of New England, and, goaded as I was with a morbid thirst, I thought with a longing desire on the crystal treasure poured in such wasteful profusion from our thousand hills. I heard, in fancy, the plunging and gurgling of waters among the shaded rocks, and saw them gleaming dark and still far down amid the crevices, the cold drops trickling from the long green mosses.

When noon came we found a little stream, with a few trees and bushes; and here we rested for an hour. Then we travelled on, guided by the sun, until, just before sunset, we reached another stream called Bitter Cottonwood Creek. A thick growth of bushes and old, storm-beaten trees grew at intervals along its bank. Near the foot of one of the trees we flung down our saddles, and hobbling our horses, turned them loose to feed. The little stream was clear and swift and ran musically over its white sands. Small water-birds were splashing in the shallows and filling the air with cries and flutterings. The sun was just sinking among gold and crimson clouds behind Mount Laramie. I lay upon a log by the margin of the water, and watched the restless motions of the little fish in a deep still nook below. Strange to say, I seemed to have gained strength since the morning, and almost felt a sense of returning health.

We built our fire. Night came, and the wolves began to howl. One deep voice began, answered in awful responses from hills, plains, and woods. Such sounds do not disturb one's sleep upon the prairie. We picketed the mare and the mule and did not awake until daylight. Then we turned them loose, still hobbled, to feed for an hour before starting. We were getting ready our breakfast when Raymond saw an antelope half a mile distant and said he would go and shoot it.

'Your business,' said I, 'is to look after the animals. I am too weak to do much if anything happens to them, and you must keep within sight of the camp.'

Raymond promised, and set out with his rifle in his hand. The mare and the mule had crossed the stream, and were feeding among the long grass on the other side, much tormented by the attacks of large, green-headed flies. As I watched them I saw them go into a hollow, and as several minutes elapsed without their reappearing, I waded through the stream to look after them. To my vexation and alarm I discovered them at a great distance, galloping away at full speed, Pauline in advance, with her hobbles broken, and the mule, still fettered, following with awkward leaps. I fired my rifle and shouted to recall Raymond. In a moment he came running through the stream, with a red handkerchief bound round his head. I pointed to the fugitives, and ordered him to pursue them. Muttering a 'Sacré,' between his teeth, he set out at full speed, still swinging his rifle in his hand. I walked up to the top of a hill, and, looking away over the prairie, could distinguish the runaways, still at full gallop. Returning to the fire, I sat down at the foot of a tree. Wearily and anxiously hour after hour passed away. The loose bark dangling from the trunk behind me flapped to and fro in the wind, and the mosquitoes kept up their drowsy hum; but other than this there was no sight nor sound of life throughout the burning landscape. The sun rose higher and higher, until I knew that it must be noon. It seemed scarcely possible that the animals could be recovered. If they were not, my situation was one of serious difficulty. Shaw, when I left him, had decided to move that morning, but whither he had not determined. To look for him would be a vain attempt. Fort Laramie was forty miles distant, and I could not walk a mile without great effort. Not then having learned the philosophy of yielding to disproportionate obstacles, I resolved, come what would, to continue the pursuit of the Indians. Only one plan occurred to me; this was, to send Raymond to the fort with an order for more horses, while I remained on the spot, awaiting his return, which might take place within three days. But to remain stationary and alone for three days, in a country full of dangerous Indians, was not the most flattering of prospects; and, protracted as my Indian hunt must be by such delay, it was not easy to foretell its result. Revolving these matters, I grew hungry; and as our stock of provisions, except four or five pounds of flour, was by this time exhausted, I left the camp to see what game I could find.

Nothing could be seen except four or five large curlews wheeling over my head, and now and then alighting upon the prairie. I shot two of them, and was about returning, when a startling sight caught my eye. A small dark object, like a human head, suddenly appeared, and vanished among the thick bushes along the stream below. In that country every stranger is a suspected enemy; and I threw forward the muzzle of my rifle. In a moment the bushes were violently shaken; two heads, but not human heads, protruded; and to my great joy I recognized the downcast, disconsolate countenance of the black mule, and the yellow visage of Pauline. Raymond came upon the mule, pale and haggard, complaining of a fiery pain in his chest. I took charge of the animals while he kneeled down by the side of the stream to drink. He had kept the runaways in sight as far as the Side Fork of Laramie Creek, a distance of more than ten miles; and here with great difficulty he had succeeded in catching them. I saw that he was unarmed, and asked him what he had done with his rifle. It had encumbered him in his pursuit, and he had dropped it on the prairie, thinking that he could find it on his return; but in this he had failed. The loss might prove a very serious one. I was too much rejoiced, however, at the recovery of the animals, and at the fidelity of Raymond, who might easily have deserted with them, to think much about it; and having made some tea for him in a tin vessel which we had brought with us, I told him that I would give him two hours for resting before we set out again. He had eaten nothing that day; but having no appetite, he lay down immediately to sleep. I picketed the animals among the best grass that I could find, and made fires of green wood to protect them from the flies; then sitting down again by the tree, I watched the slow movements of the sun, grudging every moment that passed.

The time I had mentioned expired, and I awoke Raymond. We saddled and set out again, but first we went in search of the lost rifle, and in the course of an hour were fortunate enough to find it. Then we turned westward, and moved over the hills and hollows at a slow pace towards Mount Laramie. The heat no longer tormented us, for a cloud was before the sun. The air grew fresh and cool, the distant mountains frowned more gloomily, there was a low muttering of thunder, and dense, black masses of cloud rose heavily behind the broken peaks. At first they were fringed with silver by the afternoon sun; but soon thick blackness overspread the sky, and the desert around us was wrapped in gloom.

There was an awful sublimity in the hoarse murmuring of the thunder, and the sombre shadows that involved the mountains and the plain. The storm broke with a zigzag blinding flash, a terrific crash of thunder, and a hurricane that howled over the prairie, dashing floods of water against us. Raymond looked about him and cursed the merciless elements. There seemed no shelter near, but we discerned at length a deep ravine gashed in the level prairie, and saw half-way down its side an old pine-tree, whose rough horizontal boughs formed a sort of pent-house against the tempest. We found a practicable passage, led our animals down, and fastened them to large loose stones at the bottom; then climbing up, we drew our blankets over our heads, and crouched close beneath the old tree. Perhaps I was no competent judge of time, but it seemed to me that we were sitting there a full hour, while around us poured a deluge of rain, through which the rocks on the opposite side of the gulf were barely visible. The first burst of the tempest soon subsided, but the rain poured in steady torrents. At length Raymond grew impatient, and scrambling out of the ravine, gained the level prairie above.

'What does the weather look like?' asked I from my seat under the tree.

'It looks bad,' he answered,—'dark all round;' and again he descended and sat down by my side. Some ten minutes elapsed.

'Go up again,' said I, 'and take another look;' and he clambered up the precipice. 'Well, how is it?'

'Just the same, only I see one little bright spot over the top of the mountain.'

The rain by this time had begun to abate; and going down to the bottom of the ravine we loosened the animals, who were standing up to their knees in water. Leading them up the rocky throat of the ravine, we reached the plain above. All around us was obscurity; but the bright spot above the mountains grew wider and ruddier, until at length the clouds drew apart, and a flood of sunbeams poured down, streaming along the precipices, and involving them in a thin blue haze, as soft as that which wraps the Apennines on an evening in spring. Rapidly the clouds were broken and scattered, like routed legions of evil spirits. The plain lay basking in sunbeams around us; a rainbow arched the desert from north to south, and far in front a line of woods seemed inviting us to refreshment and repose. When we reached them, they were glistening with prismatic dew-drops, and enlivened by

the songs and flutterings of birds. Strange winged insects, be-
numbed by the rain, were clinging to the leaves and the bark of
the trees.

Raymond kindled a fire with great difficulty. The animals
turned eagerly to feed on the soft rich grass, while I, wrapping
myself in my blanket, lay down and gazed on the evening landscape. The mountains, whose stern features had frowned upon us
so gloomily, seemed lighted up with a benignant smile, and the
green, waving undulations of the plain were gladdened with warm
sunshine. Wet, ill, and wearied as I was, my heart grew lighter at
the view, and I drew from it an augury of good.

When morning came Raymond awoke coughing violently,
though I had apparently received no injury. We mounted, crossed
the little stream, pushed through the trees, and began our journey
over the plain beyond. And now, as we rode slowly along, we looked
anxiously on every hand for traces of the Indians, not doubting
that the village had passed somewhere in that vicinity; but the
scanty, shrivelled grass was not more than three or four inches
high, and the ground was so hard that a host might have marched
over it and left scarcely a trace of its passage.

Up hill and down hill, and clambering through ravines, we
continued our journey. As we were passing the foot of a hill I
saw Raymond, who was some rods in advance, suddenly jerk the
reins of his mule, slide from his seat, and run in a crouching posture
up a hollow; then in an instant I heard the sharp crack of his
rifle. A wounded antelope came running on three legs over the
hill. I lashed Pauline and made after him. My fleet little mare soon
brought me by his side, and, after leaping and bounding for a
few moments in vain, he stood still, as if despairing of escape. His
glistening eyes turned up towards my face with so piteous a look
that it was with feelings of infinite compunction that I shot him
through the head with a pistol. Raymond skinned and cut him
up, and we hung the fore-quarters to our saddles, much rejoiced
that our exhausted stock of provisions was renewed in such good
time.

Gaining the top of a hill we could see along the cloudy verge of
the prairie before us the lines of trees and shadowy groves, that
marked the course of Laramie Creek. Before noon we reached its
banks, and began anxiously to search them for footprints of the
Indians. We followed the stream for several miles, now on the
shore and now wading in the water, scrutinizing every sand-bar

and every muddy bank. So long was the search that we began to fear that we had left the trail undiscovered behind us. At length I heard Raymond shouting, and saw him jump from his mule to examine some object under the bank. I rode up to his side. It was the impression of an Indian moccasin. Encouraged by this, we continued our search, till at last some appearances on a soft surface of earth not far from the shore attracted my eye; and going to examine them, I found half a dozen tracks, some made by men and some by children. Just then Raymond observed across the stream the mouth of a brook entering it from the south. He forded the water, rode in at the opening, and in a moment I heard him shouting again; so I passed over and joined him. The brook had a broad sandy bed, along which the water trickled in a scanty stream; and on either bank the bushes were so close that the view was completely intercepted. I found Raymond stooping over the footprints of three or four horses. Proceeding, we found those of a man, then those of a child, then those of more horses; till at last the bushes on each bank were beaten down and broken, and the sand ploughed up with a multitude of footsteps, and scored across with the furrows made by the lodge-poles that had been dragged through. It was now certain that we had found the trail. I pushed through the bushes, and at a little distance on the prairie beyond found the ashes of a hundred and fifty lodge-fires, with bones and pieces of buffalo-robes scattered about, and the pickets to which horses had been tied, still standing in the ground. Elated by our success, we selected a convenient tree, and, turning the animals loose, prepared to make a meal from the haunch of the antelope.

Hardship and exposure had thriven with me wonderfully. I had gained both health and strength since leaving La Bonté's camp. Raymond and I dined together in high spirits; for we rashly presumed that having found one end of the trail we should have little difficulty in reaching the other. But when the animals were led in we found that our ill-luck had not ceased to follow us. As I was saddling Pauline, I saw that her eye was dull as lead, and the hue of her yellow coat visibly darkened. I placed my foot in the stirrup to mount, when she staggered and fell flat on her side. Gaining her feet with an effort, she stood by the fire with a drooping head. Whether she had been bitten by a snake, or poisoned by some noxious plant, or attacked by a sudden disorder, it was hard to say; but at all events, her sickness was sufficiently ill-timed and unfortunate. I succeeded in a second attempt to mount her, and with a slow pace we moved forward on the trail of the Indians. It led us up a hill and over a dreary plain; and here, to our great mortification, the traces almost disappeared, for the ground was hard as adamant; and if its flinty surface had ever retained the dint of a hoof, the marks had been washed away by the deluge of yesterday. An Indian village, in its disorderly march, is scattered over the prairie often to the width of half a mile; so that its trail is nowhere clearly marked, and the task of following it is made doubly wearisome and difficult. By good fortune, many large ant-hills, a yard or more in diameter, were scattered over the plain, and these were frequently broken by the footprints of men and horses, and marked by traces of the lodge-poles. The succulent leaves of the prickly-pear, bruised from the same causes, also helped to guide us; so inch by inch we moved along. Often we lost the trail altogether, and then found it again; but late in the afternoon we were totally at fault. We stood alone, without a clew to guide us. The broken plain expanded for league after league around us, and in front the long, dark ridge of mountains stretched from north to south. Mount Laramie, a little on our right, towered high above the rest, and from a dark valley just beyond one of its lower declivities, we discerned volumes of white smoke rising slowly.

'I think,' said Raymond, 'some Indians must be there. Perhaps we had better go.' But this plan was not lightly to be adopted, and we determined still to continue our search after the lost trail. Our good stars prompted us to this decision, for we afterward had reason to believe, from information given us by the Indians, that the smoke was raised as a decoy by a Crow war-party.

Evening was coming on, and there was neither wood nor water nearer than the foot of the mountains. So thither we turned, directing our course towards the point where Laramie Creek issues upon the prairie. When we reached it, the bare tops of the mountains were still bright with sunshine. The little river was breaking, with an angry current, from its dark prison. There was something in the close vicinity of the mountains and the loud surging of the rapids wonderfully cheering and exhilarating. There was a grass-plot by the river bank, surrounded by low ridges, which would effectually screen us and our fire from the sight of wandering Indians. Here among the grass, I observed numerous circles of large stones, traces of a Dakota winter encampment. We lay down, and did not awake till the sun was up. A large rock projected from the shore, and behind it the deep water was slowly eddying round and round. The temptation was irresistible. I threw off my clothes, leaped in, suffered myself to be borne once round with the current, and then, seizing the strong root of a water-plant, drew myself to the shore. The effect was so refreshing that I mistook it for returning health. But scarcely were we mounted and on our way, before the momentary glow passed. Again I hung as usual in my seat, scarcely able to hold myself erect.

'Look yonder,' said Raymond; 'you see that big hollow there; the Indians must have gone that way, if they went anywhere about here.'

We reached the gap, which was like a deep notch cut into the mountain-ridge, and here we soon found an ant-hill furrowed with the mark of a lodge-pole. This was quite enough; there could be no doubt now. As we rode on, the opening growing narrower, the Indians had been compelled to march in closer order, and the traces became numerous and distinct. The gap terminated in a rocky gateway, leading into a rough and steep defile, between two precipitous mountains. Here grass and weeds were bruised to fragments by the throng that had passed through. We moved slowly over the rocks, up the passage; and in this toilsome manner advanced for an hour or two, bare precipices, hundreds of feet high, shooting up on either hand. Raymond, with his hardy mule, was a few rods before me when we came to the foot of an ascent steeper than the rest, and which I trusted might prove the highest point of the defile. Pauline strained upward for a few yards, moaning and stumbling, and then came to a dead stop, unable to proceed further. I dismounted, and attempted to lead her; but my own exhausted strength soon gave out; so I loosened the trail-rope from her neck, and tying it round my arm, crawled up on my hands and knees. I gained the top, totally spent, the sweat-drops trickling from my forehead. Pauline stood like a statue by my side, her shadow falling upon the scorching rock; and in this shade, for there was no other, I lay for some time, scarcely able to move a limb. All around, the black crags, sharp as needles at the top, stood baking in the sun, without tree or bush or blade of grass to cover their nakedness. The whole scene seemed parched with a pitiless, insufferable heat.

After a while I could mount again, and we moved on, descending the defile on its western side. There was something ridiculous in the situation. Man and horse were helpless alike. Pauline and I could neither fight nor run.

Raymond's saddle-girth slipped; and while I proceeded he stopped to repair the mischief. I came to the top of a little declivity, where a welcome sight greeted my eye; a nook of fresh green grass nestled among the cliffs, sunny clumps of bushes on one side, and shaggy old pine-trees leaning from the rocks on the other. A shrill, familiar voice saluted me, and recalled me to days of boyhood,—that of the insect called the 'locust' by New England schoolboys, which was clinging among the heated boughs of the old pine-trees. Then, too, as I passed the bushes, the low sound of falling water reached my ear. Pauline turned of her own accord, and pushing through the boughs we found a black rock overarched by the cool green canopy. An icy stream was pouring from its side into a wide basin of white sand, whence it had no visible outlet, but filtered through into the soil below. While I filled a tin cup at the spring, Pauline was eagerly plunging her head deep in the pool. Other visitors had been there before us. All around in the soft soil were the footprints of elk, deer, and the Rocky Mountain sheep; and the grizzly bear too had left the recent prints of his broad foot, with its frightful array of claws. Among these mountains was his home.

Soon after leaving the spring we found a little grassy plain, encircled by the mountains, and marked, to our great joy, with all the traces of an Indian camp. Raymond's practised eye detected certain signs, by which he recognized the spot where Reynal's lodge had been pitched and his horses picketed. I approached, and stood looking at the place. Reynal and I had, I believe, hardly a feeling in common, and it perplexed me a good deal to understand why I should look with so much interest on the ashes of his fire, when between him and me there was no other bond of sympathy than the slender and precarious one of a kindred race.

In half an hour from this we were free of the mountains. There was a plain before us totally barren and thickly peopled in many parts with prairie-dogs, who sat at the mouths of their burrows and yelped at us as we passed. The plain, as we thought, was about six miles wide, but it cost us two hours to cross it. Then another mountain-range rose before us. From the dense bushes that clothed the steeps for a thousand feet shot up black crags, all leaning one way, and shattered by storms and thunder into grim and threatening shapes. As we entered a narrow passage on the trail of the Indians, they impended frightfully above our heads.

Our course was through thick woods, in the shade and sunlight of overhanging boughs. As we wound from side to side of the passage to avoid its obstructions, we could see at intervals, through the foliage, the awful forms of the gigantic cliffs, that seemed to hem us in on the right and on the left, before and behind.

In an open space, fenced in by high rocks, stood two Indian forts, of a square form, rudely built of logs and branches. They were somewhat ruinous, having probably been constructed the year before. Each might have contained about twenty men. Perhaps in this gloomy spot some party had been beset by enemies, and those scowling rocks and blasted trees might not long since have looked down on a conflict, unchronicled and unknown. Yet if any traces of bloodshed remained they were hidden by the bushes and tall, rank weeds.

Gradually the mountains drew apart, and the passage expanded into a plain, where again we found traces of an Indian encampment. There were trees and bushes just before us, and we stopped here for an hour's rest and refreshment. When we had finished our meal Raymond struck fire, and lighting his pipe, sat down at the foot of a tree to smoke. For some time I observed him puffing away with a face of unusual solemnity. Then slowly taking the pipe from his lips, he looked up and remarked that we had better not go any farther.

'Why not?' asked I.

He said that the country was become very dangerous, that we were entering the range of the Snakes, Arapahoes, and Gros-ventre Blackfeet, and that if any of their wandering parties should meet us, it would cost us our lives; but he added, with blunt fidelity, that he would go anywhere I wished. I told him to bring up the animals, and mounting them we proceeded again. I confess that, as we moved forward, the prospect seemed but a doubtful one. I would have given the world for my ordinary elasticity of body and mind, and for a horse of such strength and spirit as the journey required.

Closer and closer the rocks gathered round us, growing taller and steeper, and pressing more and more upon our path. We entered at length a defile which, in its way, I never have seen rivalled. The mountain was cracked from top to bottom, and we were creeping along the bottom of the fissure, in dampness and gloom, with the clink of hoofs on the loose shingly rocks, and the hoarse murmuring of a petulant brook which kept us company. Sometimes the water, foaming among the stones, overspread the whole narrow passage; sometimes, withdrawing to one side, it gave us room to pass dry-shod. Looking up, we could see a narrow ribbon of bright blue sky between the dark edges of the opposing cliffs. This did not last long. The passage soon widened, and sunbeams found their way down, flashing upon the black waters. The defile would spread to many rods in width; bushes, trees, and flowers would spring by the side of the brook; the cliffs would be feathered with shrubbery that clung in every crevice, and fringed with trees that grew along their sunny edges. Then we would be moving again in darkness. The passage seemed about four miles long, and before we reached the end of it the unshod hoofs of our animals were broken, and their legs cut by the sharp stones. Issuing from the mountain we found another plain. All around it stood a circle of precipices, that seemed the impersonation of Silence and Solitude. Here again the Indians had encamped, as well they might after passing with their women, children, and horses, through the gulf behind us. In one day we had made a journey which it had cost them three to accomplish.

The only outlet to this amphitheatre lay over a hill some two hundred feet high, up which we moved with difficulty. Looking from the top we saw that at last we were free of the mountains. The prairie spread before us, but so wild and broken that the view was everywhere obstructed. Far on our left one tall hill swelled up against the sky, on the smooth, pale-green surface of which four slowly moving black specks were discernible. They were evidently buffalo, and we hailed the sight as a good augury; for where the buffalo were, there the Indians would probably be found. We hoped on that very night to reach the village. We were anxious to do so for a double reason, wishing to bring our journey to an end, and knowing moreover that though to enter the village in broad daylight would be perfectly safe, yet to encamp in its vicinity would be dangerous. But as we rode on, the sun was sinking, and soon was within half an hour of the horizon. We ascended a hill and looked about us for a spot for our encampment. The prairie was like a turbulent ocean suddenly congealed when its waves were at the highest, and it lay half in light and half in shadow, as the rich sunshine, yellow as gold, was pouring over it. The rough bushes of the wild sage were growing everywhere, its dull pale-green overspreading hill and hollow. Yet a little way before us a bright green belt of grass was winding along the plain, and here and there throughout its course glistened pools of water. We went down to it, kindled a fire, and turned our horses loose to feed. It was a little trickling brook, that for some yards on either side turned the barren prairie into fertility, and here and there it spread into deep pools, where the beavers had dammed it up.

We placed our last remaining piece of antelope before a scanty fire, mournfully reflecting on our exhausted stock of provisions. Just then a large gray hare, peculiar to these prairies, came jumping along, and seated himself within fifty yards to look at us. I thoughtlessly raised my rifle to shoot him, but Raymond called out to me not to fire, for fear the report should reach the ears of the Indians. That night for the first time we considered that the danger to which we were exposed was of a somewhat serious character; and to those who are unacquainted with Indians, it may seem strange that our chief apprehensions arose from the supposed proximity of the people whom we intended to visit. Had any straggling party of these faithful friends caught sight of us from the hill-top, they would probably have returned in the night to plunder us of our horses, and perhaps of our scalps. But the prairie is unfavorable to nervousness; and I presume that neither Raymond nor I thought twice of the matter that evening.

For eight hours, pillowed on our saddles, we lay insensible as logs. Pauline's yellow head was stretched over me when I awoke. I rose and examined her. Her feet were bruised and swollen by the accidents of yesterday, but her eye was brighter, her motions livelier, and her mysterious malady had visibly abated. We moved on, hoping within an hour to come in sight of the Indian village; but again disappointment awaited us. The trail disappeared upon a hard and stony plain. Raymond and I rode from side to side, scrutinizing every yard of ground, until at length I found traces of the lodge-poles, by the side of a ridge of rocks. We began to follow them.

'What is that black spot out there on the prairie?'

'It looks like a dead buffalo,' answered Raymond.

We rode to it, and found it to be the huge carcass of a bull killed by the hunters as they had passed. Tangled hair and scraps of hide were scattered on all sides, for the wolves had made merry over it, and hollowed out the entire carcass. It was covered with myriads of large black crickets, and from its appearance must have lain there four or five days. The sight was a disheartening one, and I observed to Raymond that the Indians might still be fifty or sixty miles off. But he shook his head, and replied that they dared not go so far for fear of their enemies the Snakes.

Soon after this we lost the trail again, and ascended a neighboring ridge, totally at a loss. Before us lay a plain perfectly flat, spreading on the right and left, without apparent limit, and bounded in front by a long, broken line of hills, ten or twelve miles distant. All was open and exposed to view, yet not a buffalo nor an Indian was visible.

'Do you see that?' said Raymond; 'now we had better turn round.'

But as Raymond's *bourgeois* thought otherwise, we descended the hill and began to cross the plain. We had come so far that neither Pauline's limbs nor my own could carry me back to Fort Laramie. I considered that the lines of expediency and inclination tallied exactly, and that the most prudent course was to keep forward. The ground immediately around us was thickly strewn with the skulls and bones of buffalo, for here, a year or two before, the Indians had made a 'surround;' yet no living game was in sight. At length an antelope sprang up and gazed at us. We fired together, and both missed, although the animal stood, a fair mark, within eighty yards. This ill-success might perhaps be charged to our own eagerness, for by this time we had no provisions left except a little flour. We could see several pools of water, glistening in the distance. As we approached, wolves and antelopes bounded away through the tall grass around them, and flocks of large white plover flew screaming over their surface. Having failed of the antelope Raymond tried his hand at the birds, with the same ill-success. The water also disappointed us. Its margin was so mired by the crowd of buffalo that our timorous animals were afraid to approach. So we turned away and moved towards the hills. The rank grass, where it was not trampled down by the buffalo, fairly swept our horses' necks.

Again we found the same execrable barren prairie, offering no clew by which to guide our way. As we drew near the hills an opening appeared, through which the Indians must have gone if they had passed that way at all. Slowly we began to ascend it. I felt the most dreary forebodings of ill-success when on looking round I could discover neither dent of hoof, nor footprint, nor trace of lodge-pole, though the passage was encumbered by the skulls of buffalo. We heard thunder muttering; another storm was coming on.

As we gained the top of the gap the prospect beyond began to disclose itself. First, we saw a long dark line of ragged clouds upon the horizon, while above them rose the peaks of the Medicine-Bow range, the vanguard of the Rocky Mountains; then little by little the plain came into view, a vast green uniformity, forlorn and tenantless, though Laramie Creek glistened in a waving line over its surface, without a bush or a tree upon its banks. As yet, the round projecting shoulder of a hill intercepted a part of the view. I rode in advance, when suddenly I could distinguish a few dark spots on the prairie, along the bank of the stream.

'Buffalo!' said I.

'Horses, by God!' exclaimed Raymond, lashing his mule forward as he spoke. More and more of the plain disclosed itself, and more and more horses appeared scattered along the river bank, or feeding in bands over the prairie. Then, standing in a circle by the stream, swarming with their savage inhabitants, we saw, a mile or more off, the tall lodges of the Ogillallah. Never did the heart of wanderer more gladden at the sight of home than did mine at the sight of that Indian camp.

14. The Ogillallah Village

This is hardly the place for portraying the mental features of the Indians. The same picture, slightly changed in shade and coloring, would serve with very few exceptions for all the tribes north of the Mexican territories. But with this similarity in their modes of thought, the tribes of the lake and ocean shores, of the forests and of the plains, differ greatly in their manner of life. Having been domesticated for several weeks among one of the wildest of the hordes that roam over the remote prairies, I had unusual opportunities of observing them, and flatter myself that a sketch of the scenes that passed daily before my eyes may not be without interest. They were thorough savages. Neither their manners nor their ideas were in the slightest degree modified by contact with civilization. They knew nothing of the power and real character of the white men, and their children would scream in terror when they saw me. Their religion, superstitions, and prejudices were those handed down to them from immemorial time. They fought with the weapons that their fathers fought with, and wore the same garments of skins. They were living representatives of the 'stone age;' for though their lances and arrows were tipped with iron procured from the traders, they still used the rude stone mallet of the primeval world.

Great changes are at hand in that region. With the stream of emigration to Oregon and California, the buffalo will dwindle away, and the large wandering communities who depend on them for support must be broken and scattered. The Indians will soon be abased by whiskey and overawed by military posts; so that within a few years the traveller may pass in tolerable security through their country. Its danger and its charm will have disappeared together.

As soon as Raymond and I discovered the village from the gap in the hills, we were seen in our turn; keen eyes were constantly on the watch. As we rode down upon the plain, the side of the village nearest us was darkened with a crowd of naked figures. Several men came forward to meet us. I could distinguish among them the green blanket of the Frenchman Reynal. When we came up the ceremony of shaking hands had to be gone through in due form, and then all were eager to know what had become of the rest of my party. I satisfied them on this point, and we all moved together towards the village.

'You 've missed it,' said Reynal; 'if you 'd been here day before yesterday, you 'd have found the whole prairie over yonder black with buffalo as far as you could see. There were no cows, though,— nothing but bulls. We made a "surround" every day till yesterday. See the village there; don't that look like good living?'

In fact I could see, even at that distance, long cords stretched from lodge to lodge, over which the meat, cut by the squaws into thin sheets, was hanging to dry in the sun. I noticed too that the village was somewhat smaller than when I had last seen it, and I asked Reynal the cause. He said that old Le Borgne had felt too weak to pass over the mountains, and so had remained behind with all his relations, including Mahto-Tatonka and his brothers. The Whirlwind too had been unwilling to come so far, because, as Reynal said, he was afraid. Only half a dozen lodges had adhered to him, the main body of the village setting their chief's authority

at naught, and taking the course most agreeable to their in-
clinations.

'What chiefs are there in the village now?' asked I.

'Well,' said Reynal, 'there's old Red-Water, and the Eagle-
Feather, and the Big Crow, and the Mad Wolf, and The Panther,
and the White-Shield, and—what's his name?—the half-breed
Cheyenne.'

By this time we were close to the village, and I observed that
while the greater part of the lodges were very large and neat in
their appearance, there was at one side a cluster of squalid, miserable huts. I looked towards them and made some remark about
their wretched appearance. But I was touching upon delicate
ground.

'My squaw's relations live in those lodges,' said Reynal, very
warmly; 'and there isn't a better set in the whole village.'

'Are there any chiefs among them?'

'Chiefs?' said Reynal; 'yes, plenty!'

'What are their names?'

'Their names? Why, there's the Arrow-Head. If he isn't a
chief he ought to be one. And there's the Hail-Storm. He's
nothing but a boy, to be sure; but he's bound to be a chief one of
these days.'

Just then we passed between two of the lodges, and entered the
great area of the village. Superb naked figures stood silently gazing
on us.

'Where's the Bad Wound's lodge?' said I to Reynal.

'There you've missed it again! The Bad Wound is away with
The Whirlwind. If you could have found him here, and gone to
live in his lodge, he would have treated you better than any man
in the village. But there's the Big Crow's lodge yonder, next to
old Red-Water's. He's a good Indian for the whites, and I advise
you to go and live with him.'

'Are there many squaws and children in his lodge?' said I.

'No, only one squaw and two or three children. He keeps the
rest in a separate lodge by themselves.'

So, still followed by a crowd of Indians, Raymond and I rode
up to the entrance of the Big Crow's lodge. A squaw came out
immediately and took our horses. I put aside the leather flap that
covered the low opening, and stooping, entered the Big Crow's
dwelling. There I could see the chief in the dim light, seated at one
side, on a pile of buffalo-robes. He greeted me with a guttural

'How, colà!' I requested Reynal to tell him that Raymond and I
were come to live with him. The Big Crow gave another low exclamation. The announcement may seem intrusive, but, in fact,
every Indian in the village would have deemed himself honored
that white men should give such preference to his hospitality.

The squaw spread a buffalo-robe for us in the guest's place at
the head of the lodge. Our saddles were brought in, and scarcely
were we seated upon them before the place was thronged with
Indians, crowding in to see us. The Big Crow produced his pipe
and filled it with the mixture of tobacco and *shongsasha*, or red
willow bark. Round and round it passed, and a lively conversation went forward. Meanwhile a squaw placed before the two
guests a wooden bowl of boiled buffalo-meat; but unhappily this
was not the only banquet destined to be inflicted on us. One after
another, boys and young squaws thrust their heads in at the opening, to invite us to various feasts in different parts of the village.
For half an hour or more we were actively engaged in passing from
lodge to lodge, tasting in each of the bowl of meat set before us,
and inhaling a whiff or two from our entertainer's pipe. A thunder-
storm that had been threatening for some time now began in good
earnest. We crossed over to Reynal's lodge, though it hardly deserved the name, for it consisted only of a few old buffalo-robes,
supported on poles, and was quite open on one side. Here we sat
down, and the Indians gathered round us.

'What is it?' said I, 'that makes the thunder?'

'It 's my belief,' said Reynal, 'that it 's a big stone rolling over
the sky.'

'Very likely,' I replied; 'but I want to know what the Indians
think about it.'

So he interpreted my question, which produced some debate.
There was a difference of opinion. At last old Mene-Seela, or Red-
Water, who sat by himself at one side, looked up with his withered
face, and said he had always known what the thunder was. It was
a great black bird; and once he had seen it, in a dream, swooping
down from the Black Hills, with its loud-roaring wings; and when
it flapped them over a lake, they struck lightning from the water.

'The thunder is bad,' said another old man, who sat muffled
in his buffalo-robe; 'he killed my brother last summer.'

Reynal, at my request, asked for an explanation; but the old
man remained doggedly silent and would not look up. Some time
after, I learned how the accident occurred. The man who was

killed belonged to an association which, among other mystic
functions, claimed the exclusive power and privilege of fighting the
thunder. Whenever a storm which they wished to avert was
threatening, the thunder-fighters would take their bows and
arrows, their guns, their magic drum, and a sort of whistle made
out of the wing-bone of the war-eagle, and, thus equipped, run
out and fire at the rising cloud, whooping, yelling, whistling, and
beating their drum to frighten it down again. One afternoon a
heavy black cloud was coming up, and they repaired to the top
of a hill, where they brought all their magic artillery into play
against it. But the undaunted thunder, refusing to be terrified,
darted out a bright flash, which struck one of the party dead as
he was in the very act of shaking his long iron-pointed lance against
it. The rest scattered and ran, yelling in an ecstasy of superstitious terror, back to their lodges.

The lodge of my host Kongra Tonga, or the Big Crow, presented
a picturesque spectacle that evening. A score or more of Indians
were seated round it in a circle, their dark naked forms just visible
by the dull light of the smouldering fire in the middle. The pipe
glowed brightly in the gloom as it passed from hand to hand. Then
a squaw would drop a piece of buffalo-fat on the dull embers.
Instantly a bright flame would leap up, darting its light to the
very apex of the tall, conical structure, where the tops of the
slender poles that supported the covering of hide were gathered
together. It gilded the features of the Indians, as with animated
gestures they sat, telling their endless stories of war and hunting,
and displayed rude garments of skins that hung round the lodge,
—the bow, quiver, and lance, suspended over the resting-place
of the chief, and the rifles and powder-horns of the two white
guests. For a moment all would be bright as day; then the flames
would die out; fitful flashes from the embers would illumine the
lodge, and then leave it in darkness. Then the light would wholly
fade, and the lodge and all within it be involved again in obscurity.

As I left the lodge next morning I was saluted by howling and
yelping all around the village, and half its canine population
rushed forth to the attack. Being as cowardly as they were
clamorous, they kept jumping about me at the distance of a few
yards, only one little cur, about ten inches long, having spirit
enough to make a direct assault. He dashed valiantly at the
leather tassel which in the Dakota fashion was trailing behind the

heel of my moccasin, and kept his hold, growling and snarling all the while, though every step I made almost jerked him over on his back. As I knew that the eyes of the whole village were on the watch to see if I showed any sign of fear, I walked forward without looking to the right or left, surrounded wherever I went by this magic circle of dogs. When I came to Reynal's lodge I sat down by it; on which the dogs dispersed growling to their respective quarters. Only one large white one remained, running about me and showing his teeth. I called him, but he only growled the more. I looked at him well. He was fat and sleek; just such a dog as I wanted. 'My friend,' thought I, 'you shall pay for this! I will have you eaten this very morning!'

I intended that day to give the Indians a feast, by way of conveying a favorable impression of my character and dignity; and a white dog is the dish which the customs of the Dakota prescribe for all occasions of formality and importance. I consulted Reynal: he soon discovered that an old woman in the next lodge was owner of the white dog. I took a gaudy cotton handkerchief, and, laying it on the ground, arranged some vermilion, beads, and other trinkets upon it. Then the old squaw was summoned. I pointed to the dog and to the handkerchief. She gave a scream of delight, snatched up the prize, and vanished with it into her lodge. For a few more trifles, I engaged the services of two other squaws, each of whom took the white dog by one of his paws, and led him away behind the lodges. Having killed him they threw him into a fire to singe; then chopped him up and put him into two large kettles to boil. Meanwhile I told Raymond to fry in buffalo-fat what little flour we had left, and also to make a kettle of tea as an additional luxury.

The Big Crow's squaw was briskly at work sweeping out the lodge for the approaching festivity. I confided to my host himself the task of inviting the guests, thinking that I might thereby shift from my own shoulders the odium of neglect and oversight.

When feasting is in question one hour of the day serves an Indian as well as another. My entertainment came off at about eleven o'clock. At that hour Reynal and Raymond walked across the area of the village, to the admiration of the inhabitants, carrying the two kettles of dog meat slung on a pole between them. These they placed in the centre of the lodge, and then went back for the bread and the tea. Meanwhile I had put on a pair of brilliant moccasins, and substituted for my old buckskin frock a coat which I had brought with me in view of such public occasions. I also made careful use of the razor, an operation which no man will neglect who desires to gain the good opinion of Indians. Thus attired, I seated myself between Reynal and Raymond at the head of the lodge. Only a few minutes elapsed before all the guests had come in and were seated on the ground, wedged together in a close circle. Each brought with him a wooden bowl to hold his share of the repast. When all were assembled, two of the officials, called 'soldiers' by the white men, came forward with ladles made of the horn of the Rocky Mountain sheep, and began to distribute the feast, assigning a double share to the old men and chiefs. The dog vanished with astonishing celerity, and each guest turned his dish bottom upward to show that all was gone. Then the bread was distributed in its turn, and finally the tea. As the 'soldiers' poured it out into the same wooden bowls that had served for the substantial part of the meal, I thought it had a particularly curious and uninviting color.

'Oh,' said Reynal, 'there was not tea enough, so I stirred some soot in the kettle, to make it look strong.'

Fortunately an Indian's palate is not very discriminating. The tea was well sweetened, and that was all they cared for.

Now the feast being over, the time for speech-making was come. The Big Crow produced a flat piece of wood, on which he cut up tobacco and *shongsasha*, and mixed them in due proportions. The pipes were filled and passed from hand to hand around the company. Then I began my speech, each sentence being interpreted by Reynal as I went on, and echoed by the whole audience with the usual exclamations of assent and approval. As nearly as I can recollect, it was as follows:—

'I had come,' I told them, 'from a country so far distant that at the rate they travel, they could not reach it in a year.'

'How! how!'

'There the Meneaska were more numerous than the blades of grass on the prairie. The squaws were far more beautiful than any they had ever seen, and all the men were brave warriors.'

'How! how! how!'

I was assailed by twinges of conscience as I uttered these last words. But I recovered myself and began again.

'While I was living in the Meneaska lodges, I had heard of the Ogillallah, how great and brave a nation they were, how they loved the whites, and how well they could hunt the buffalo and

strike their enemies. I resolved to come and see if all that I heard
was true.'

'How! how! how! how!'

'As I had come on horseback through the mountains, I had been
able to bring them only a very few presents.'

'How!'

'But I had enough tobacco to give them all a small piece. They
might smoke it and see how much better it was than the tobacco
which they got from the traders.'

'How! how! how!'

'I had plenty of powder, lead, knives, and tobacco at Fort
Laramie. These I was anxious to give them, and if any of them
should come to the fort before I went away, I would make them
handsome presents.'

'How! how! how! how!'

Raymond then cut up and distributed among them two or
three pounds of tobacco, and old Mene-Seela began to make a
reply. It was long, but the following was the pith of it.

'He had always loved the whites. They were the wisest people
on earth. He believed they could do anything, and he was always
glad when any of them came to live in the Ogillallah lodges. It was
true I had not made them many presents, but the reason of it was
plain. It was clear that I liked them, or I never should have come
so far to find their village.'

Several other speeches of similar import followed, and then, this
more serious matter being disposed of, there was an interval of
smoking, laughing, and conversation. Old Mene-Seela suddenly
interrupted it with a loud voice:—

'Now is a good time,' he said, 'when all the old men and chiefs
are here together, to decide what the people shall do. We came
over the mountains to make our lodges for next year. Our old
ones are good for nothing; they are rotten and worn out. But we
have been disappointed. We have killed buffalo-bulls enough, but
we have found no herds of cows, and the skins of bulls are too
thick and heavy for our squaws to make lodges of. There must be
plenty of cows about the Medicine-Bow Mountain. We ought to
go there. To be sure it is farther westward than we have ever
been before, and perhaps the Snakes will attack us, for those
hunting-grounds belong to them. But we must have new lodges
at any rate; our old ones will not serve for another year. We ought
not to be afraid of the Snakes. Our warriors are brave, and they are

all ready for war. Besides, we have three white men with their rifles to help us.'

This speech produced a good deal of debate. As Reynal did not interpret what was said, I could only judge of the meaning by the features and gestures of the speakers. At the end of it however the greater number seemed to have fallen in with Mene-Seela's opinion. A short silence followed, and then the old man struck up a discordant chant, which I was told was a song of thanks for the entertainment I had given them.

'Now,' said he, 'let us go, and give the white men a chance to breathe.'

So the company all dispersed into the open air, and for some time the old chief was walking round the village, singing his song in praise of the feast, after the custom of the nation.

At last the day drew to a close, and as the sun went down the horses came trooping from the surrounding plains to be picketed before the dwellings of their respective masters. Soon within the great circle of lodges appeared another concentric circle of restless horses; and here and there fires glowed around them. I went over and sat by the lodge of Reynal. The Eagle-Feather, who was a son of Mene-Seela, and brother of my host the Big Crow, was seated there already, and I asked him if the village would move in the morning. He shook his head, and said that nobody could tell, for since old Mahto-Tatonka had died, the people had been like children that did not know their own minds. They were no better than a body without a head. So I, as well as the Indians them-selves, fell asleep that night without knowing whether we should set out in the morning towards the country of the Snakes.

At daybreak, however, as I was coming up from the river after my morning's ablutions, I saw that a movement was contem-plated. Some of the lodges were reduced to nothing but bare skeletons of poles; the leather covering of others was flapping in the wind as the squaws pulled it off. One or two chiefs of note had resolved, it seemed, on moving; and they having set their squaws to work, the example was followed by the rest of the village. One by one the lodges were sinking down in rapid succession, and where the great circle of the village had been only a few moments before, nothing now remained but a ring of horses and Indians, crowded in confusion together. The ruins of the lodges were spread over the ground, together with kettles, stone mallets, great ladles of horn, buffalo-robes, and cases of painted hide, filled with

dried meat. Squaws bustled about in busy preparation, the old
hags screaming to one another at the stretch of their leathern
lungs. The shaggy horses were patiently standing while the lodge-
poles were lashed to their sides, and the baggage piled upon their
backs. The dogs, with tongues lolling out, lay lazily panting, and
waiting for the time of departure. Each warrior sat on the ground
by the decaying embers of his fire, unmoved amid the confusion,
holding in his hand the long trail-rope of his horse.

As their preparations were completed, each family moved off
the ground. The crowd was rapidly melting away. I could see
them crossing the river, and passing in quick succession along the
profile of the hill on the farther side. When all were gone I mounted
and set out after them, followed by Raymond, and, as we gained
the summit, the whole village came in view at once, straggling
away for a mile or more over the barren plains before us. Everywhere glittered the iron points of lances. The sun never shone upon
a more strange array. Here were the heavy-laden pack-horses,
some wretched old woman leading them, and two or three children
clinging to their backs. Here were mules or ponies covered from
head to tail with gaudy trappings, and mounted by some gay
young squaw, grinning bashfulness and pleasure as the Meneaska
looked at her. Boys with miniature bows and arrows wandered
over the plains, little naked children ran along on foot, and numberless dogs scampered among the feet of the horses. The young
braves, gaudy with paint and feathers, rode in groups among the
crowd, often galloping, two or three at once along the line, to try
the speed of their horses. Here and there you might see a rank of
sturdy pedestrians stalking along in their white buffalo-robes.
These were the dignitaries of the village, the old men and warriors,
to whose age and experience that wandering democracy yielded
a silent deference. With the rough prairie and the broken hills for
its background, the restless scene was striking and picturesque
beyond description. Days and weeks made me familiar with it,
but never impaired its effect upon my fancy.

As we moved on, the broken column grew yet more scattered
and disorderly, until, as we approached the foot of a hill, I saw the
old men before mentioned seating themselves in a line upon the
ground, in advance of the whole. They lighted a pipe and sat
smoking, laughing, and telling stories, while the people, stopping
as they successively came up, were soon gathered in a crowd
behind them. Then the old men rose, drew their buffalo-robes

over their shoulders, and strode on as before. Gaining the top of
the hill, we found a steep declivity before us. There was not a
minute's pause. The whole descended in a mass, amid dust and
confusion. The horses braced their feet as they slid down, women
and children screamed, dogs yelped as they were trodden upon,
while stones and earth went rolling to the bottom. In a few
moments I could see the village from the summit, spreading again
far and wide over the plain below.

At our encampment that afternoon I was attacked anew by my
old disorder. In half an hour the strength that I had been gaining
for a week past had vanished again, and I became like a man in a
dream. But at sunset I lay down in the Big Crow's lodge and
slept, totally unconscious till the morning. The first thing that
awakened me was a hoarse flapping over my head, and a sudden
light that poured in upon me. The camp was breaking up, and
the squaws were moving the covering from the lodge. I arose
and shook off my blanket with the feeling of perfect health; but
scarcely had I gained my feet when a sense of my helpless condition was once more forced upon me, and I found myself scarcely
able to stand. Raymond had brought up Pauline and the mule,
and I stooped to raise my saddle from the ground. My strength
was unequal to the task. 'You must saddle her,' said I to Raymond as I sat down again on a pile of buffalo-robes. He did so,
and with a painful effort I mounted. As we were passing over a
great plain, surrounded by long broken ridges, I rode slowly in
advance of the Indians, with thoughts that wandered far from
the time and the place. Suddenly the sky darkened, and thunder
began to mutter. Clouds were rising over the hills, as dark as the
first forebodings of an approaching calamity; and in a moment all
around was wrapped in shadow. I looked behind. The Indians
had stopped to prepare for the approaching storm, and the dense
mass of savages stretched far to the right and left. Since the first
attack of my disorder the effects of rain upon me had usually been
injurious in the extreme. I had no strength to spare, having at
that moment scarcely enough to keep my seat on horseback. Then,
for the first time, it pressed upon me as a strong probability that I
might never leave those deserts. 'Well,' thought I to myself, 'the
prairie makes quick and sharp work. Better to die here, in the
saddle to the last, than to stifle in the hot air of a sick chamber;
and a thousand times better than to drag out life, as many have
done, in the helpless inaction of lingering disease.' So, drawing

the buffalo-robe on which I sat, over my head, I waited till the storm should come. It broke at last with a sudden burst of fury, and passing away as rapidly as it came, left the sky clear again. My reflections served me no other purposes than to look back upon as a piece of curious experience; for the rain did not produce the ill effects that I had expected. We encamped within an hour. Having no change of clothes, I contrived to borrow a curious kind of substitute from Reynal; and this done, I went home, that is, to the Big Crow's lodge, to make the entire transfer that was necessary. Half a dozen squaws were in the lodge, and one of them taking my arm held it against her own, while a general laugh and scream of admiration was raised at the contrast in the color of the skin.

Our encampment that afternoon was not far from a spur of the Black Hills, whose ridges, bristling with fir-trees, rose from the plains a mile or two on our right. That they might move more rapidly towards their proposed hunting-grounds, the Indians determined to leave at this place their stock of dried meat and other superfluous articles. Some left even their lodges, and contented themselves with carrying a few hides to make a shelter from the sun and rain. Half the inhabitants set out in the afternoon, with loaded pack-horses, towards the mountains. Here they suspended the dried meat upon trees, where the wolves and grizzly bears could not get at it. All returned at evening. Some of the young men declared that they had heard the reports of guns among the mountains to the eastward, and many surmises were thrown out as to the origin of these sounds. For my part, I was in hopes that Shaw and Henry Chatillon were coming to join us. I little suspected that at that very moment my unlucky comrade was lying on a buffalo-robe at Fort Laramie, fevered with ivy poison, and solacing his woes with tobacco and Shakspeare.

As we moved over the plains on the next morning, several young men rode about the country as scouts; and at length we began to see them occasionally on the tops of the hills, shaking their robes as a signal that they saw buffalo. Soon after, some bulls came in sight. Horsemen darted away in pursuit, and we could see from the distance that one or two of the buffalo were killed. Raymond suddenly became inspired.

'This is the country for me!' he said; 'if I could only carry the buffalo that are killed here every month down to St Louis, I'd make my fortune in one winter. I'd grow as rich as old Papin, or

Mackenzie either. I call this the poor man's market. When I 'm
hungry, I 've only got to take my rifle and go out and get better
meat than the rich folks down below can get, with all their
money. You won't catch me living in St Louis another winter.'

'No,' said Reynal, 'you had better say that, after you and your
Spanish woman almost starved to death there. What a fool you
were ever to take her to the settlements!'

'Your Spanish woman?' said I; 'I never heard of her before.
Are you married to her?'

'No,' answered Raymond; 'the priests don't marry their
women, and why should I marry mine?'

This honorable mention of the Mexican clergy introduced the
subject of religion, and I found that my two associates, in common with other white men in that country, were as indifferent to
their future welfare as men whose lives are in constant peril are
apt to be. Raymond had never heard of the Pope. A certain bishop,
who lived at Taos or at Santa Fé, embodied his loftiest idea of an
ecclesiastical dignitary. Reynal observed that a priest had been
at Fort Laramie two years ago, on his way to the Nez Percé
mission, and that he had confessed all the men there, and given
them absolution. 'I got a good clearing out myself that time,' said
Reynal, 'and I reckon that will do for me till I go down to the
settlements again.'

Here he interrupted himself with an oath, and exclaimed:
'Look! look! The Panther is running an antelope!'

The Panther, on his black-and-white horse, one of the best in
the village, came at full speed over the hill in hot pursuit of an
antelope, that darted away like lightning before him. The attempt
was made in mere sport and bravado, for very few are the horses
that can for a moment compete in swiftness with this little animal.
The antelope ran down the hill towards the main body of the
Indians, who were moving over the plain below. Sharp yells were
given, and horsemen galloped out to intercept his flight. At this he
turned sharply to the left, and scoured away with such speed that
he distanced all his pursuers, even the vaunted horse of the
Panther himself. A few moments after, we witnessed a more
serious sport. A shaggy buffalo-bull bounded out from a neighboring hollow, and close behind him came a slender Indian boy,
riding without stirrups or saddle, and lashing his eager little horse
to full speed. Yard after yard he drew closer to his gigantic victim,
though the bull, with his short tail erect and his tongue lolling out

a foot from his foaming jaws, was straining his unwieldy strength to the utmost. A moment more, and the boy was close alongside. It was our friend the Hail-Storm. He dropped the rein on his horse's neck and jerked an arrow from the quiver at his shoulder.

'I tell you,' said Reynal, 'that in a year's time that boy will match the best hunter in the village. There, he has given it to him! and there goes another! You feel well now, old bull, don't you, with two arrows stuck in your lights! There, he has given him another! Hear how the Hail-Storm yells when he shoots! Yes, jump at him; try it again, old fellow! You may jump all day before you get your horns into that pony!'

The bull sprang again and again at his assailant, but the horse kept dodging with wonderful celerity. At length the bull followed up his attack with a furious rush, and the Hail-Storm was put to flight, the shaggy monster following close behind. The boy clung in his seat like a leech, and secure in the speed of his little pony, looked round towards us and laughed. In a moment he was again alongside the bull, who was now driven to desperation. His eyeballs glared through his tangled mane, and the blood flew from his mouth and nostrils. Thus still battling with each other, the two enemies disappeared over the hill.

Many of the Indians rode at full gallop towards the spot. We followed at a more moderate pace, and soon saw the bull lying dead on the side of the hill. The Indians were gathered around him, and several knives were already at work. These little instruments were plied with such wonderful address that the twisted sinews were cut apart, the ponderous bones fell asunder as if by magic, and in a moment the vast carcass was reduced to a heap of bloody ruins. The surrounding group of savages offered no very attractive spectacle to a civilized eye. Some were cracking the huge thighbones and devouring the marrow within; others were cutting away pieces of the liver and other approved morsels, and swallowing them on the spot with the appetite of wolves. The faces of most of them, besmeared with blood from ear to ear, looked grim and horrible enough. My friend the White Shield proffered me a marrow-bone, so skilfully laid open that all the rich substance within was exposed to view at once. Another Indian held out a large piece of the delicate lining of the paunch; but these courteous offerings I begged leave to decline. I noticed one little boy who was very busy with his knife about the jaws and throat of the buffalo, from which he extracted some morsel of peculiar delicacy. It is

but fair to say that only certain parts of the animal are considered
eligible in these extempore banquets.

We encamped that night, and marched westward through the
greater part of the following day. On the next morning we again
resumed our journey. It was the seventeenth of July, unless my
note-book misleads me. At noon we stopped by some pools of
rain-water, and in the afternoon again set forward. This double
movement was contrary to the usual practice of the Indians, but all
were very anxious to reach the hunting-ground, kill the necessary
number of buffalo, and retreat as soon as possible from the dangerous neighborhood. I pass by for the present some curious
incidents that occurred during these marches and encampments.
Late in the afternoon of the last-mentioned day we came upon the
banks of a little sandy stream, of which the Indians could not tell
the name; for they were very ill acquainted with that part of the
country. So parched and arid were the prairies around that they
could not supply grass enough for the horses to feed upon, and we
were compelled to move farther and farther up the stream in
search of ground for encampment. The country was much wilder
than before. The plains were gashed with ravines and broken into
hollows and steep declivities, which flanked our course, as, in
long scattered array, the Indians advanced up the side of the
stream. Mene-Seela consulted an extraordinary oracle to instruct
him where the buffalo were to be found. When he with the other
chiefs sat down on the grass to smoke and converse, as they often
did during the march, the old man picked up one of those enormous black-and-green crickets, which the Dakota call by a name
that signifies 'They who point out the buffalo.' The 'Root-Diggers,'
a wretched tribe beyond the mountains, turn them to good
account by making them into a sort of soup, pronounced by
certain unscrupulous trappers to be extremely rich. Holding the
bloated insect respectfully between his fingers and thumb, the
old Indian looked attentively at him and inquired, 'Tell me, my
father, where must we go to-morrow to find the buffalo?' The
cricket twisted about his long horns in evident embarrassment.
At last he pointed, or seemed to point, them westward. Mene-
Seela, dropping him gently on the grass, laughed with great glee,
and said that if we went that way in the morning we should be
sure to kill plenty of game.

Towards evening we came upon a fresh, green meadow, traversed
by the stream, and deep-set among tall, sterile bluffs. The Indians

descended its steep bank; and as I was at the rear, I was one of the last to reach this point. Lances were glittering, feathers fluttering, and the water below me was crowded with men and horses passing through, while the meadow beyond swarmed with the restless crowd of Indians. The sun was just setting, and poured its softened light upon them through an opening in the hills.

I remarked to Reynal that at last we had found a good 'camping-ground.

'Oh, it 's very good,' replied he, ironically, 'especially if there is a Snake war-party about, and they take it into their heads to shoot down at us from the top of these hills. It 's no plan of mine, 'camping in such a hole as this.'

The Indians also seemed anxious. High up on the top of the tallest bluff, conspicuous in the bright evening sunlight, sat a naked warrior on horseback, looking around over the neighboring country; and Raymond told me that many of the young men had gone out in different directions as scouts.

The shadows had reached to the very summit of the bluffs before the lodges were erected, and the village reduced again to quiet and order. A cry was suddenly raised, and men, women, and children came running out with animated faces, and looked eagerly through the opening in the hills by which the stream entered from the westward. I could discern afar off some dark, heavy masses, passing over the sides of a low hill. They disappeared and then others followed. These were bands of buffalo cows. The hunting-ground was reached at last, and everything promised well for the morrow's chase. Being fatigued and exhausted, I lay down in Kongra-Tonga's lodge, when Raymond thrust in his head, and called upon me to come and see some sport. A number of Indians were gathered, laughing, along the line of lodges on the western side of the village, and at some distance I could plainly see in the twilight two huge black monsters stalking, heavily and solemnly, directly towards us. They were buffalo-bulls. The wind blew from them to the village, and such was their blindness and stupidity, that they were advancing upon the enemy without the least consciousness of his presence. Raymond told me that two young men had hidden themselves with guns in a ravine about twenty yards in front of us. The two bulls walked slowly on, heavily swinging from side to side in their peculiar gait of stupid dignity. They approached within four or five rods of the ravine where the Indians lay in ambush. Here at last they seemed conscious that something was wrong, for they both stopped and stood perfectly still, without looking either to the right or to the left. Nothing of them was to be seen but two black masses of shaggy mane, with horns, eyes, and nose in the centre, and a pair of hoofs visible at the bottom. At last the more intelligent of them seemed to have concluded that it was time to retire. Very slowly, and with an air of the gravest and most majestic deliberation, he began to turn round, as if he were revolving on a pivot. Little by little his ugly brown side was exposed to view. A white smoke sprang out, as it were from the ground; a sharp report came with it. The old bull gave a very undignified jump, and galloped off. At this his comrade wheeled about with considerable expedition. The other Indian shot at him from the ravine, and then both the bulls ran away at full speed, while half the juvenile population of the village raised a yell and ran after them. The first bull soon stopped, and while the crowd stood looking at him at a respectful distance he reeled and rolled over on his side. The other, wounded in a less vital part, galloped away to the hills and escaped.

In half an hour it was totally dark. I lay down to sleep, and ill as I was, there was something very animating in the prospect of the general hunt that was to take place on the morrow.

15. The Hunting Camp

Long before daybreak the Indians broke up their camp. The women of Mene-Seela's lodge were as usual among the first that were ready for departure, and I found the old man himself sitting by the embers of the decayed fire, over which he was warming his withered fingers, as the morning was chill and damp. The preparations for moving were even more confused and disorderly than usual. While some families were leaving the ground the lodges of others were still standing untouched. At this old Mene-Seela grew impatient, and walking out to the middle of the village, he stood with his robe wrapped close around him, and harangued the people in a loud, sharp voice. Now, he said, when they were on an enemy's hunting-grounds, was not the time to behave like children; they ought to be more active and united than ever. His speech had some effect. The delinquents took down their lodges and loaded their pack-horses; and when the sun rose, the last of the men, women, and children had left the deserted camp.

This movement was made merely for the purpose of finding a better and safer position. So we advanced only three or four miles up the little stream, when each family assumed its relative place in the great ring of the village, and the squaws set actively at work in preparing the camp. But not a single warrior dismounted from his horse. All the men that morning were mounted on inferior animals, leading their best horses by a cord, or confiding them to the care of boys. In small parties they began to leave the ground and ride rapidly away over the plains to the westward. I had taken no food, and not being at all ambitious of farther abstinence, I went into my host's lodge, which his squaws had set up with wonderful despatch, and sat down in the centre, as a gentle hint that I was hungry. A wooden bowl was soon set before me, filled with the nutritious preparation of dried meat called *pemmican* by the northern voyagers, and *wasna* by the Dakota. Taking a handful to break my fast upon, I left the lodge just in time to see the last band of hunters disappear over the ridge of the neighboring hill. I mounted Pauline and galloped in pursuit, riding rather by the balance than by any muscular strength that remained to me. From the top of the hill I could overlook a wide extent of desolate prairie, over which, far and near, little parties of naked horsemen were rapidly passing. I soon came up to the nearest, and we had not ridden a mile before all were united into one large and compact body. All was haste and eagerness. Each hunter whipped on his horse as if anxious to be the first to reach the game. In such movements among the Indians this is always more or less the case; but it was especially so in the present instance, because the head chief of the village was absent, and there were but few 'soldiers,' a sort of Indian police, who among their other functions usually assume the direction of a buffalo hunt. No man turned to the right hand or to the left. We rode at a swift canter straight forward, up hill and down hill, and through the stiff, obstinate growth of the endless wild-sage bushes. For an hour and a half the same red shoulders, the same long black hair rose and fell with the motion of the horses before me. Very little was said, though once I observed an old man severely reproving Raymond for having left his rifle behind him, when there was some probability of encountering an enemy before the day was over. As we galloped across a plain thickly set with sage bushes, the foremost riders vanished suddenly from sight, as if diving into the earth. The arid soil was cracked into a deep ravine. Down we all went in succession and galloped in a line along the bottom, until we found a point where, one by one, the horses could scramble out. Soon after, we came upon a wide, shallow stream, and as we rode swiftly over the hard sand-beds and through the thin sheets of rippling water, many of the savage horsemen threw themselves to the ground, knelt on the sand, snatched a hasty draught, and leaping back again to their seats, galloped on as before.

Meanwhile scouts kept in advance of the party; and now we began to see them on the ridges of the hills, waving their robes in token that buffalo were visible. These however proved to be nothing more than old straggling bulls, feeding upon the neighboring plains, who would stare for a moment at the hostile array and then gallop clumsily off. At length we could discern several of these scouts making their signals to us at once,—no longer waving their robes boldly from the top of the hill, but standing lower down, so that they could not be seen from the plains beyond. Game worth pursuing had evidently been discovered. The excited Indians now urged forward their tired horses even more rapidly than before. Pauline, who was still sick and jaded, began to groan heavily; and her yellow sides were darkened with sweat. As we were crowding together over a lower intervening hill, I heard Reynal and Raymond shouting to me from the left; and, looking in that direction, I saw them riding away behind a party of about twenty mean-looking Indians. These were the relatives of Reynal's squaw, Margot, who, not wishing to take part in the general hunt, were riding towards a distant hollow, where they saw a small band of buffalo which they meant to appropriate to themselves. I answered to the call by ordering Raymond to turn back and follow me. He reluctantly obeyed, though Reynal, who had relied on his assistance in skinning, cutting up, and carrying to camp the buffalo that he and his party should kill, loudly protested, and declared that we should see no sport if we went with the rest of the Indians. Followed by Raymond, I pursued the main body of hunters, while Reynal, in a great rage, whipped his horse over the hill after his ragamuffin relatives. The Indians, still about a hundred in number, galloped in a dense body at some distance in advance, a cloud of dust flying in the wind behind them. I could not overtake them until they had stopped on the side of the hill where the scouts were standing. Here each hunter sprang in haste from the tired animal he had ridden, and leaped upon the fresh horse he had brought with him. There was not a saddle or a bridle in the whole party. A piece of buffalo-robe, girthed over the horse's back, served in the place of the one, and a cord of twisted hair, lashed round his lower jaw, answered for the other. Eagle feathers dangled from every mane and tail, as marks of courage and speed. As for the rider, he wore no other clothing than a light cincture at his waist, and a pair of moccasins. He had a heavy whip, with a handle of solid elk-horn, and a lash of knotted bull-hide fastened to his wrist by a band. His bow was in his hand and his quiver of otter or panther skin hung at his shoulder. Thus equipped, some thirty of the hunters galloped away towards the left, in order to make a circuit under cover of the hills, that the buffalo might be assailed on both sides at once. The rest impatiently waited until time enough had elapsed for their companions to reach the required position. Then riding upward in a body, we gained the ridge of the hill, and for the first time came in sight of the buffalo on the plain beyond.

They were a band of cows, four or five hundred in number, crowded together near the bank of a wide stream that was soaking across the sand-beds of the valley. This valley was a large circular basin, sun-scorched and broken, scantily covered with herbage and surrounded with high, barren hills, from an opening in which we could see our allies galloping out upon the plain. The wind blew from that direction. The buffalo, aware of their approach, had begun to move, though very slowly and in a compact mass. I have no farther recollection of seeing the game until we were in the midst of them, for as we rode down the hill other objects engrossed my attention. Numerous old bulls were scattered over the plain, and ungallantly deserting their charge at our approach began to wade and plunge through the quicksands of the stream, and gallop towards the hills. One old veteran was straggling behind the rest, with one of his fore-legs, which had been broken by some accident, dangling about uselessly. His appearance, as he went shambling along on three legs, was so ludicrous that I could not help pausing for a moment to look at him. As I came near he would try to rush upon me, nearly throwing himself down at every awkward attempt. Looking up, I saw the whole body of Indians full a hundred yards in advance. I lashed Pauline in pursuit, and reached them just in time; for at that moment each hunter, as if by a common impulse, violently struck his horse, each horse sprang forward, and, scattering in the charge in order to assail the entire herd at once, we all rushed headlong upon the buffalo. We were among them in an instant. Amid the trampling and the yells I could see their dark figures running hither and thither through clouds of dust, and the horsemen darting in pursuit. While we were charging on one side, our companions attacked the bewildered and panic-stricken herd on the other. The uproar and confusion lasted but a moment. The dust cleared away, and the buffalo could be seen scattering as from a common centre, flying over the plain singly, or in long files and small compact bodies. while behind them followed the Indians riding at furious speed, and yelling as they launched arrow after arrow into their sides. The carcasses were strewn thickly over the ground. Here and there stood wounded buffalo, their bleeding sides feathered with arrows; and as I rode by them their eyes would glare, they would bristle like gigantic cats, and feebly attempt to rush up and gore my horse. Others, less disabled, were feebly staggering away, destined to the maws of wolves.

I left camp that morning with a philosophic resolution. Neither I nor my horse were at that time fit for such sport, and I had determined to remain a quiet spectator; but amid the rush of horses and buffalo, the uproar and the dust, I found it impossible to sit still; and as four or five buffalo ran past me in a line, I lashed Pauline in pursuit. We went plunging through the water and the quicksands, and clambering the bank, chased them through the wild-sage bushes that covered the rising ground beyond. But neither her native spirit nor the blows of the knotted bull-hide could supply the place of poor Pauline's exhausted strength. We could not gain an inch upon the fugitives. At last, however, they came full upon a ravine too wide to leap over; and as this compelled them to turn abruptly to the left, I contrived to get within ten or twelve yards of the hindmost. At this she faced about, bristled angrily, and made a show of charging. I shot at her, and hit her in the neck. Down she tumbled into the ravine whither her companions had descended before her. I saw their dark backs appearing and disappearing as they galloped along the bottom; then, one by one, they scrambled out on the other side, and ran off as before, the wounded animal following with the rest.

Turning back, I saw Raymond coming on his black mule to meet me; and as we rode over the field together, we counted scores of carcasses lying on the plain, in the ravines, and on the sandy bed of the stream. Far away in the distance, horsemen and buffalo were still scouring along, with clouds of dust rising behind them; and over the sides of the hills long files of the frightened animals were rapidly ascending. The hunters began to return. The boys, who had held the horses behind the hill, made their appearance, and the work of flaying and cutting up began in earnest all over the field. I noticed my host Kongra-Tonga beyond the stream, just alighting by the side of a cow which he had killed. Riding up to him, I found him in the act of drawing out an arrow, which, with the exception of the notch at the end, had entirely disappeared in the animal. I asked him to give it to me, and I still retain it as a proof, though by no means the most striking one that could be offered, of the force and dexterity with which the Indians shoot their arrows.

The hides and meat were piled upon the horses, and the hunters began to leave the ground. Raymond and I, too, getting tired of the scene, set out for the village, riding straight across the intervening desert. There was no path, and as far as I could see, no landmark sufficient to guide us; but Raymond seemed to have an instinctive perception of the point on the horizon towards which we ought to direct our course. Antelope were bounding on all sides, and as is always the case in the presence of buffalo, they seemed to have lost their natural shyness. Bands of them would run lightly up the rocky declivities, and stand gazing down upon us from the summit. At length we could distinguish the tall white rocks and the old pine-trees that, as we well remembered, were just above the site of the encampment. Still we could see nothing of the camp itself, until, mounting a grassy hill, we saw the circle of lodges, dingy with storms and smoke, standing on the plain at our feet.

I entered the lodge of my host. His squaw instantly brought me food and water, and spread a buffalo-robe for me to lie upon; and being much fatigued I lay down and fell asleep. In about an hour the entrance of Kongra-Tonga, with his arms smeared with blood to the elbows, awoke me; he sat down in his usual seat, on the left side of the lodge. His squaw gave him a vessel of water for washing, set before him a bowl of boiled meat, and, as he was eating, pulled off his bloody moccasins and placed fresh ones on his feet; then outstretching his limbs, my host composed himself to sleep.

And now the hunters, two or three at a time, came rapidly in, and each consigning his horses to the squaws, entered his lodge with the air of a man whose day's work was done. The squaws flung down the load from the burdened horses, and vast piles of meat and hides were soon gathered before every lodge. By this time it was darkening fast, and the whole village was illumined by the glare of fires. All the squaws and children were gathered about the piles of meat, exploring them in search of the daintiest portions. Some of these they roasted on sticks before the fires, but often they dispensed with this superfluous operation. Late into the night the fires were still glowing upon the groups of feasters engaged in this savage banquet around them.

Several hunters sat down by the fire in Kongra-Tonga's lodge to talk over the day's exploits. Among the rest, Mene-Seela came in. Though he must have seen full eighty winters, he had taken an active share in the day's sport. He boasted that he had killed two cows that morning, and would have killed a third if the dust had not blinded him so that he had to drop his bow and arrows and press both hands against his eyes to stop the pain. The fire-light fell upon his wrinkled face and shrivelled figure as he sat telling his story, with such inimitable gesticulation that every man in the lodge broke into a laugh.

Old Mene-Seela was one of the few Indians in the village with whom I would have trusted myself alone without suspicion, and the only one from whom I should have received a gift or a service without the certainty that it proceeded from an interested motive. He was a great friend to the whites. He liked to be in their company, and was very vain of the favors he had received from them. He told me one afternoon, as we were sitting together in his son's lodge, that he considered the beaver and the whites the wisest people on earth; indeed, he was convinced they were the same; and an incident which had happened to him long before had assured him of this. So he began the following story, and as the pipe passed in turn to him, Reynal availed himself of these interruptions to translate what had preceded. But the old man accompanied his words with such admirable pantomime that translation was hardly necessary.

He said that when he was very young, and had never yet seen a white man, he and three or four of his companions were out on a beaver hunt, and he crawled into a large beaver-lodge, to see what was there. Sometimes he crept on his hands and knees, sometimes he was obliged to swim, and sometimes to lie flat on his face and drag himself along. In this way he crawled a great distance under ground. It was very dark, cold, and close, so that at last he was almost suffocated, and fell into a swoon. When he began to recover, he could just distinguish the voices of his companions outside, who had given him up for lost, and were singing his death-song. At first he could see nothing, but soon discerned something white before him, and at length plainly distinguished three people, entirely white, one man and two women, sitting at the edge of a black pool of water. He became alarmed, and thought it high time to retreat. Having succeeded, after great trouble, in reaching daylight again, he went to the spot directly above the pool of water where he had seen the three mysterious beings. Here he beat a hole with his war-club in the ground, and sat down to watch. In a moment the nose of an old male beaver appeared at the opening. Mene-Seela instantly seized him and dragged him up, when two other beavers, both females, thrust out their heads, and these he served in the same way. 'These,' said the old man, concluding his story, for which he was probably indebted to a dream, 'must have been the three white people whom I saw sitting at the edge of the water.'

Mene-Seela was the grand depositary of the legends and traditions of the village. I succeeded, however, in getting from him only a few fragments. Like all Indians, he was excessively superstitious, and continually saw some reason for withholding his stories. 'It is a bad thing,' he would say, 'to tell the tales in summer. Stay with us till next winter, and I will tell you everything I know; but now our war-parties are going out, and our young men will be killed if I sit down to tell stories before the frost begins.'

But to leave this digression. We remained encamped on this spot five days, during three of which the hunters were at work incessantly, and immense quantities of meat and hides were brought in. Great alarm, however, prevailed in the village. All were on the alert. The young men ranged the country as scouts, and the old men paid careful attention to omens and prodigies, and especially to their dreams. In order to convey to the enemy (who, if they were in the neighborhood, must inevitably have

known of our presence) the impression that we were constantly on
the watch, piles of sticks and stones were erected on all the
surrounding hills, in such a manner as to appear at a distance like
sentinels. Often, even to this hour, that scene will rise before my
mind like a visible reality,—the tall white rocks; the old pine-
trees on their summits; the sandy stream that ran along their
bases and half encircled the village; and the wild-sage bushes,
with their dull green hue and their medicinal odor, that covered
all the neighboring declivities. Hour after hour the squaws
would pass and repass with their vessels of water between the
stream and the lodges. For the most part, no one was to be seen
in the camp but women and children, two or three superannuated
old men, and a few lazy and worthless young ones. These, together with the dogs, now grown fat and good-natured with the
abundance in the camp, were its only tenants. Still it presented a
busy and bustling scene. In all quarters the meat, hung on cords
of hide, was drying in the sun, and around the lodges the squaws,
young and old, were laboring on the fresh hides stretched upon
the ground, scraping the hair from one side and the still adhering
flesh from the other, and rubbing into them the brains of the
buffalo, in order to render them soft and pliant.

In mercy to myself and my horse I did not go out with the
hunters after the first day. Of late, however, I had been gaining
strength rapidly, as was always the case upon every respite of
my disorder. I was soon able to walk with ease. Raymond and I
would go out upon the neighboring prairies to shoot antelope, or
sometimes to assail straggling buffalo, on foot; an attempt in
which we met with rather indifferent success. As I came out of
Kongra-Tonga's lodge one morning, Reynal called to me from
the opposite side of the village, and asked me over to breakfast.
The breakfast was a substantial one. It consisted of the rich,
juicy hump-ribs of a fat cow; a repast unrivalled in its way. It was
roasting before the fire, impaled upon a stout stick, which Reynal
took up and planted in the ground before his lodge, when he, with
Raymond and myself, taking our seats around it, unsheathed our
knives and assailed it with good will. In spite of all medical
experience, this solid fare, without bread or salt, seemed to agree
with me admirably.

'We shall have strangers here before night,' said Reynal.

'How do you know that?' I asked.

'I dreamed so. I am as good at dreaming as an Indian. There's the Hail-Storm; he dreamed the same thing, and he and his crony, the Rabbit, have gone out on discovery.'

I laughed at Reynal for his credulity, went over to my host's odge, took down my rifle, walked out a mile or two on the prairie, saw an old bull standing alone, crawled up a ravine, shot him, and saw him escape. Then, exhausted and rather ill-humored, I walked back to the village. By a strange coincidence, Reynal's prediction had been verified; for the first persons whom I saw were the two trappers, Rouleau and Saraphin, coming to meet me. These men, as the reader may possibly recollect, had left our party about a fortnight before. They had been trapping among the Black Hills, and were now on their way to the Rocky Mountains, intending in a day or two to set out for the neighboring Medicine Bow. They were not the most elegant or refined of companions, yet they made a very welcome addition to the limited society of the village. For the rest of that day we lay smoking and talking in Reynal's lodge. This indeed was no better than a hut, made of hides stretched on poles, and entirely open in front. It was well carpeted with soft buffalo-robes, and here we remained, sheltered from the sun, surrounded by the domestic utensils of Madame Margot's household. All was quiet in the village. Though the hunters had not gone out that day, they lay sleeping in their lodges, and most of the women were silently engaged in their heavy tasks. A few young men were playing at a lazy game of ball in the area of the village; and when they became tired, some girls supplied their place with a more boisterous sport. At a little distance, among the lodges, some children and half-grown squaws were playfully tossing one of their number in a buffalo-robe, an exact counterpart of the ancient pastime from which Sancho Panza suffered so much. Farther out on the prairie, a host of little naked boys were roaming about, engaged in various rough games, or pursuing birds and ground-squirrels with their bows and arrows; and woe to the unhappy little animals that fell into their merciless, torture-loving hands. A squaw from the next lodge, a notable housewife, named Weah Washtay, or the Good Woman, brought us a large bowl of *wasna*, and went into an ecstasy of delight when I presented her with a green glass ring, such as I usually wore with a view to similar occasions.

The sun went down, and half the sky was glowing fiery red, reflected on the little stream as it wound away among the sage-bushes. Some young men left the village, and soon returned, driving in before them all the horses, hundreds in number, and of every size, age, and color. The hunters came out and each securing those that belonged to him, examined their condition, and tied them fast by long cords to stakes driven in front of his lodge. It was half an hour before the bustle subsided and tranquillity was restored again. By this time it was nearly dark. Kettles were hung over the fires, around which the squaws were gathered with their children, laughing and talking merrily. A circle of a different kind was formed in the centre of the village. This was composed of the old men and warriors of repute, who sat together with their white buffalo-robes drawn close around their shoulders; and as the pipe passed from hand to hand, their conversation had not a particle of the gravity and reserve usually ascribed to Indians. I sat down with them as usual. I had in my hand half a dozen squibs and serpents, which I had made one day when encamped upon Laramie Creek, with gunpowder and charcoal, and the leaves of 'Fremont's Expedition,' rolled round a stout lead-pencil. I waited till I could get hold of the large piece of burning *bois-de-vache* which the Indians kept by them on the ground for lighting their pipes. With this I lighted all the fireworks at once, and tossed them whizzing and sputtering into the air, over the heads of the company. They all jumped up and ran off with yelps of astonishment and consternation. After a moment or two they ventured to come back one by one, and some of the boldest, picking up the cases of burnt paper, examined them with eager curiosity to discover their mysterious secret. From that time forward I enjoyed great repute as a 'fire-medicine.'

The camp was filled with the low hum of cheerful voices. There were other sounds, however, of a different kind; for from a large lodge, lighted up like a gigantic lantern by the blazing fire within, came a chorus of dismal cries and wailings, long drawn out, like the howling of wolves, and a woman almost naked, was crouching close outside, crying violently, and gashing her legs with a knife till they were covered with blood. Just a year before, a young man belonging to this family had been slain by the enemy, and his relatives were thus lamenting his loss. Still other sounds might be heard; loud earnest cries often repeated from amid the gloom, at a distance beyond the village. They proceeded from some young men, who, being about to set out in a few days on a war-party, were standing at the top of a hill, calling on the Great Spirit to aid them in their enterprise. While I was listening Rouleau, with a

laugh on his careless face, called to me and directed my attention
to another quarter. In front of the lodge where Weah Washtay
lived, another squaw was standing, angrily scolding an old yellow
dog, who lay on the ground with his nose resting between his
paws, and his eyes turned sleepily up to her face, as if pretending
to give respectful attention, but resolved to fall asleep as soon as
it was all over.

'You ought to be ashamed of yourself!' said the old woman.
'I have fed you well, and taken care of you ever since you were
small and blind, and could only crawl about and squeal a little,
instead of howling as you do now. When you grew old I said you
were a good dog. You were strong and gentle when the load was
put on your back, and you never ran among the feet of the horses
when we were all travelling together over the prairie. But you
had a bad heart! Whenever a rabbit jumped out of the bushes you
were always the first to run after him and lead away all the other
dogs behind you. You ought to have known that it was very
dangerous to act so. When you had got far out on the prairie,
and no one was near to help you, perhaps a wolf would jump out
of the ravine; and then what could you do? You would certainly
have been killed, for no dog can fight well with a load on his back.
Only three days ago you ran off in that way, and turned over the
bag of wooden pins with which I used to fasten up the front of the
lodge. Look up there, and you will see that it is all flapping
open. And now to-night you have stolen a great piece of fat meat
which was roasting before the fire for my children. I tell you, you
have a bad heart, and you must die!'

So saying, the squaw went into the lodge, and coming out with
a large stone mallet, killed the unfortunate dog at one blow. This
speech is worthy of notice, as illustrating a curious characteristic
of the Indians, who ascribe intelligence and a power of under-
standing speech to the inferior animals; to whom, indeed, according to many of their traditions, they are linked in close affinity;
and they even claim the honor of a lineal descent from bears,
wolves, deer, or tortoises.

As it grew late, I walked across the village to the lodge of my
host Kongra-Tonga. As I entered I saw him, by the blaze of the
fire in the middle, reclining half asleep in his usual place. His
couch was by no means an uncomfortable one. It consisted of
buffalo-robes, laid together on the ground, and a pillow made of
whitened deer-skin, stuffed with feathers and ornamented with

beads. At his back was a light frame-work of poles and slender reeds, against which he could lean with ease when in a sitting posture; and at the top of it, just above his head, hung his bow and quiver. His squaw, a laughing, broad-faced woman, apparently had not yet completed her domestic arrangements, for she was bustling about the lodge, pulling over the utensils and the bales of dried meat that were ranged carefully around it. Unhappily, she and her partner were not the only tenants of the dwelling; for half a dozen children were scattered about, sleeping in every imaginable posture. My saddle was in its place at the head of the lodge, and a buffalo-robe was spread on the ground before it. Wrapping myself in my blanket, I lay down; but had I not been extremely fatigued, the noise in the next lodge would have prevented my sleeping. There was the monotonous thumping of the Indian drum, mixed with occasional sharp yells, and a chorus chanted by twenty voices. A grand scene of gambling was going forward, with all the appropriate formalities. The players were staking on the chances of the game, their ornaments, their horses, and as the excitement rose, their garments, and even their weapons; for desperate gambling is not confined to the hells of Paris. The men of the plains and forests no less resort to it as a relief to the tedious monotony of their lives, which alternate between fierce excitement and listless inaction. I fell asleep with the dull notes of the drum still sounding on my ear; but these orgies lasted without intermission till daylight. I was soon awakened by one of the children crawling over me, while another larger one was tugging at my blanket and nestling himself in a very disagreeable proximity. I immediately repelled these advances by punching the heads of these miniature savages with a short stick which I always kept by me for the purpose; and as sleeping half the day and eating much more than is good for them makes them extremely restless, this operation usually had to be repeated four or five times in the course of the night. My host himself was the author of another formidable annoyance. All these Indians, and he among the rest, think themselves bound to the constant performance of certain acts as the condition on which their success in life depends, whether in war, love, hunting, or any other employment. These 'medicines,' as they are called, which are usually communicated in dreams, are often absurd enough. Some Indians will strike the butt of the pipe against the ground every time they smoke; others will insist that everything they say shall be interpreted by contraries; and Shaw once met an old man who conceived that all would be lost unless he compelled every white man he met to drink a bowl of cold water. My host was particularly unfortunate in his allotment. The spirits had told him in a dream that he must sing a certain song in the middle of every night; and regularly at about twelve o'clock his dismal monotonous chanting would awaken me, and I would see him seated bolt upright on his couch, going through his dolorous performance with a most business-like air. There were other voices of the night, still more inharmonious. Twice or thrice, between sunset and dawn, all the dogs in the village, and there were hundreds of them, would bay and yelp in chorus; a horrible clamor, resembling no sound that I have ever heard, except perhaps the frightful howling of wolves that we used sometimes to hear, long afterward, when descending the Arkansas on the trail of General Kearney's army. This canine uproar is, if possible, more discordant than that of the wolves. Heard at a distance slowly rising on the night, it has a strange, unearthly effect, and would fearfully haunt the dreams of a nervous man; but when you are sleeping in the midst of it the din is outrageous. One long, loud howl begins it, and voice after voice takes up the sound, till it passes around the whole circumference of the village, and the air is filled with confused and discordant cries, at once fierce and mournful. It lasts a few moments, and then dies away into silence.

Morning came, and Kongra-Tonga, mounting his horse, rode out with the hunters. It may not be amiss to glance at him for an instant in his character of husband and father. Both he and his squaw, like most other Indians, were very fond of their children, whom they indulged to excess, and never punished, except in extreme cases, when they would throw a bowl of cold water over them. Their offspring became sufficiently undutiful and disobedient under this system of education, which tends not a little to foster that wild idea of liberty and utter intolerance of restraint which lie at the foundation of the Indian character. It would be hard to find a fonder father than Kongra-Tonga. There was one urchin in particular, rather less than two feet high, to whom he was exceedingly attached; and sometimes spreading a buffalo-robe in the lodge, he would seat himself upon it, place his small favorite upright before him and chant in a low tone some of the words used as an accompaniment to the war-dance. The little fellow, who could just manage to balance himself by stretching out both arms, would lift his feet and turn slowly round and round in time to his father's music, while my host would laugh with delight, and look smiling up into my face to see if I were admiring this precocious performance of his offspring. In his capacity of husband he was less tender. The squaw who lived in the lodge with him had been his partner for many years. She took good care of his children and his household concerns. He liked her well enough, and as far as I could see, they never quarrelled; but his warmer affections were reserved for younger and more recent favorites. Of these he had at present only one, who lived in a lodge apart from his own. One day while in this camp, he became displeased with her, pushed her out, threw after her her ornaments, dresses, and everything she had, and told her to go home to her father. Having consummated this summary divorce, for which he could show good reasons, he came back, seated himself in his usual place, and began to smoke with an air of the utmost tranquillity and self-satisfaction.

I was sitting in the lodge with him on that very afternoon when I felt some curiosity to learn the history of the numerous scars that appeared on his naked body. Of some of them, however, I did not venture to inquire, for I already understood their origin. Each of his arms was marked as if deeply gashed with a knife at regular intervals, and there were other scars also, of a different character, on his back and on either breast. They were the traces of the tortures which these Indians, in common with a few other tribes, inflict upon themselves at certain seasons; in part, it may be, to gain the glory of courage and endurance, but chiefly as an act of self-sacrifice to secure the favor of the spirits. The scars upon the breast and back were produced by running through the flesh strong splints of wood, to which heavy buffalo-skulls are fastened by cords of hide, and the wretch runs forward with all his strength, assisted by two companions, who take hold of each arm, until the flesh tears apart and the skulls are left behind. Others of Kongra-Tonga's scars were the result of accidents; but he had many received in war. He was one of the most noted warriors in the village. In the course of his life he had slain, as he boasted to me, fourteen men; and though, like other Indians, he was a braggart and liar, yet in this statement common report bore him out. Being flattered by my inquiries, he told me tale after tale, true or false, of his warlike exploits; and there was one among the rest illustrating the worst features of Indian character too well for me to omit it. Pointing out of the opening of the lodge towards the Medicine-Bow Mountain, not many miles distant, he said that he was there a few summers ago with a war-party of his young men. Here they found two Snake Indians hunting. They shot one of them with arrows, and chased the other up the side of the mountain till they surrounded him, and Kongra-Tonga himself, jumping forward among the trees, seized him by the arm. Two of his young men then ran up and held him fast while he scalped him alive. They then built a great fire, and cutting the tendons of their captive's wrists and feet, threw him in, and held him down with long poles until he was burnt to death. He garnished his story with descriptive particulars much too revolting to mention. His features were remarkably mild and open, without the fierceness of expression common among these Indians; and as he detailed these devilish cruelties, he looked up into my face with the air of earnest simplicity which a little child would wear in relating to its mother some anecdote of its youthful experience.

Old Mene-Seela's lodge could offer another illustration of the ferocity of Indian warfare. A bright-eyed, active little boy was living there who had belonged to a village of the Gros-Ventre Blackfeet, a small but bloody and treacherous band, in close alliance with the Arapahoes. About a year before, Kongra-Tonga and a party of warriors had found about twenty lodges of these Indians upon the plains a little to the eastward of our present camp; and surrounding them in the night, they butchered men, women, and children, preserving only this little boy alive. He was adopted into the old man's family, and was now fast becoming identified with the Ogillallah children, among whom he mingled on equal terms. There was also a Crow warrior in the village, a man of gigantic stature and most symmetrical proportions. Having been taken prisoner many years before and adopted by a squaw in place of a son whom she had lost, he had forgotten his old nationality, and was now both in act and inclination an Ogillallah.

It will be remembered that the scheme of the grand war-party against the Snake and Crow Indians originated in this village; and though this plan had fallen to the ground, the embers of martial ardor continued to glow. Eleven young men had prepared to go out against the enemy, and the fourth day of our stay in this camp was fixed upon for their departure. At the head of this party was a well-built, active little Indian, called the White

Shield, whom I had always noticed for the neatness of his dress and appearance. His lodge too, though not a large one, was the best in the village, his squaw was one of the prettiest, and altogether his dwelling was the model of an Ogillallah domestic establishment. I was often a visitor there, for the White Shield, being rather partial to white men, used to invite me to continual feasts at all hours of the day. Once, when the substantial part of the entertainment was over, and he and I were seated crosslegged on a buffalo-robe smoking together very amicably, he took down his warlike equipments, which were hanging round the lodge, and displayed them with great pride and self-importance. Among the rest was a superb head-dress of feathers. Taking this from its case, he put it on and stood before me, perfectly conscious of the gallant air which it gave to his dark face and his vigorous, graceful figure. He told me that upon it were the feathers of three war-eagles, equal in value to the same number of good horses. He took up also a shield gayly painted and hung with feathers. The effect of these barbaric ornaments was admirable. His quiver was made of the spotted skin of a small panther, common among the Black Hills, from which the tail and distended claws were still allowed to hang. The White Shield concluded his entertainment in a manner characteristic of an Indian. He begged of me a little powder and ball, for he had a gun as well as a bow and arrows; but this I was obliged to refuse, because I had scarcely enough for my own use. Making him however a parting present of a paper of vermilion, I left him quite contented.

On the next morning the White Shield took cold, and was attacked with an inflammation of the throat. Immediately he seemed to lose all spirit, and though before no warrior in the village had borne himself more proudly, he now moped about from lodge to lodge with a forlorn and dejected air. At length he sat down, close wrapped in his robe, before the lodge of Reynal, but when he found that neither he nor I knew how to relieve him, he arose and stalked over to one of the medicine-men of the village. This old imposter thumped him for some time with both fists, howled and yelped over him, and beat a drum close to his ear to expel the evil spirit. This treatment failing of the desired effect, the White Shield withdrew to his own lodge, where he lay disconsolate for some hours. Making his appearance once more in the afternoon, he again took his seat on the ground before Reynal's lodge, holding his throat with his hand. For some time he sat silent, with his eyes fixed mournfully on the ground. At last he began to speak in a low tone.

'I am a brave man,' he said; 'all the young men think me a great warrior and ten of them are ready to go with me to the war. I will go and show them the enemy. Last summer the Snakes killed my brother. I cannot live unless I revenge his death. To-morrow we will set out and I will take their scalps.'

The White Shield, as he expressed this resolution, seemed to have lost all the accustomed fire and spirit of his look, and hung his head as if in a fit of despondency.

As I was sitting that evening at one of the fires, I saw him arrayed in his splendid war-dress, his cheeks painted with vermilion, leading his favorite war-horse to the front of his lodge. He mounted and rode round the village, singing his war-song in a loud, hoarse voice amid the shrill acclamations of the women. Then dismounting, he remained for some minutes prostrate upon the ground, as if in an act of supplication. On the following morning I looked in vain for the departure of the warriors. All was quiet in the village until late in the forenoon, when the White Shield came and seated himself in his old place before us. Reynal asked him why he had not gone out to find the enemy.

'I cannot go,' he answered in a dejected voice. 'I have given my war-arrows to the Meneaska' (the American).

'You have only given him two of your arrows,' said Reynal. 'If you ask him he will give them back again.'

For some time the White Shield said nothing. At last he spoke in a gloomy tone,—

'One of my young men has had bad dreams. The spirits of the dead came and threw stones at him in his sleep.'

If such a dream had actually taken place it might have broken up this or any other war-party, but both Reynal and I were convinced at the time that it was a mere fabrication to excuse his remaining at home.

The White Shield was a warrior of noted prowess. Very probably he would have received a mortal wound without the show of pain, and endured without flinching the worst tortures that an enemy could inflict upon him. The whole power of an Indian's nature would be summoned to encounter such a trial; every influence of his education from childhood would have prepared him for it; the cause of his suffering would have been visibly and palpably before him, and his spirit would rise to set his enemy at defiance, and gain the highest glory of a warrior by meeting death with fortitude. But when he feels himself attacked by a mysterious evil, before whose assaults his manhood is wasted, and his strength drained away, when he can see no enemy to resist and defy, the boldest warrior falls prostrate at once. He believes that a bad spirit has taken possession of him, or that he is the victim of some charm. When suffering from a protracted disorder, an Indian will often abandon himself to his supposed destiny, pine away and die, the victim of his own imagination. The same effect will often follow a series of calamities, or a long run of ill-luck, and Indians have been known to ride into the midst of an enemy's camp, or attack a grizzly bear single-handed, to get rid of a life supposed to lie under the doom of fate.

Thus, after all his fasting, dreaming, and calling upon the Great Spirit, the White Shield's war-party came to nought.

16. The Trappers

In speaking of the Indians, I have almost forgotten two bold adventurers of another race, the trappers Rouleau and Saraphin. These men were bent on a hazardous enterprise. They were on their way to the country ranged by the Arapahoes, a day's journey west of our camp. These Arapahoes, of whom Shaw and I afterwards fell in with a large number, are ferocious savages, who of late had declared themselves enemies to the whites, and threatened death to the first who should venture within their territory. The occasion of the declaration was as follows:—

In the preceding spring, 1845, Colonel Kearney left Fort Leavenworth with several companies of dragoons, marched to Fort Laramie, passed along the foot of the mountains to Bent's Fort, and then, turning eastward again, returned to the point whence he set out. While at Fort Laramie, he sent a part of his command as far westward as Sweetwater, while he himself remained at the fort, and despatched messages to the surrounding Indians to meet him there in council. Then for the first time the tribes of that vicinity saw the white warriors, and, as might have been expected, they were lost in astonishment at their regular order, their gay attire, the completeness of their martial equipment, and the size and strength of their horses. Among the rest, the Arapahoes came in considerable numbers to the Fort. They had lately committed numerous murders, and Colonel Kearney threatened that if they killed any more white men he would turn loose his dragoons upon them and annihilate their nation. In the evening, to add effect to his speech, he ordered a howitzer to be fired and a rocket to be thrown up. Many of the Arapahoes fell flat on the ground, while others ran away screaming with amazement and terror. On the following day they withdrew to their mountains, confounded at the appearance of the dragoons, at their big gun which went off twice at one shot and the fiery messenger which they had sent up to the Great Spirit. For many months they remained quiet, and did no farther mischief. At length, just before we came into the country, one of them, by an act of the basest treachery, killed two white men, Boot and May, who were trapping among the mountains. For this act it was impossible to discover a motive. It seemed to spring from one of those inexplicable impulses which often possess Indians, and which appear to be mere outbreaks of native ferocity. No sooner was the murder committed than the whole tribe were in consternation. They expected every day that the avenging dragoons would come, little thinking that a desert of nine hundred miles lay between them and their enemy. A large deputation of them came to Fort Laramie, bringing a valuable present of horses, in atonement. These Bordeaux refused to accept. They then asked if he would be satisfied with their delivering up the murderer himself; but he declined this offer also. The Arapahoes went back more terrified than ever. Weeks passed away, and still no dragoons appeared. A result followed which those best acquainted with Indians had predicted. They imagined that fear had prevented Bordeaux from accepting their gifts, and that they had nothing to apprehend from the vengeance of the whites. From terror they rose to the height of insolence. They called the white men cowards and old women; and a friendly Dakota came to Fort Laramie with the report that they were determined to kill the first white dog they could lay hands on.

Had a military officer, with suitable powers, been stationed at Fort Laramie; had he accepted the offer of the Arapahoes to deliver up the murderer, and ordered him to be led out and shot, in presence of his tribe, they would have been awed into tranquillity, and much danger averted; but now the neighborhood of the Medicine-Bow Mountain was perilous in the extreme. Old Mene-Seela, a true friend of the whites, and many other of the Indians, gathered about the two trappers, and vainly endeavored to turn them from their purpose; but Rouleau and Saraphin only laughed at the danger. On the morning preceding that on which they were to leave the camp, we could all see faint white columns of smoke rising against the dark base of the Medicine Bow. Scouts were sent out immediately, and reported that these proceeded from an Arapahoe camp, abandoned only a few hours before. Still the two trappers continued their preparations for departure.

Saraphin was a tall, powerful fellow, with a sullen and sinister countenance. His rifle had very probably drawn other blood than that of buffalo or Indians. Rouleau had a broad, ruddy face, marked with as few traces of thought or care as a child's. His figure was square and strong, but the first joints of both his feet were frozen off, and his horse had lately thrown and trampled upon him, by which he had been severely injured in the chest. But nothing could subdue his gayety. He went all day rolling about the camp on his stumps of feet, talking, singing, and frolicking with the Indian women. Rouleau had an unlucky partiality for squaws. He always had one, whom he must needs bedizen with beads, ribbons, and all the finery of an Indian wardrobe; and though he was obliged to leave her behind him during his expeditions, this hazardous necessity did not at all trouble him, for his disposition was the reverse of jealous. If at any time he had not lavished the whole of the precarious profits of his vocation upon his dark favorite, he devoted the rest to feasting his comrades. If liquor was not to be had—and this was usually the case— strong coffee would be substituted. As the men of that region are by no means remarkable for providence or self-restraint, whatever was set before them on these occasions, however extravagant in price or enormous in quantity, was sure to be disposed of at one sitting. Like other trappers, Rouleau's life was one of contrast and variety. It was only at certain seasons, and for a limited time, that he was absent on his expeditions. For the rest of the year he would lounge about the fort, or encamp with his friends in its vicinity, hunting, or enjoying all the luxury of inaction; but when once in pursuit of the beaver, he was involved in extreme privations and perils. Hand and foot, eye and ear must be always alert. Frequently he must content himself with devouring his evening meal uncooked, lest the light of his fire should attract the eyes of some wandering Indian; and sometimes, having made his rude repast, he must leave his fire still blazing, and withdraw to a distance under cover of the darkness, that his disappointed enemy, drawn thither by the light, may find his victim gone, and be unable to trace his footsteps in the gloom. This is the life led by scores of men among the Rocky Mountains. I once met a trapper whose breast was marked with the scars of six bullets and arrows, one of his arms broken by a shot, and one of his knees shattered; yet still, with the mettle of New England, whence he had come, he continued to follow his perilous calling.

On the last day of our stay in this camp the trappers were ready for departure. When in the Black Hills they had caught seven beavers, and they now left their skins in charge of Reynal, to be kept until their return. Their strong, gaunt horses were equipped with rusty Spanish bits, and rude Mexican saddles, to which wooden stirrups were attached, while a buffalo-robe was rolled up behind, and a bundle of beaver-traps slung at the pommel. These, together with their rifles, knives, powder-horns and bullet-pouches, flint and steel, and a tin cup, composed their whole travelling equipment. They shook hands with us, and rode away; Saraphin, with his grim countenance, was in advance; but Rouleau, clambering gayly into his seat, kicked his horse's sides, flourished his whip, and trotted briskly over the prairie, trolling forth a Canadian song at the top of his voice. Reynal looked after them, with his face of brutal selfishness.

'Well,' he said, 'if they are killed, I shall have the beaver. They'll fetch me fifty dollars at the fort, anyhow.'

This was the last I saw of them.

We had been five days in the hunting-camp, and the meat, which all this time had hung drying in the sun, was now fit for transportation. Buffalo-hides also had been procured in sufficient quantities for making the next season's lodges; but it remained to provide the long poles on which they were to be supported.

These were only to be had among the tall pine woods of the Black Hills, and in that direction therefore our next move was to be made. Amid the general abundance which during this time had prevailed in the camp, there were no instances of individual privation, for although the hide and the tongue of the buffalo belong by exclusive right to the hunter who has killed it, yet any one else is equally entitled to help himself from the rest of the carcass. Thus the weak, the aged, and even the indolent come in for a share of the spoils, and many a helpless old woman, who would otherwise perish from starvation, is sustained in abundance.

On the twenty-fifth of July, late in the afternoon, the camp broke up, with the usual tumult and confusion, and we all moved once more, on horseback and on foot, over the plains. We advanced, however, but a few miles. The old men, who during the whole march had been stoutly striding along on foot in front of the people, now seated themselves in a circle on the ground, while the families, erecting their lodges in the prescribed order around them, formed the usual great circle of the camp; meanwhile these village patriarchs sat smoking and talking. I threw my bridle to Raymond, and sat down as usual along with them. There was none of that reserve and apparent dignity which an Indian always assumes when in council, or in the presence of white men whom he distrusts. The party, on the contrary, was an extremely merry one, and as in a social circle of a quite different character, 'if there was not much wit, there was at least a great deal of laughter.'

When the first pipe was smoked out, I rose and withdrew to the lodge of my host. Here I was stooping, in the act of taking off my powder-horn and bullet-pouch, when suddenly, and close at hand, pealing loud and shrill, and in right good earnest, came the terrific yell of the war-whoop. Kongra-Tonga's squaw snatched up her youngest child and ran out of the lodge. I followed, and found the whole village in confusion, resounding with cries and yells. The circle of old men in the centre had vanished. The warriors, with glittering eyes, came darting, weapons in hand, out of the low openings of the lodges, and running with wild yells towards the farther end of the village. Advancing a few rods in that direction, I saw a crowd in furious agitation. Just then I distinguished the voices of Raymond and Reynal, shouting to me from a distance, and looking back, I saw the latter with his rifle in his hand, standing on the farther bank of a little stream that

ran along the outskirts of the camp. He was calling to Raymond
and me to come over and join him, and Raymond, with his usual
deliberate gait and stolid countenance, was already moving in that
direction.

This was clearly the wisest course, unless we wished to involve
ourselves in the fray; so I turned to go, but just then a pair of
eyes, gleaming like a snake's, and an aged familiar countenance
was thrust from the opening of a neighboring lodge, and out
bolted Mene-Seela, full of fight, clutching his bow and arrows in
one hand and his knife in the other. At that instant he tripped and
fell sprawling on his face, while his weapons flew scattering in
every direction. The women with loud screams were hurrying with
their children in their arms to place them out of danger, and I
observed some hastening to prevent mischief by carrying away
all the weapons they could lay hands on. On a rising ground close
to the camp stood a line of old women singing a medicine-song
to allay the tumult. As I approached the side of the brook, I
heard gun-shots behind me, and turning back saw that the crowd
had separated into two long lines of naked warriors confronting
each other at a respectful distance, and yelling and jumping about
to dodge the shot of their adversaries, while they discharged
bullets and arrows against each other. At the same time certain
sharp, humming sounds in the air over my head, like the flight of
beetles on a summer evening, warned me that the danger was not
wholly confined to the immediate scene of the fray. So, wading
through the brook, I joined Reynal and Raymond, and we sat
down on the grass, in the posture of an armed neutrality, to watch
the result.

Happily it may be for ourselves, though contrary to our ex-
pectation, the disturbance was quelled almost as soon as it began.
When I looked again, the combatants were once more mingled
together in a mass. Though yells sounded occasionally from the
throng, the firing had entirely ceased, and I observed five or six
persons moving about, as if acting the part of peace-makers. One
of the village heralds or criers proclaimed in a loud voice something which my two companions were too much engrossed in their
own observations to translate for me. The crowd began to disperse, though many a deep-set black eye still glittered with an
unnatural lustre, as the warriors slowly withdrew to their lodges.
This fortunate suppression of the disturbance was owing to a few
of the old men, less pugnacious than Mene-Seela, who boldly

ran in between the combatants, and aided by some of the 'soldiers,' or Indian police, succeeded in effecting their object.

It seemed very strange to me that although many arrows and bullets were discharged, no one was mortally hurt, and I could only account for this by the fact that both the marksman and the object of his aim were leaping about incessantly. By far the greater part of the villagers had joined in the fray, for although there were not more than a dozen guns in the whole camp, I heard at least eight or ten shots fired.

In a quarter of an hour all was comparatively quiet. A group of warriors was again seated in the middle of the village, but this time I did not venture to join them, because I could see that the pipe, contrary to the usual order, was passing from the left hand to the right around the circle; a sure sign that a 'medicine-smoke' of reconciliation was going forward, and that a white man would be an intruder. When I again entered the still agitated camp it was nearly dark, and mournful cries, howls, and wailings resounded from many female voices. Whether these had any connection with the late disturbance, or were merely lamentations for relatives slain in some former war expeditions, I could not distinctly ascertain.

To inquire too closely into the cause of the quarrel was by no means prudent, and it was not until some time after that I discovered what had given rise to it. Among the Dakota there are many associations or fraternities, superstitious, warlike, or social. Among them was one called 'The Arrow-Breakers,' now in great measure disbanded and dispersed. In the village there were, however, four men belonging to it, distinguished by the peculiar arrangement of their hair, which rose in a high, bristling mass above their foreheads, adding greatly to their apparent height, and giving them a most ferocious appearance. The principal among them was the Mad Wolf, a warrior of remarkable size and strength, great courage, and the fierceness of a demon. I had always looked upon him as the most dangerous man in the village; and though he often invited me to feasts, I never entered his lodge unarmed. The Mad Wolf had taken a fancy to a fine horse belonging to another Indian, called the Tall Bear; and anxious to get the animal into his possession, he made the owner a present of another horse nearly equal in value. According to the customs of the Dakota, the acceptance of this gift involved a sort of obligation to make a return; and the Tall Bear well understood that the other had his favorite buffalo-horse in view. He however accepted the present without a word of thanks, and having picketed the horse before his lodge, suffered day after day to pass without making the expected return. The Mad Wolf grew impatient; and at last, seeing that his bounty was not likely to produce the desired result, he resolved to reclaim it. So this evening, as soon as the village was encamped, he went to the lodge of the Tall Bear, seized upon the horse he had given him, and led him away. At this the Tall Bear broke into one of those fits of sullen rage not uncommon among Indians, ran up to the unfortunate horse, and gave him three mortal stabs with his knife. Quick as lightning the Mad Wolf drew his bow to its utmost tension and held the arrow quivering close to the breast of his adversary. The Tall Bear, as the Indians who were near him said, stood with his bloody knife in his hand facing the assailant with the utmost calmness. Some of his friends and relatives, seeing his danger, ran hastily to his assistance. The remaining three Arrow-Breakers on the other hand, came to the aid of their associate. Their friends joined them, the war-cry was raised, and the tumult became general.

The 'soldiers,' who lent their timely aid in putting it down, are the most important executive functionaries in an Indian village. The office is one of considerable honor, being confided only to men of courage and repute. They derive their authority from the old men and chief warriors of the village, who elect them in councils occasionally convened for the purpose, and thus they can exercise a degree of authority which no one else in the village would dare to assume. While very few Ogillallah chiefs could venture without risk of their lives to strike or lay hands upon the meanest of their people, the 'soldiers,' in the discharge of their appropriate functions, have full license to make use of these and similar acts of coercion.

17. The Black Hills

We travelled eastward for two days, and then the gloomy ridges of the Black Hills rose before us. The village passed along for some miles beneath their declivities, trailing out to a great length over the arid prairie, or winding among small detached hills of distorted shapes. Turning sharply to the left, we entered a wide defile of the mountains, down the bottom of which a brook came winding, lined with tall grass and dense copses, amid which were hidden many beaver dams and lodges. We passed along between two lines of high precipices and rocks piled in disorder one upon another, with scarcely a tree, a bush, or a clump of grass. The restless Indian boys wandered along their edges and clambered up and down their rugged sides, and sometimes a group of them would stand on the verge of a cliff and look down on the procession as it passed beneath. As we advanced, the passage grew more narrow; then it suddenly expanded into a round grassy meadow, completely encompassed by mountains; and here the families stopped as they came up in turn, and the camp rose like magic.

The lodges were hardly pitched when, with their usual precipitation, the Indians set about accomplishing the object that had brought them there; that is, obtaining poles for their new lodges. Half the population, men, women, and boys, mounted their horses and set out for the depths of the mountains. It was a strange cavalcade, as they rode at full gallop over the shingly rocks and into the dark opening of the defile beyond. We passed between precipices, sharp and splintering at the tops, their sides beetling over the defile or descending in abrupt declivities, bristling with fir-trees. On our left they rose close to us like a wall, but on the right a winding brook with a narrow strip of marshy soil intervened. The stream was clogged with old beaver-dams and spread frequently into wide pools. There were thick bushes and many dead and blasted trees along its course, though frequently nothing remained but stumps cut close to the ground by the beaver, and marked with the sharp chisel-like teeth of those indefatigable laborers. Sometimes we dived among trees, and then emerged upon open spots, over which, Indian-like, all galloped at full speed. As Pauline bounded over the rocks I felt her saddle-girth slipping, and alighted to draw it tighter; when the whole cavalcade swept by me in a moment, the women with their gaudy ornaments tinkling as they rode, the men whooping, laughing, and lashing forward their horses. Two black-tailed deer bounded away among the rocks; Raymond shot at them from horseback; the sharp report of his rifle was answered by another equally sharp from the opposing cliffs, and then the echoes, leaping in rapid succession from side to side died away rattling far amid the mountains.

After having ridden in this manner six or eight miles the scene changed, and all the declivities were covered with forests of tall, slender spruce and pine trees. The Indians began to fall off to the right and left, dispersing with their hatchets and knives to cut the poles which they had come to seek. I was soon left almost alone; but in the stillness of those lonely mountains, the stroke of hatchets and the sound of voices might be heard from far and near.

Reynal, who imitated the Indians in their habits as well as the worst features of their character, had killed buffalo enough to make a lodge for himself and his squaw, and now he was eager to get the poles necessary to complete it. He asked me to let Raymond go with him, and assist in the work. I assented, and the two men immediately entered the thickest part of the wood. Having left my horse in Raymond's keeping, I began to climb the mountain. I was weak and weary, and made slow progress, often pausing to rest; but after an hour I gained a height whence the little valley out of which I had climbed seemed like a deep, dark gulf, though the inaccessible peak of the mountain was still towering to a much greater distance above. Objects familiar from childhood surrounded me,—crags and rocks, a black and sullen brook that gurgled with a hollow voice deep among the crevices, a wood of mossy, distorted trees and prostrate trunks flung down by age and storms, scattered among the rocks, or damming the foaming waters of the brook.

Wild as they were, these mountains were thickly peopled. As I climbed farther, I found the broad, dusty paths made by the elk, as they filed across the mountain side. The grass on all the terraces was trampled down by deer; there were numerous tracks of wolves, and in some of the rougher and more precipitous parts of the ascent I found footprints different from any that I had ever seen, and which I took to be those of the Rocky Mountain sheep. I sat down on a rock; there was a perfect stillness. No wind was stirring, and not even an insect could be heard. I remembered the danger of becoming lost in such a place, and fixed my eye upon one of the tallest pinnacles of the opposite mountain. It rose sheer upright from the woods below, and, by an extraordinary freak of nature, sustained aloft on its very summit a large, loose rock. Such a landmark could never be mistaken, and feeling once more secure, I began again to move forward. A white wolf jumped up from among some bushes and leaped clumsily away; but he stopped for a moment and turned back his keen eye and grim, bristling muzzle. I longed to take his scalp and carry it back with me as a trophy of the Black Hills, but before I could fire, he was gone among the rocks. Soon after I heard a rustling sound, with a cracking of twigs at a little distance, and saw moving above the tall bushes the branching antlers of an elk. I was in a hunter's paradise.

Such are the Black Hills, as I found them in July; but they wear a different garb when winter sets in, when the broad boughs of the fir-trees are bent to the ground by the load of snow, and the dark mountains are white with it. At that season the trappers, returned from their autumn expeditions, often build their cabins in the midst of these solitudes, and live in abundance and luxury on the game that harbors there. I have heard them tell how, with their tawny mistresses, and perhaps a few young Indian companions, they had spent months in total seclusion. They would dig pitfalls, and set traps for the white wolves, sables, and martens, and though through the whole night the awful chorus of the wolves would resound from the frozen mountains around them, yet within their massive walls of logs they would lie in careless ease before the blazing fire, and in the morning shoot the elk and deer from their very door.

18. A Mountain Hunt

The camp was full of the newly cut lodge-poles; some, already prepared, were stacked together, white and glistening, to dry and harden in the sun; others were lying on the ground, and the squaws, the boys, and even some of the warriors were busily at work peeling off the bark and paring them with their knives to the proper dimensions. Most of the hides obtained at the last camp were dressed and scraped thin enough for use, and many of the squaws were engaged in fitting them together and sewing them with sinews, to form the coverings for the lodges. Men were wandering among the bushes that lined the brook along the margin of the camp, cutting sticks of red willow, or *shongsasha*, the bark of which, mixed with tobacco, they use for smoking. Reynal's squaw was hard at work with her awl and buffalo sinews upon

her lodge, while her proprietor, having just finished an enormous
breakfast of meat, was smoking a social pipe with Raymond and
myself. He proposed at length that we should go out on a hunt.
'Go to the Big Crow's lodge,' said he, 'and get your rifle. I 'll
bet the gray Wyandot pony against your mare that we start an
elk or a black-tailed deer, or likely as not a big-horn, before we
are two miles out of camp. I 'll take my squaw's old yellow
horse; you can't whip him more than four miles an hour, but he is
as good for the mountains as a mule.'

I mounted the black mule which Raymond usually rode. She
was a powerful animal, gentle and manageable enough by nature;
but of late her temper had been soured by misfortune. About a
week before, I had chanced to offend some one of the Indians, who
out of revenge went secretly into the meadow and gave her a
severe stab in the haunch with his knife. The wound, though
partially healed, still galled her extremely, and made her even
more perverse and obstinate than the rest of her species.

The morning was a glorious one, and I was in better health than
I had been at any time for the last two months. We left the little
valley and ascended a rocky hollow in the mountain. Very soon
we were out of sight of the camp, and of every living thing, man,
beast, bird, or insect. I had never before, except on foot, passed
over such execrable ground, and I desire never to repeat the experiment. The black mule grew indignant, and even the redoubtable yellow horse stumbled every moment, and kept
groaning to himself as he cut his feet and legs among the sharp
rocks.

It was a scene of silence and desolation. Little was visible except
beetling crags and the bare shingly sides of the mountains,
relieved by scarcely a trace of vegetation. At length, however, we
came upon a forest tract, and had no sooner done so than we
heartily wished ourselves back among the rocks again; for we
were on a steep descent, among trees so thick that we could see
scarcely a rod in any direction.

If one is anxious to place himself in a situation where the hazardous and the ludicrous are combined in about equal proportions,
let him get upon a vicious mule, with a snaffle bit, and try to drive
her through the woods down a slope of forty-five degrees. Let him
have a long rifle, a buckskin frock with long fringes, and a head
of long hair. These latter appendages will be caught every
moment and twitched away in small portions by the twigs,

which will also whip him smartly across the face, while the large branches above thump him on the head. His mule, if she be a true one, will alternately stop short and dive violently forward, and his positions upon her back will be somewhat diversified. At one time he will clasp her affectionately, to avoid the blow of a bough overhead; at another, he will throw himself back and fling his knee forward against her neck, to keep it from being crushed between the rough bark of a tree and the ribs of the animal. Reynal was cursing incessantly during the whole way down. Neither of us had the remotest idea where we were going; and though I have seen rough riding, I shall always retain an evil recollection of that five minutes' scramble.

At last we left our troubles behind us, emerging into the channel of a brook that circles along the foot of the descent; and here, turning joyfully to the left, we rode at ease over the white pebbles and the rippling water, shaded from the glaring sun by an over-arching green transparency. These halcyon moments were of short duration. The friendly brook, turning sharply to one side, went brawling and foaming down the rocky hill into an abyss, which, as far as we could see, had no bottom; so once more we betook ourselves to the detested woods. When next we came out from their shadow we found ourselves standing in the broad glare of day, on a high jutting point of the mountain. Before us stretched a long, wide, desert valley, winding away far amid the mountains. Reynal gazed intently; he began to speak at last:—

'Many a time, when I was with the Indians, I have been hunting for gold all through the Black Hills. There 's plenty of it here; you may be certain of that. I have dreamed about it fifty times, and I never dreamed yet but what it came out true. Look over yonder at those black rocks piled up against that other big rock. Don't it look as if there might be something there? It won't do for a white man to be rummaging too much about these mountains; the Indians say they are full of bad spirits; and I believe myself that it's no good luck to be hunting about here after gold. Well, for all that, I would like to have one of those fellows up here, from down below, to go about with his witch-hazel rod, and I 'll guarantee that it would not be long before he would light on a gold-mine. Never mind; we 'll let the gold alone for to-day. Look at those trees down below us in the hollow; we 'll go down there, and I reckon we 'll get a black-tailed deer.'

But Reynal's predictions were not verified. We passed

mountain after mountain, and valley after valley; we explored deep ravines; yet still, to my companion's vexation and evident surprise, no game could be found. So, in the absence of better, we resolved to go out on the plains and look for an antelope. With this view we began to pass down a narrow valley, the bottom of which was covered with the stiff wild-sage bushes and marked with deep paths, made by the buffalo, who, for some inexplicable reason, are accustomed to penetrate, in their long grave processions, deep among the gorges of these sterile mountains.

Reynal's eye ranged incessantly among the rocks and along the edges of the precipices, in hopes of discovering the mountain-sheep peering down upon us from that giddy height. Nothing was visible for some time. At length we both detected something in motion near the foot of one of the mountains, and a moment afterward a black-tailed deer stood gazing at us from the top of a rock, and then, slowly turning away, disappeared behind it. In an instant Reynal was out of his saddle, and running towards the spot. I, being too weak to follow, sat holding his horse and waiting the result. I lost sight of him; then heard the report of his rifle, deadened among the rocks, and finally saw him reappear, with a surly look, that plainly betrayed his ill-success. Again we moved forward down the long valley, till we came full upon what seemed a wide and very shallow ditch, incrusted at the bottom with white clay, dried and cracked in the sun. Under this fair outside Reynal's eye detected the signs of lurking mischief. He called to me to stop, and then alighting, picked up a stone and threw it into the ditch. To my amazement it fell with a dull splash, breaking at once through the thin crust, and spattering round the hole a yellowish, creamy fluid, into which it sank and disappeared. A stick five or six feet long lay on the ground, and with this we sounded the insidious abyss close to its edge. It was just possible to touch the bottom. Places like this are numerous among the Rocky Mountains. The buffalo, in his blind and heedless walk, often plunges into them unawares. Down he sinks; one snort of terror, one convulsive struggle, and the slime calmly flows above his shaggy head, the languid undulations of its sleek and placid surface alone betraying how the powerful monster writhes in his death-throes below.

We found after some trouble a point where we could pass the abyss, and now the valley began to open upon plains which spread to the horizon before us. On one of their distant swells we discerned three or four black specks, which Reynal pronounced to be buffalo.

'Come,' said he, 'we must get one of them. My squaw wants more sinews to finish her lodge with, and I want some glue myself.'

He immediately put the yellow horse to such a gallop as he was capable of executing, while I set spurs to the mule, who soon far outran her plebeian rival. When we had galloped a mile or more, a large rabbit, by ill-luck, sprang up just under the feet of the mule, which bounded violently aside in full career. Weakened as I was, I was flung forcibly to the ground, and my rifle, falling close to my head, went off with the shock. Its sharp, spiteful report rang for some moments in my ear. Being slightly stunned, I lay for an instant motionless, and Reynal, supposing me to be shot, rode up and began to curse the mule. Soon recovering myself, I rose, picked up the rifle, and anxiously examined it. It was badly injured. The stock was cracked, and the main screw broken, so that the lock had to be tied in its place with a string; yet happily it was not rendered totally unserviceable. I wiped it out, reloaded it, and handing it to Reynal, who meanwhile had caught the mule and led her up to me, I mounted again. No sooner had I done so than the brute began to rear and plunge with extreme violence; but being now well prepared for her, and free from incumbrance, I soon reduced her to submission. Then, taking the rifle again from Reynal, we galloped forward as before.

We were now free of the mountains and riding far out on the broad prairie. The buffalo were still some two miles in advance of us. When we came near them, we stopped where a gentle swell of the plain concealed us, and while I held his horse Reynal ran forward with his rifle, till I lost sight of him beyond the rising ground. A few minutes elapsed: I heard the report of his piece, and saw the buffalo running away at full speed on the right; immediately after, the hunter himself, unsuccessful as before, came up and mounted his horse in excessive ill-humor. He cursed the Black Hills and the buffalo, swore that he was a good hunter, which indeed was true, and that he had never been out before among those mountains without killing two or three deer at least.

We now turned towards the distant encampment. As we rode along, antelope in considerable numbers were flying lightly in all directions over the plain, but not one of them would stand and be shot at. When we reached the foot of the mountain-ridge that lay

between us and the village, we were too impatient to take the
smooth and circuitous route; so turning short to the left we
drove our wearied animals upward among the rocks. Still more
antelope were leaping about among these flinty hillsides. Each of
us shot at one, though from a great distance, and each missed his
mark. At length we reached the summit of the last ridge. Looking
down we saw the bustling camp in the valley at our feet, and in-
gloriously descended to it. As we rode among the lodges, the
Indians looked in vain for the fresh meat that should have hung
behind our saddles, and the squaws uttered various suppressed
ejaculations, to the great indignation of Reynal. Our mortification
was increased when we rode up to his lodge. Here he saw his
young Indian relative, the Hail-Storm, his light, graceful figure
reclining on the ground in an easy attitude, while with his friend
the Rabbit, who sat by his side, he was making an abundant
meal from a wooden bowl of *wasna*, which the squaw had placed
between them. Near him lay the fresh skin of a female elk, which
he had just killed among the mountains, only a mile or two from
the camp. No doubt the boy's heart was elated with triumph,
but he betrayed no sign of it. He even seemed totally unconscious
of our approach, and his handsome face had all the tranquillity
of Indian self-control,—a self-control which prevents the exhibition of emotion without restraining the emotion itself. It was
about two months since I had known the Hail-Storm, and within
that time his character had remarkably developed. When I first
saw him he was just emerging from the habits and feelings of the
boy into the ambition of the hunter and warrior. He had lately
killed his first deer, and this had excited his aspirations for distinction. Since that time he had been continually in search of
game, and no young hunter in the village had been so active or so
fortunate as he. All this success had produced a marked change
in his character. As I first remembered him he always shunned
the society of the young squaws, and was extremely bashful and
sheepish in their presence; but now, in the confidence of his new
reputation he began to assume the air and arts of a man of gal-
lantry. He wore his red blanket dashingly over his left shoulder,
painted his cheeks every day with vermilion, and hung pendants
of shells in his ears. If I observed aright, he met with very good
success in his new pursuits; still the Hail-Storm had much to
accomplish before he attained the full standing of a warrior.
Gallantly as he began to bear himself among the women and

girls, he was still timid and abashed in the presence of the chiefs
and old men; for he had never yet killed a man, or stricken the
dead body of an enemy in battle. I have no doubt that the handsome, smooth-faced boy burned with desire to flesh his maiden
scalping-knife, and I would not have encamped alone with him
without watching his movements with a suspicious eye.

His elder brother, the Horse, was of a different character. He
was nothing but a lazy dandy. He knew very well how to hunt,
but preferred to live by the hunting of others. He had no appetite
for distinction, and the Hail-Storm already surpassed him in
reputation. He had a dark and ugly face, and passed a great part
of his time in adorning it with vermilion, and contemplating it
by means of a little pocket looking-glass which I had given him.
As for the rest of the day, he divided it between eating, sleeping,
and sitting in the sun on the outside of a lodge. Here he would
remain for hour after hour arrayed in all his finery, with an old
dragoon's sword in his hand, evidently flattering himself that he
was the centre of attraction to the eyes of the surrounding
squaws. Yet he sat looking straight forward with a face of the
utmost gravity, as if wrapped in profound meditation, and it was
only by the occasional sidelong glances which he shot at his
supposed admirers that one could detect the true course of his
thoughts.

Both he and his brother may represent classes in the Indian
community; neither should the Hail-Storm's friend the Rabbit,
be passed by without notice. The Hail-Storm and he were in-
separable; they ate, slept, and hunted together, and shared with
one another almost all that they possessed. If there be anything
that deserves to be called romantic in the Indian character, it is
to be sought for in friendships such as this, which are common
among many of the prairie tribes.

Slowly, hour after hour, that weary afternoon dragged away.
I lay in Reynal's lodge, overcome by the listless torpor that per-
vaded the encampment. The day's work was finished, or if it were
not, the inhabitants had resolved not to finish it at all, and were
dozing quietly within the shelter of the lodges. A profound
lethargy, the very spirit of indolence, seemed to have sunk upon
the village. Now and then I could hear the low laughter of some
girl from within a neighboring lodge, or the small shrill voices of
a few restless children who alone were moving in the deserted
area. The spirit of the place infected me; I could not think

consecutively; I was fit only for musing and revery, when at last, like the rest, I fell asleep.

When evening came, and the fires were lighted round the lodges, a select family circle convened in the neighborhood of Reynal's domicile. It was composed entirely of his squaw's relatives, a mean and ignoble clan, among whom none but the Hail-Storm held forth any promise of future distinction. Even his prospects were rendered not a little dubious by the character of the family, less however from any principle of aristocratic distinction than from the want of powerful supporters to assist him in his under-takings and help to avenge his quarrels. Raymond and I sat down along with them. There were eight or ten men gathered round the fire, together with about as many women, old and young, some of whom were tolerably good-looking. As the pipe passed round among the men, a lively conversation went forward, more merry than delicate, and at length two or three of the elder women (for the girls were somewhat diffident and bashful) began to assail Raymond with various pungent witticisms. Some of the men took part, and an old squaw concluded by bestowing on him a ludicrous and indecent nickname, at which a general laugh followed at his expense. Raymond grinned and giggled and made several futile attempts at repartee. Knowing the impolicy and even danger of suffering myself to be placed in a ludicrous light among the Indians, I maintained a rigid, inflexible countenance, and wholly escaped their sallies.

In the morning I found, to my great disgust, that the camp was to remain where it was for another day. I dreaded its languor and monotony, and, to escape it, set out to explore the surrounding mountains. I was accompanied by a faithful friend, my rifle, the only friend indeed on whose prompt assistance in time of trouble I could wholly rely. Most of the Indians in the village, it is true, professed good-will towards the whites, but the experience of others and my own observation had taught me the extreme folly of confidence, and the utter impossibility of foreseeing to what sudden acts the strange, unbridled impulses of an Indian may urge him. When among this people danger is never so near as when you are unprepared for it, never so remote as when you are armed and on the alert to meet it at any moment. Nothing offers so strong a temptation to their ferocious instincts as the appearance of timidity, weakness, or security.

Many deep and gloomy gorges, choked with trees and bushes,

opened from the sides of the hills, which were shaggy with
forests wherever the rocks permitted vegetation to spring. A
great number of Indians were stalking along the edges of the
woods, and boys were whooping and laughing on the mountains,
practising eye and hand, and indulging their destructive propen-
sities by killing birds and small animals with their little bows and
arrows. There was one glen, stretching up between steep cliffs
far into the bosom of the mountain. I began to ascend along its
bottom, pushing my way onward among the rocks, trees, and
bushes that obstructed it. A slender thread of water trickled
through it, which since issuing from the heart of its native rock
could scarcely have been warmed or gladdened by a ray of
sunshine. After advancing for some time, I conceived myself to
be entirely alone; but coming to a part of the glen in a great
measure free of trees and undergrowth, I saw at some distance
the black head and red shoulders of an Indian among the bushes
above. The reader need not prepare himself for a startling adventure, for I have none to relate. The head and shoulders
belonged to Mene-Seela, my best friend in the village. As I had
approached noiselessly with my moccasined feet, the old man
was quite unaware of my presence; and turning to a point where
I could gain an unobstructed view of him, I saw him seated alone,
immovable as a statue, among the rocks and trees. His face was
turned upward, and his eyes seemed riveted on a pine tree
springing from a cleft in the precipice above. The crest of the pine
was swaying to and fro in the wind, and its long limbs waved
slowly up and down, as if the tree had life. Looking for a while
at the old man, I was satisfied that he was engaged in an act of
worship, or prayer, or communion of some kind with a supernatural being. I longed to penetrate his thoughts, but I could do
nothing more than conjecture and speculate. I knew that though
the intellect of an Indian can embrace the idea of an all-wise,
all-powerful Spirit, the supreme Ruler of the universe, yet his
mind will not always ascend into communion with a being that
seemed to him so vast, remote, and incomprehensible; and when
danger threatens, when his hopes are broken, and trouble over-
shadows him, he is prone to turn for relief to some inferior agency,
less removed from the ordinary scope of his faculties. He has a
guardian spirit, on whom he relies for succor and guidance. To
him all nature is instinct with mystic influence. Among those
mountains not a wild beast was prowling, a bird singing, or a leaf

fluttering, that might not tend to direct his destiny, or give
warning of what was in store for him; and he watches the world of
nature around him as the astrologer watches the stars. So closely
is he linked with it that his guardian spirit, no unsubstantial
creation of the fancy, is usually embodied in the form of some
living thing,—a bear, a wolf, an eagle, or a serpent; and Mene-
Seela, as he gazed intently on the old pine-tree, might believe it
to inshrine the fancied guide and protector of his life.

Whatever was passing in the mind of the old man, it was no
part of good sense to disturb him. Silently retracing my footsteps, I descended the glen till I came to a point where I could
climb the precipices that shut it in, and gain the side of the
mountain. Looking up, I saw a tall peak rising among the woods.
Something impelled me to climb; I had not felt for many a day
such strength and elasticity of limb. An hour and a half of slow
and often intermitted labor brought me to the summit; and
emerging from the dark shadows of the rocks and pines, I stepped
out into the light, and walking along the sunny verge of a precipice, seated myself on its extreme point. Looking between the
mountain-peaks to the westward, the pale-blue prairie was
stretching to the farthest horizon, like a serene and tranquil
ocean. The surrounding mountains were in themselves sufficiently
striking and impressive, but this contrast gave redoubled effect
to their stern features.

19. Passage of the Mountains

When I took leave of Shaw at La Bonté's camp, I promised to meet him at Fort Laramie on the first of August. The Indians, too, intended to pass the mountains and move towards the fort. To do so at this point was impossible, because there was no passage; and in order to find one we were obliged to go twelve or fourteen miles southward. Late in the afternoon the camp broke up. I rode in company with three or four young Indians at the rear, and the moving swarm stretched before me, in the ruddy light of sunset, or the deep shadow of the mountains, far beyond my sight. It was an ill-omened spot they chose to encamp upon. When they were there just a year before, a war-party of ten men, led by the Whirlwind's son, had gone out against the enemy, and not one had ever returned. This was the immediate cause of this

season's warlike preparations. I was not a little astonished, when
I came to the camp, at the confusion of horrible sounds with
which it was filled; howls, shrieks, and wailings rose from all the
women present, many of whom, not content with this exhibition
of grief for the loss of their friends and relatives, were gashing
their legs deeply with knives. A warrior in the village, who had
lost a brother in the expedition, chose another mode of displaying
his sorrow. The Indians, who though often rapacious, are devoid
of avarice, will sometimes, when in mourning, or on other
solemn occasions, give away the whole of their possessions, and
reduce themselves to nakedness and want. The warrior in
question led his best horses into the middle of the village, and
gave them away to his friends; upon which songs and acclamations in praise of his generosity mingled with the cries of the
women.

On the next morning we entered again among the mountains.
There was nothing in their appearance either grand or picturesque,
though they were desolate to the last degree, being mere piles of
black and broken rocks, without trees or vegetation of any kind.
As we passed among them along a wide valley, I noticed Raymond
riding by the side of a young squaw, to whom he was addressing
various compliments. All the old squaws in the neighborhood
watched his proceedings in great admiration, and the girl herself
would turn aside her head and laugh. Just then his mule thought
proper to display her vicious pranks, and began to rear and plunge
furiously. Raymond was an excellent rider, and at first he stuck
fast in his seat; but the moment after, I saw the mule's hind-
legs flourishing in the air and my unlucky follower pitching head
foremost over her ears. There was a burst of screams and laughter
from all the women, in which his mistress herself took part, and
Raymond was assailed by such a shower of witticisms that he
was glad to ride forward out of hearing.

Not long after, as I rode near him, I heard him shouting to me.
He was pointing towards a detached rocky hill that stood in the
middle of the valley before us, and from behind it a long file of elk
came out at full speed and entered an opening in the mountain.
They had scarcely disappeared, when whoops and exclamations
came from fifty voices around me. The young men leaped from
their horses, flung down their heavy buffalo-robes and ran at full
speed towards the foot of the nearest mountain. Reynal also
broke away at a gallop in the same direction. 'Come on! come on!'

he called to us. 'Do you see that band of big-horn up yonder? If there 's one of them, there 's a hundred!'

In fact, near the summit of the mountain I could see a large number of small white objects, moving rapidly upwards among the precipices, while others were filing along its rocky profile. Anxious to see the sport, I galloped forward, and entering a passage in the side of the mountain, ascended among the loose rocks as far as my horse could carry me. Here I fastened her to an old pine-tree. At that moment Raymond called to me from the right that another band of sheep was close at hand in that direction. I ran up to the top of the opening, which gave me a full view into the rocky gorge beyond; and here I plainly saw some fifty or sixty sheep, almost within rifle-shot, clattering upwards among the rocks, and endeavoring, after their usual custom, to reach the highest point. The naked Indians bounded up lightly in pursuit. In a moment the game and hunters disappeared. Nothing could be seen or heard but the occasional report of a gun, more and more distant, reverberating among the rocks.

I turned to descend, and as I did so, could see the valley below alive with Indians passing rapidly through it, on horseback and on foot. A little farther on, all were stopping as they came up; the camp was preparing and the lodges rising. I descended to this spot, and soon after Reynal and Raymond returned. They bore between them a sheep which they had pelted to death with stones from the edge of a ravine, along the bottom of which it was attempting to escape. One by one the hunters came dropping in; yet such is the activity of the Rocky Mountain sheep, that although sixty or seventy men were out in pursuit, not more than half a dozen animals were killed. Of these only one was a full-grown male. He had a pair of horns, the size of which was almost beyond belief. I have seen among the Indians ladles with long handles, capable of containing more than a quart, cut out from such horns.

Through the whole of the next morning we were moving forward among the hills. On the following day the heights closed around us, and the passage of the mountains began in earnest. Before the village left its 'camping-ground, I set forward in company with the Eagle-Feather, a man of powerful frame, but with a bad and sinister face. His son, a light-limbed boy, rode with us, and another Indian, named the Panther, was also of the party. Leaving the village out of sight behind us, we rode together up a rocky defile. After a while, however, the Eagle-Feather discovered

in the distance some appearance of game, and set off with his
son in pursuit of it, while I went forward with the Panther. This
was a mere *nom de guerre*; for, like many Indians, he concealed
his real name out of some superstitious notion. He was a noble-
looking fellow. As he suffered his ornamented buffalo-robe to fall
in folds about his loins, his stately and graceful figure was fully
displayed; and while he sat his horse in an easy attitude the long
feathers of the prairie-cock fluttering from the crown of his head,
he seemed the very model of a wild prairie-rider. He had not the
same features with those of other Indians. Unless his face greatly
belied him, he was free from the jealousy, suspicion, and malignant cunning of his people. For the most part, a civilized white
man can discover very few points of sympathy between his own
nature and that of an Indian. With every disposition to do justice
to their good qualities, he must be conscious that an impassable
gulf lies between him and his red brethren. Nay, so alien to himself
do they appear that, after breathing the air of the prairie for a
few months or weeks, he begins to look upon them as a troublesome and dangerous species of wild beast. Yet, in the countenance
of the Panther, I gladly read that there were at least some points
of sympathy between him and me. We were excellent friends, and
as we rode forward together through rocky passages, deep dells,
and little barren plains, he occupied himself very zealously in
teaching me the Dakota language. After a while we came to a
grassy recess, where some gooseberry-bushes were growing at the
foot of a rock; and these offered such temptation to my companion
that he gave over his instructions, and stopped so long to gather
the fruit that before we were in motion again the van of the village
came in view. An old woman appeared, leading down her packhorse among the rocks above. Savage after savage followed, and
the little dell was soon crowded with the throng.

That morning's march was one not to be forgotten. It led us
through a sublime waste, a wilderness of mountains and pine-
forests, over which the spirit of loneliness and silence seemed
brooding. Above and below, little could be seen but the same dark,
green foliage. It overspread the valleys, and enveloped the
mountains, from the black rocks that crowned their summits to
the streams that circled round their bases. I rode to the top of a
hill whence I could look down on the savage procession as it
passed beneath my feet, and, far on the left, could see its thin and
broken line, visible only at intervals, stretching away for miles

among the mountains. On the farthest ridge, horsemen were still descending like mere specks in the distance.

I remained on the hill till all had passed, and then descending followed after them. A little farther on I found a very small meadow, set deeply among steep mountains; and here the whole village had encamped. The little spot was crowded with the confused and disorderly host. Some of the lodges were already set up, or the squaws perhaps were busy in drawing the heavy coverings of skin over the bare poles. Others were as yet mere skeletons, while others still, poles, covering, and all, lay scattered in disorder on the ground among buffalo-robes, bales of meat, domestic utensils, harness, and weapons. Squaws were screaming to one another, horses rearing and plunging, dogs yelping, eager to be disburdened of their loads, while the fluttering of feathers and the gleam of savage ornaments added liveliness to the scene. The small children ran about amid the crowd, while many of the boys were scrambling among the overhanging rocks, and standing with their little bows in their hands, looking down upon the restless throng. In contrast with the general confusion, a circle of old men and warriors sat in the midst, smoking in profound indifference and tranquillity. The disorder at length subsided. The horses were driven away to feed along the adjacent valley, and the camp assumed an air of listless repose. It was scarcely past noon; a vast white canopy of smoke from a burning forest to the eastward overhung the place, and partially obscured the rays of the sun; yet the heat was almost insupportable. The lodges stood crowded together without order in the narrow space. Each was a hot-house, within which the lazy proprietor lay sleeping. The camp was silent as death. Nothing stirred except now and then an old woman passing from lodge to lodge. The girls and young men sat together in groups, under the pine-trees upon the surrounding heights. The dogs lay panting on the ground, too languid even to growl at the white man. At the entrance of the meadow, there was a cold spring among the rocks, completely overshadowed by tall trees and dense undergrowth. In this cool and shady retreat a number of girls were assembled, sitting together on rocks and fallen logs, discussing the latest gossip of the village, or laughing and throwing water with their hands at the intruding Meneaska. The minutes seemed lengthened into hours. I lay for a long time under a tree studying the Ogillallah tongue, with the aid of my friend the Panther. When we were both tired of this, I lay down

by the side of a deep, clear pool, formed by the water of the
spring. A shoal of little fishes of about a pin's length were playing
in it, sporting together, as it seemed, very amicably; but on closer
observation I saw that they were engaged in cannibal warfare
among themselves. Now and then one of the smallest would fall
a victim, and immediately disappear down the maw of his conqueror. Every moment, however, the tyrant of the pool, a goggle-
eyed monster about three inches long, would slowly emerge with
quivering fins and tail from under the shelving bank. The small
fry at this would suspend their hostilities, and scatter in a panic
at the appearance of overwhelming force.

'Soft-hearted philanthropists,' thought I, 'may sigh long for
their peaceful millennium; for, from minnows to men, life is
incessant war.'

Evening approached at last; the crests of the mountains were
still bright in sunshine, while our deep glen was completely
shadowed. I left the camp, and climbed a neighboring hill. The
sun was still glaring through the stiff pines on the ridge of the
western mountain. In a moment he was gone, and, as the landscape darkened, I turned again towards the village. As I descended,
the howling of wolves and the barking of foxes came up out of the
dim woods from far and near. The camp was glowing with a multitude of fires, and alive with dusky naked figures, whose tall
shadows flitted, weird and ghost-like, among the surrounding
crags.

I found a circle of smokers seated in their usual place; that is,
on the ground before the lodge of a certain warrior who seemed to
be generally known for his social qualities. I sat down to smoke a
parting pipe with my savage friends. That day was the first of
August on which I had promised to meet Shaw at Fort Laramie.
The fort was less than two days' journey distant, and that my
friend need not suffer anxiety on my account, I resolved to push
forward as rapidly as possible to the place of meeting. I went to
look after the Hail-Storm, and having found him I offered him
a handful of hawks'-bells and a paper of vermilion, on condition
that he would guide me in the morning through the mountains.

The Hail-Storm ejaculated 'How!' and accepted the gift.
Nothing more was said on either side; the matter was settled, and
I lay down to sleep in Kongra-Tonga's lodge.

Long before daylight, Raymond shook me by the shoulder.

'Everything is ready,' he said.

I went out. The morning was chill, damp, and dark; and the whole camp seemed asleep. The Hail-Storm sat on horseback before the lodge, and my mare Pauline and the mule which Raymond rode were picketed near it. We saddled and made our other arrangements for the journey, but before these were completed the camp began to stir, and the lodge-coverings fluttered and rustled as the squaws pulled them down in preparation for departure. Just as the light began to appear we left the ground, passing up through a narrow opening among the rocks which led eastward out of the meadow. Gaining the top of this passage, I turned and sat looking back upon the camp, dimly visible in the gray light of morning. All was alive with the bustle of preparation. I turned away, half unwilling to take a final leave of my savage associates. We passed among rocks and pine-trees so dark that for a while we could scarcely see our way. The country in front was wild and broken, half hill, half plain, partly open and partly covered with woods of pine and oak. Barriers of lofty mountains encompassed it; the woods were fresh and cool in the early morning, the peaks of the mountains were wreathed with mist, and sluggish vapors were entangled among the forests upon their sides. At length the black pinnacle of the tallest mountain was tipped with gold by the rising sun. The Hail-Storm, who rode in front, gave a low exclamation. Some large animal leaped up from among the bushes, and an elk, as I thought, his horns thrown back over his neck, darted past us across the open space, and bounded like a mad thing away among the adjoining pines. Raymond was soon out of his saddle, but before he could fire the animal was full two hundred yards distant. The ball struck its mark, though much too low for mortal effect. The elk, however, wheeled in his flight, and ran at full speed among the trees, nearly at right angles to his former course. I fired and broke his shoulder; still he moved on, limping down into a neighboring woody hollow, whither the young Indian followed, and killed him. When we reached the spot we discovered him to be no elk, but a black-tailed deer, an animal nearly twice as large as the common deer, and quite unknown in the East. The reports of the rifles had reached the ears of the Indians, and several of them came to the spot. Leaving the hide of the deer to the Hail-Storm, we hung as much of the meat as we wanted behind our saddles left the rest to the Indians, and resumed our journey. Meanwhile the village was on its way, and had gone so far that to get in advance of it was impossible. We directed our course so as to strike its line of march at the nearest point. In a short time, through the dark trunks of the pines, we could see the figures of the Indians as they passed. Once more we were among them. They were moving with even more than their usual precipitation, crowded together in a narrow pass between rocks and old pine-trees. We were on the eastern descent of the mountain, and soon came to a rough and difficult defile, leading down a steep declivity. The whole swarm poured down together, filling the rocky passage-way like some turbulent mountain-stream. The mountains before us were on fire, and had been so for weeks. The view in front was obscured by a vast, dim sea of smoke, while on either hand rose the tall cliffs, bearing aloft their crests of pines, and the sharp pinnacles and broken ridges of the mountains beyond were faintly traceable as through a veil. The scene in itself was grand and imposing, but with the savage multitude, the armed warriors, the naked children, the gayly apparelled girls, pouring impetuously down the heights, it would have formed a noble subject for a painter, and only the pen of a Scott could have done it justice in description.

We passed over a burnt tract where the ground was hot beneath the horses' feet, and between the blazing sides of two mountains. Before long we had descended to a softer region, where we found a succession of little valleys watered by a stream, along the borders of which grew abundance of wild gooseberries and currants, and the children and many of the men straggled from the line of march to gather them as we passed along. Descending still farther, the view changed rapidly. The burning mountains were behind us, and through the open valleys in front we could see the prairie, stretching like an ocean beyond the sight. After passing through a line of trees that skirted the brook, the Indians filed out upon the plains. I was thirsty and knelt down by the little stream to drink. As I mounted again, I very carelessly left my rifle among the grass, and my thoughts being otherwise absorbed, I rode for some distance before discovering its absence. I lost no time in turning about and galloping back in search of it. Passing the line of Indians, I watched every warrior as he rode by me at a canter, and at length discovered my rifle in the hands of one of them, who, on my approaching to claim it, immediately gave it up. Having no other means of acknowledging the obligation, I took off one of my spurs and gave it to him. He was greatly delighted, looking upon it as a distinguished mark of favor, and immediately held out his foot for me to buckle it on. As soon as I had done so, he struck it with all his force into the side of his horse, which gave a violent leap. The Indian laughed and spurred harder than before. At this the horse shot away like an arrow, amid the screams and laughter of the squaws, and the ejaculations of the men, who exclaimed: 'Washtay!—Good!' at the potent effect of my gift. The Indian had no saddle, and nothing in place of a bridle except a leather string tied round the horse's jaw. The animal was of course wholly uncontrollable, and stretched away at full speed over the prairie, till he and his rider vanished behind a distant swell. I never saw the man again, but I presume no harm came to him. An Indian on horseback has more lives than a cat.

The village encamped on the scorching prairie, close to the foot of the mountains. The heat was intense and penetrating. The coverings of the lodges were raised a foot or more from the ground, in order to procure some circulation of air; and Reynal thought proper to lay aside his trapper's dress of buckskin and assume the very scanty costume of an Indian. Thus elegantly attired, he stretched himself in his lodge on a buffalo-robe, alternately cursing the heat and puffing at the pipe which he and I passed between us. There was present also a select circle of Indian friends and relatives. A small boiled puppy was served up as a parting feast, to which was added, by way of dessert, a wooden bowl of gooseberries from the mountains.

'Look there,' said Reynal, pointing out of the opening of his lodge; 'do you see that line of buttes about fifteen miles off? Well, now do you see that farthest one, with the white speck on the face of it? Do you think you ever saw it before?'

'It looks to me,' said I, 'like the hill that we were 'camped under when we were on Laramie Creek, six or eight weeks ago.'

'You 've hit it,' answered Reynal.

'Go and bring in the animals, Raymond,' said I; 'we 'll camp there to-night, and start for the fort in the morning.'

The mare and the mule were soon before the lodge. We saddled them, and in the mean time a number of Indians collected about us. The virtues of Pauline, my strong, fleet, and hardy little mare, were well known in camp, and several of the visitors were mounted upon good horses which they had brought me as presents. I promptly declined their offers, since accepting them would have involved the necessity of transferring Pauline into their barbarous

hands. We took leave of Reynal, but not of the Indians, who are
accustomed to dispense with such superfluous ceremonies. Leaving
the camp we rode straight over the prairie towards the white-faced
bluff, whose pale ridges swelled gently against the horizon, like a
cloud. An Indian went with us, whose name I forget, though the
ugliness of his face and the ghastly width of his mouth dwell
vividly in my recollection. The antelope were numerous, but we
did not heed them. We rode directly towards our destination, over
the arid plains and barren hills; until, late in the afternoon, half
spent with heat, thirst, and fatigue, we saw a gladdening sight,—
the long line of trees and the deep gulf that mark the course of
Laramie Creek. Passing through the growth of huge, dilapidated
old cotton-wood trees that bordered the creek, we rode across to
the other side. The rapid and foaming waters were filled with fish
playing and splashing in the shallows. As we gained the farther
bank, our horses turned eagerly to drink, and we, kneeling on the
sand, followed their example. We had not gone far before the
scene began to grow familiar.

'We are getting near home, Raymond,' said I.

There stood the big tree under which we had encamped so
long; there were the white cliffs that used to look down upon our
tent when it stood at the bend of the creek; there was the meadow
in which our horses had grazed for weeks, and a little farther on,
the prairie-dog village where I had beguiled many a languid hour
in shooting the unfortunate inhabitants.

'We are going to catch it now,' said Raymond, turning his broad
face up towards the sky.

In truth the cliffs and the meadow, the stream and the groves,
were darkening fast. Black masses of cloud were swelling up in the
south, and the thunder was growling ominously.

'We will 'camp there,' I said, pointing to a grove of trees
lower down the stream. Raymond and I turned towards it, but the
Indian stopped and called earnestly after us. When we demanded
what was the matter he said that the ghosts of two warriors were
always among those trees, and that if we slept there they would
scream and throw stones at us all night, and perhaps steal our
horses before morning. Thinking it as well to humor him, we
left behind us the haunt of these extraordinary ghosts, and passed
on towards Chugwater, riding at full gallop, for the big drops
began to patter down. Soon we came in sight of the poplar saplings
that grew about the mouth of the little stream. We leaped to the

ground, threw off our saddles, turned our horses loose, and drawing our knives began to slash among the bushes to cut twigs and branches for making a shelter against the rain. Bending down the taller saplings as they grew, we piled the young shoots upon them, and thus made a convenient pent-house; but our labor was needless. The storm scarcely touched us. Half a mile on our right the rain was pouring down like a cataract, and the thunder roared over the prairie like a battery of cannon; while we by good fortune received only a few heavy drops from the skirt of the passing cloud. The weather cleared and the sun set gloriously. Sitting close under our leafy canopy we proceeded to discuss a substantial meal of *wasna* which Weah-Washtay had given me. The Indian had brought with him his pipe and a bag of *shongsasha*; so before lying down to sleep we sat for some time smoking together. First, however, our wide-mouthed friend had taken the precaution of carefully examining the neighborhood. He reported that eight men, counting them on his fingers, had been encamped there not long before,—Bisonette, Paul Dorion, Antoine Le Rouge, Richardson, and four others, whose names he could not tell. All this proved strictly correct. By what instinct he had arrived at such accurate conclusions, I am utterly at a loss to divine.

It was still quite dark when I awoke and called Raymond. The Indian was already gone, having chosen to go on before us to the fort. Setting out after him, we rode for some time in complete darkness and when the sun at length rose, glowing like a fiery ball of copper, we were within ten miles of the fort. At length, from the summit of a sandy bluff we could see Fort Laramie, miles before us, standing by the side of the stream like a little gray speck, in the midst of the boundless desolation. I stopped my horse, and sat for a moment looking down upon it. It seemed to me the very centre of comfort and civilization. We were not long in approaching it, for we rode at speed the greater part of the way. Laramie Creek still intervened between us and the friendly walls. Entering the water at the point where we had struck upon the bank, we raised our feet to the saddle behind us, and thus kneeling as it were on horseback, passed dry-shod through the swift current. As we rode up the bank a number of men appeared in the gateway. Three of them came forward to meet us. In a moment I distinguished Shaw; Henry Chatillon followed, with his face of manly simplicity and frankness, and Deslauriers came last, with a broad grin of welcome. The meeting was not on either side one of mere ceremony. For my own part, the change was a most agreeable one, from the society of savages and men little better than savages, to that of my gallant and high-minded companion, and our noble-hearted guide. My appearance was equally welcome to Shaw, who was beginning to entertain some uncomfortable surmises concerning me.

Bordeaux greeted me cordially, and shouted to the cook. This functionary was a new acquisition, having lately come from Fort Pierre with the trading wagons. Whatever skill he might have boasted, he had not the most promising materials to exercise it upon. He set before me, however, a breakfast of biscuit, coffee, and salt pork. It seemed like a new phase of existence to be seated once more on a bench with a knife and fork, a plate and teacup, and something resembling a table before me. The coffee seemed delicious, and the bread was a most welcome novelty, since for three weeks I had tasted scarcely anything but meat, and that for the most part without salt. The meal also had the relish of good company, for opposite to me sat Shaw in elegant dishabille. If one is anxious thoroughly to appreciate the value of a congenial companion, he has only to spend a few weeks by himself in an Ogillallah village. And if he can contrive to add to his seclusion a debilitating and somewhat critical illness, his perceptions upon this subject will be rendered considerably more vivid.

Shaw had been two or three weeks at the fort. I found him established in his old quarters, a large apartment usually occupied by the absent *bourgeois*. In one corner was a soft pile of excellent buffalo-robes, and here I lay down. Shaw brought me three books.

'Here,' said he, 'is your Shakspeare and Byron, and here is the Old Testament, which has as much poetry in it as the other two put together.'

I chose the worst of the three, and for the greater part of that day I lay on the buffalo-robes, fairly revelling in the creations of that resplendent genius which has achieved no more signal triumph than that of half beguiling us to forget the unmanly character of its possessor.

20. The Lonely Journey

On the day of my arrival at Fort Laramie, Shaw and I were lounging on two buffalo-robes in the large apartment hospitably assigned
to us; Henry Chatillon also was present, busy about the harness
and weapons, which had been brought into the room, and two or
three Indians were crouching on the floor, eying us with their
fixed, unwavering gaze.

'I have been well off here,' said Shaw, 'in all respects but one;
there is no good *shongsasha* to be had for love or money.'

I gave him a small leather bag containing some of excellent
quality which I had brought from the Black Hills. 'Now, Henry,'
said he, 'hand me Papin's chopping-board, or give it to that
Indian, and let him cut the mixture; they understand it better
than any white man.'

The Indian, without saying a word, mixed the bark and the tobacco in due proportions, filled the pipe, and lighted it. This done, my companion and I proceeded to deliberate on our future course of proceeding; first, however, Shaw acquainted me with some incidents which had occurred at the fort during my absence.

About a week before, four men had arrived from beyond the mountains: Sublette, Reddick, and two others. Just before reaching the fort they had met a large party of Indians, chiefly young men. All of them belonged to the village of our old friend Smoke, who, with his whole band of adherents, professed the greatest friendship for the whites. The travellers therefore approached and began to converse without the least suspicion. Suddenly, however, their bridles were seized, and they were ordered to dismount. Instead of complying, they lashed their horses, and broke away from the Indians. As they galloped off they heard a yell behind them, with a burst of derisive laughter, and the reports of several guns. None of them were hurt, though Reddick's bridle-rein was cut by a bullet within an inch of his hand. After this taste of Indian manners, they felt for the moment no disposition to encounter farther risks. They intended to pursue the route southward along the foot of the mountains to Bent's Fort; and as our plans coincided with theirs, they proposed to join forces. Finding, however, that I did not return, they grew impatient of inaction, forgot their late danger, and set out without us, promising to wait our arrival at Bent's Fort. From thence we were to make the long journey to the settlements in company, as the path was not a little dangerous, being infested by hostile Pawnees and Camanches.

We expected, on reaching Bent's Fort, to find there still another reinforcement. A young Kentuckian had come out to the mountains with Russel's party of California emigrants. One of his chief objects, as he gave out, was to kill an Indian; an exploit which he afterwards succeeded in achieving, much to the jeopardy of ourselves, and others who had to pass through the country of the dead Pawnee's enraged relatives. Having become disgusted with his emigrant associates, he left them, and had some time before set out with a party of companions for the head of the Arkansas. He left us a letter, to say that he would wait until we arrived at Bent's Fort, and accompany us thence to the settlements. When however he came to the fort, he found there a party of forty men about to make the homeward journey, and wisely preferred to avail himself of so strong an escort. Sublette and his companions also joined this company; so that on reaching Bent's Fort, some six weeks after, we found ourselves deserted by our allies and thrown once more upon our own resources.

On the fourth of August, early in the afternoon, we bade a final adieu to the hospitable gateway of Fort Laramie. Again Shaw and I were riding side by side on the prairie. For the first fifty miles we had companions with us: Troché, a trapper, and Rouville, a nondescript in the employ of the Fur Company, who were going to join the trader Bisonette at his encampment near the head of Horse Creek. We rode only six or eight miles that afternoon before we came to a little brook traversing the barren prairie. All along its course grew copses of young wild-cherry trees, loaded with ripe fruit, and almost concealing the gliding thread of water with their dense growth. Here we encamped; and being too indolent to pitch our tent, we flung our saddles on the ground, spread a pair of buffalo-robes, lay down upon them, and began to smoke. Meanwhile Deslauriers busied himself with his frying-pan, and Raymond stood guard over the band of grazing horses. Deslauriers had an active assistant in Rouville, who professed great skill in the culinary art, and seizing upon a fork, began to lend his aid in cooking supper. Indeed, according to his own belief, Rouville was a man of universal knowledge, and he lost no opportunity to display his manifold accomplishments. He had been a circus-rider at St Louis, and once he rode round Fort Laramie on his head, to the utter bewilderment of the Indians. He was also noted as the wit of the fort, and as he had considerable humor and abundant vivacity, he contributed more that night to the liveliness of the camp than all the rest of the party put together. At one instant he would kneel by Deslauriers, instructing him in the true method of frying antelope-steaks, then he would come and seat himself at our side, dilating upon the correct fashion of braiding up a horse's tail, telling apocryphal stories how he had killed a buffalo-bull with a knife, having first cut off his tail when at full speed, or relating whimsical anecdotes of the *bourgeois* Papin. At last he snatched up a volume of Shakspeare that was lying on the grass, and halted and stumbled through a line or two to prove that he could read. He went gambolling about the camp, chattering like some frolicsome ape; and whatever he was doing at one moment, the presumption was a sure one that he would

not be doing it the next. His companion Troché sat silently on
the grass, not speaking a word, but keeping a vigilant eye on
a very ugly little Utah squaw, of whom he was extremely
jealous.

On the next day we travelled farther, crossing the wide, sterile
basin called 'Goché's Hole.' Towards night we became involved
among ravines; and being unable to find water, our journey was
protracted to a very late hour. On the next morning we had to
pass a long line of bluffs, whose raw sides, wrought upon by rains
and storms, were of a ghastly whiteness most oppressive to the
sight. As we ascended a gap in these hills, the way was marked by
huge footprints, like those of a human giant. They were the tracks
of the grizzly bear, of which we had also seen abundance on the
day before. Immediately after this we were crossing a barren
plain, spreading in long and gentle undulations to the horizon.
Though the sun was bright, there was a light haze in the atmosphere. The distant hills assumed strange, distorted forms in the
mirage, and the edge of the horizon was continually changing its
aspect. Shaw and I were riding together, and Henry Chatillon
was a few rods before us, when he stopped his horse suddenly,
and turning round with the peculiar earnest expression which he
always wore when excited, called us to come forward. We galloped to his side. Henry pointed towards a black speck on the
gray swell of the prairie, apparently about a mile off. 'It must be
a bear,' said he; 'come, now we shall all have some sport. Better
fun to fight him than to fight an old buffalo-bull; grizzly bear so
strong and smart.'

So we all galloped forward together, prepared for a hard fight;
for these bears, though clumsy in appearance, are incredibly
fierce and active. The swell of the prairie concealed the black object
from our view. Immediately after, it appeared again. But now it
seemed very near to us; and as we looked at it in astonishment, it
suddenly separated into two parts, each of which took wing and
flew away. We stopped our horses and looked at Henry, whose face
exhibited a curious mixture of mirth and mortification. His eye
had been so completely deceived by the peculiar atmosphere
that he had mistaken two large crows at the distance of fifty
rods for a grizzly bear a mile off. To the journey's end Henry never
heard the last of the grizzly bear with wings.

In the afternoon we came to the foot of a considerable hill. As
we ascended it Rouville began to ask questions concerning our

condition and prospects at home, and Shaw was edifying him with an account of an imaginary wife and child, to which he listened with implicit faith. Reaching the top of the hill, we saw the windings of Horse Creek on the plains below us, and a little on the left we could distinguish the camp of Bisonette among the trees and copses along the course of the stream. Rouville's face assumed just then a ludicrously blank expression. We inquired what was the matter; when it appeared that Bisonette had sent him from this place to Fort Laramie with the sole object of bringing back a supply of tobacco. Our rattlebrain friend, from the time of his reaching the fort up to the present moment, had entirely forgotten the object of his journey, and had ridden a dangerous hundred miles for nothing. Descending to Horse Creek we forded it, and on the opposite bank a solitary Indian sat on horseback under a tree. He said nothing, but turned and led the way towards the camp. Bisonette had made choice of an admirable position. The stream, with its thick growth of trees, inclosed on three sides a wide green meadow, where about forty Dakota lodges were pitched in a circle, and beyond them a few lodges of the friendly Cheyennes. Bisonette himself lived in the Indian manner. Riding up to his lodge, we found him seated at the head of it, surrounded by various appliances of comfort not common on the prairie. His squaw was near him, and rosy children were scrambling about in printed calico gowns; Paul Dorion, also, with his leathery face and old white capote, was seated in the lodge, together with Antoine Le Rouge, a half-breed Pawnee, Sibille, a trader, and several other white men.

'It will do you no harm,' said Bisonette, 'to stay here with us for a day or two, before you start for the Pueblo.'

We accepted the invitation, and pitched our tent on a rising ground above the camp and close to the trees. Bisonette soon invited us to a feast, and we suffered abundance of the same sort of attention from his Indian associates. The reader may possibly recollect that when I joined the Indian village, beyond the Black Hills, I found that a few families were absent, having declined to pass the mountains along with the rest. The Indians in Bisonette's camp consisted of these very families, and many of them came to me that evening to inquire after their relatives and friends. They were not a little mortified to learn that while they, from their own timidity and indolence, were almost in a starving condition, the rest of the village had provided their lodges for the next season, laid in a great stock of provisions, and were living in abundance. Bisonette's companions had been sustaining themselves for some time on wild cherries, which the squaws pounded, stones and all, and spread on buffalo-robes to dry in the sun; they were then eaten without further preparation, or used as an ingredient in various delectable compounds.

On the next day the camp was in commotion with a new arrival. A single Indian had come with his family from the Arkansas. As he passed among the lodges he put on an expression of unusual dignity and importance, and gave out that he had brought great news to tell the whites. Soon after the squaws had pitched his lodge, he sent his little son to invite all the white men, and all the more distinguished Indians to a feast. The guests arrived and sat wedged together, shoulder to shoulder, within the hot and suffocating lodge. The Stabber, for that was our entertainer's name, had killed an old buffalo-bull on his way. This veteran's boiled tripe, tougher than leather, formed the main item of the repast. For the rest, it consisted of wild cherries and grease boiled together in a large copper kettle. The feast was distributed, and for a moment all was silent, strenuous exertion; then each guest, though with one or two exceptions, turned his wooden dish bottom upwards to prove that he had done full justice to his entertainer's hospitality. The Stabber next produced his chopping-board, on which he prepared the mixture for smoking, and filled several pipes, which circulated among the company. This done, he seated himself upright on his couch, and began with much gesticulation to tell his story. I will not repeat his childish jargon. It was so entangled, like the greater part of an Indian's stories, with absurd and contradictory details, that it was almost impossible to disengage from it a single particle of truth. All that we could gather was the following:—

He had been on the Arkansas, and there he had seen six great war-parties of whites. He had never believed before that the whole world contained half so many white men. They all had large horses, long knives, and short rifles, and some of them were dressed alike, in the most splendid war-dresses he had ever seen. From this account it was clear that bodies of dragoons and perhaps also of volunteer cavalry had passed up the Arkansas. The Stabber had also seen a great many of the white lodges of the Meneaska, drawn by their long-horned buffalo. These could be nothing else than covered ox-wagons used no doubt in transporting

stores for the troops. Soon after seeing this, our host had met an
Indian who had lately come from among the Camanches, who
had told him that all the Mexicans had gone out to a great buffalo
hunt; that the Americans had hid themselves in a ravine; and
that when the Mexicans had shot away all their arrows, the
Americans fired their guns, raised their war-whoop, rushed out,
and killed them all. We could only infer from this that war had
been declared with Mexico, and a battle fought in which the
Americans were victorious. When, some weeks after, we arrived
at the Pueblo, we heard of General Kearney's march up the
Arkansas, and of General Taylor's victories at Matamoras.

As the sun was setting that evening a crowd gathered on the
plain by the side of our tent, to try the speed of their horses.
These were of every shape, size, and color. Some came from
California, some from the States, some from among the mountains,
and some from the wild bands of the prairie. They were of every
hue, white, black, red, and gray, or mottled and clouded with a
strange variety of colors. They all had a wild and startled look,
very different from the sober aspect of a well-bred city steed.
Those most noted for swiftness and spirit were decorated with
eagle feathers dangling from their manes and tails. Fifty or sixty
Dakota were present, wrapped from head to foot in their heavy
robes of whitened hide. There was also a considerable number of
the Cheyennes, many of whom wore gaudy Mexican ponchos,
swathed around their shoulders, but leaving the right arm bare.
Mingled among the crowd of Indians was a number of Canadians,
chiefly in the employ of Bisonette,—men whose home is the wilderness, and who love the camp-fire better than the domestic hearth.
They are contented and happy in the midst of hardship, privation,
and danger. Their cheerfulness and gaiety is irrepressible, and no
people on earth understand better how 'to daff the world aside
and bid it pass.' Besides these, were two or three half-breeds, a
race of rather extraordinary composition, being, according to the
common saying, half Indian, half white man, and half devil.
Antoine Le Rouge was the most conspicuous among them, with
his loose trousers and fluttering calico shirt. A handkerchief was
bound round his head to confine his black, snaky hair, and his
small eyes twinkled beneath it with a mischievous lustre. He
had a fine cream-colored horse, whose speed he must needs try
along with the rest. So he threw off the rude high-peaked saddle,
and substituting a piece of buffalo-robe, leaped lightly into his

seat. The space was cleared, the word was given, and he and his Indian rival darted out like lightning from among the crowd, each stretching forward over his horse's neck and plying his heavy Indian whip with might and main. A moment, and both were lost in the gloom; but Antoine soon came riding back victorious, exultingly patting the neck of his quivering and panting horse.

About midnight, as I lay asleep, wrapped in a buffalo-robe on the ground by the side of our cart, Raymond came and woke me. Something, he said, was going forward which I would like to see. Looking down into the camp, I saw on the farther side of it a great number of Indians gathered about a fire, the bright glare of which made them visible through the thick darkness; while from the midst proceeded a loud, measured chant, which would have killed Paganini outright, broken occasionally by a burst of sharp yells. I gathered the robe around me, for the night was cold, and walked down to the spot. The dark throng of Indians was so dense that they almost intercepted the light of the flame. As I was pushing among them with little ceremony, a chief interposed himself, and I was given to understand that a white man must not approach the scene of their solemnities too closely. By passing round to the other side, where there was a little opening in the crowd, I could see clearly what was going forward, without in-truding my unhallowed presence into the inner circle. The society of the 'Strong Hearts' were engaged in one of their dances. The 'Strong Hearts' are a warlike association, comprising men of both the Dakota and Cheyenne nations, and entirely composed, or supposed to be so, of young braves of the highest mettle. Its fundamental principle is the admirable one of never retreating from any enterprise once begun. All these Indian associations have a tutelary spirit. That of the 'Strong Hearts' is embodied in the fox, an animal which white men would hardly have selected for a similar purpose, though his subtle character agrees well enough with an Indian's notions of what is honorable in warfare. The dancers were circling round and round the fire, each figure brightly illumined at one moment by the yellow light, and at the next drawn in blackest shadow as it passed between the flame and the spectator. They would imitate with the most ludicrous exact-ness the motions and voice of their sly patron the fox. Then a startling yell would be given. Many other warriors would leap into the ring, and with faces upturned towards the starless sky, they would all stamp and whoop, and brandish their weapons like so many frantic devils.

We remained here till the next afternoon. My companion and I with our three attendants then set out for the Pueblo, a distance of three hundred miles, and we supposed the journey would occupy about a fortnight. During this time we all hoped that we might not meet a single human being, for should we encounter any, they would in all probability be enemies, in whose eyes our rifles would be our only passports. For the first two days nothing worth mentioning took place. On the third morning, however, an untoward incident occurred. We were encamped by the side of a little brook in an extensive hollow of the plain. Deslauriers was up long before daylight, and before he began to prepare breakfast he turned loose all the horses, as in duty bound. There was a cold mist clinging close to the ground, and by the time the rest of us were awake the animals were invisible. It was only after a long and anxious search that we could discover by their tracks the direction they had taken. They had all set off for Fort Laramie, following the guidance of a mutinous old mule; and though many of them were hobbled, they travelled three miles before they could be overtaken and driven back.

For two or three days we were passing over an arid desert. The only vegetation was a few tufts of short grass, dried and shrivelled by the heat. There was abundance of strange insects and reptiles. Huge crickets, black and bottle-green, and wingless grasshoppers of the most extravagant dimensions, were tumbling about our horses' feet, and lizards without number darting like lightning among the tufts of grass. The most curious animal, however, was that commonly called the horned-frog. I caught one of them and consigned him to the care of Deslauriers, who tied him up in a moccasin. About a month after this I examined the prisoner's condition, and finding him still lively and active, I provided him with a cage of buffalo-hide, which was hung up in the cart. In this manner he arrived safely at the settlements. From thence he travelled the whole way to Boston, packed closely in a trunk, being regaled with fresh air regularly every night. When he reached his destination he was deposited under a glass case, where he sat for some months in great tranquillity, alternately dilating and contracting his white throat to the admiration of his visitors. At length, one morning about the middle of winter, he gave up the ghost, and he now occupies a bottle of alcohol in the Agassiz

Museum. His death was attributed to starvation,—a very probable conclusion, since for six months he had taken no food whatever, though the sympathy of his juvenile admirers had tempted his palate with a great variety of delicacies. We found also animals of a somewhat larger growth. The number of prairie-dogs was astounding. Frequently the hard and dry plain was thickly covered, for miles together, with the little mounds which they make at the mouth of their burrows, and small squeaking voices yelped at us as we passed along. The noses of the inhabitants were just visible at the mouth of their holes, but no sooner was their curiosity satisfied than they would instantly vanish. Some of the bolder dogs—though in fact they are no dogs at all, but little marmots rather smaller than a rabbit—would sit yelping at us on the top of their mounds, jerking their tails emphatically with every shrill cry they uttered. As the danger drew nearer they would wheel about, toss their heels into the air, and dive in a twinkling into their burrows. Towards sunset, and especially if rain was threatening, the whole community made their appearance above ground. We saw them gathered in large knots around the burrow of some favorite citizen. There they would all sit erect, their tails spread out on the ground, and their paws hanging down before their white breasts, chattering and squeaking with the utmost vivacity upon some topic of common interest, while the proprietor of the burrow sat on the top of his mound, looking down with a complacent countenance on the enjoyment of his guests. Meanwhile others ran about from burrow to burrow, as if on some errand of the last importance to their subterranean commonwealth. The snakes are apparently the prairie-dog's worst enemies; at least I think too well of the latter to suppose that they associate on friendly terms with these slimy intruders, which may be seen at all times basking among their holes, into which they always retreat when disturbed. Small owls, with wise and grave countenances, also make their abode with the prairie-dogs, though on what terms they live together I could never ascertain.

On the fifth day after leaving Bisonette's camp, we saw, late in the afternoon, what we supposed to be a considerable stream, but on approaching it, we found to our disappointment, nothing but a dry bed of sand, into which the water had sunk and disappeared. We separated, some riding in one direction and some in another, along its course. Still we found no traces of water, not even so much as a wet spot in the sand. The old cotton-wood trees that grew along the bank, lamentably abused by lightning and tempest, were withering with the drought, and on the dead limbs, at the summit of the tallest, half a dozen crows were hoarsely cawing, like birds of evil omen. We had no alternative but to keep on. There was no water nearer than the South Fork of the Platte, about ten miles distant. We moved forward, angry and silent, over a desert as flat as the outspread ocean.

The sky had been obscured since the morning by thin mists and vapors, but now vast piles of clouds were gathered together in the west. They rose to a great height above the horizon, and looking up at them I distinguished one mass darker than the rest, and of a peculiar conical form. I happened to look again, and still could see it as before. At some moments it was dimly visible, at others its outline was sharp and distinct; but while the clouds around it were shifting, changing, and dissolving away, it still towered aloft in the midst of them, fixed and immovable. It must, thought I, be the summit of a mountain; and yet its height staggered me. My conclusion was right, however. It was Long's Peak, once believed to be one of the highest of the Rocky Mountain chain, though more recent discoveries have proved the contrary. The thickening gloom soon hid it from view, and we never saw it again, for on the following day, and for some time after, the air was so full of mist that the view of distant objects was entirely cut off.

It grew very late. Turning from our direct course, we made for the river at its nearest point, though in the utter darkness it was not easy to direct our way with much precision. Raymond rode on one side and Henry on the other. We heard each of them shouting that he had come upon a deep ravine. We steered at random between Scylla and Charybdis, and soon after became as it seemed inextricably involved, with deep chasms all around us, while the darkness was such that we could not see a rod in any direction. We partially extricated ourselves by scrambling, cart and all, through a shallow ravine. We came next to a steep descent, down which we plunged without well knowing what was at the bottom. There was a great crackling of sticks and dry twigs. Over our heads were certain large shadowy objects; and in front something like the faint gleaming of a dark sheet of water. Raymond ran his horse against a tree; Henry alighted, and, feeling on the ground, declared that there was grass enough for the horses. Before taking off his saddle, each man led his own horses down to the water in the best way he could. Then picketing two or three of the evil-disposed, we turned the rest loose, and lay down among the dry sticks to sleep. In the morning we found ourselves close to the South Fork of the Platte, on a spot surrounded by bushes and rank grass. Compensating ourselves with a hearty breakfast for the ill-fare of the previous night, we set forward again on our journey. When only two or three rods from the camp I saw Shaw stop his mule, level his gun, and fire at some object in the grass. Deslauriers next jumped forward, and began to dance about, belaboring the unseen enemy with a whip. Then he stooped down, and drew out of the grass by the neck a large rattlesnake, with his head completely shattered by Shaw's bullet. As Deslauriers held him out at arm's length with an exulting grin, his tail, which still kept slowly writhing about, almost touched the ground; and his body in the largest part was as thick as a stout man's arm. He had fourteen rattles, but the end of his tail was blunted, as if he could once have boasted of many more. From this time till we reached the Pueblo, we killed at least four or five of these snakes every day, as they lay coiled and rattling on the hot sand. Shaw was the Saint Patrick of the party, and whenever he killed a snake he pulled off his tail and stored it away in his bullet-pouch, which was soon crammed with an edifying collection of rattles, great and small. Deslauriers with his whip also came in for a share of praise. A day or two after this, he triumphantly produced a small snake about a span and a half long, with one infant rattle at the end of his tail.

We forded the South Fork of the Platte. On its farther bank were the traces of a very large camp of Arapahoes. The ashes of some three hundred fires were visible among the scattered trees, together with the remains of sweating lodges, and all the other appurtenances of a permanent camp. The place, however, had been for some months deserted. A few miles farther on we found more recent signs of Indians,—the trail of two or three lodges which had evidently passed the day before; every footprint was perfectly distinct in the dry, dusty soil. We noticed in particular the track of one moccasin, upon the sole of which its economical proprietor had placed a large patch. These signs gave us but little uneasiness, as the number of the warriors scarcely exceeded that of our own party. At noon we rested under the walls of a large fort, built in these solitudes some years since by M. St Vrain. It was now abandoned and fast falling into ruin. The walls of unbaked bricks were cracked from top to bottom. Our horses recoiled in terror from the neglected entrance, where the heavy gates were torn from their hinges and flung down. The area within was overgrown with weeds, and the long ranges of apartments once occupied by the motley concourse of traders, Canadians, and squaws, were now miserably dilapidated. Twelve miles farther on, near the spot where we encamped, were the remains of another fort, standing in melancholy desertion and neglect.

Early on the following morning we made a startling discovery. We passed close by a large deserted encampment of Arapahoes. There were about fifty fires still smouldering on the ground, and it was evident from numerous signs that the Indians must have left the place within two hours of our reaching it. Their trail crossed our own, at right angles, and led in the direction of a line of hills, half a mile on our left. There were women and children in the party, which would have greatly diminished the danger of encountering them. Henry Chatillon examined the encampment and the trail with a very professional and business-like air.

'Supposing we had met them, Henry?' said I.

'Why,' said he, 'we hold out our hands to them, and give them all we 've got; they take away everything and then I believe they no kill us. Perhaps,' added he, looking up with a quiet, unchanged face, 'perhaps we no let them rob us. Maybe before they come near, we have a chance to get into a ravine, or under the bank of the river; then, you know, we fight them.'

About noon on that day we reached Cherry Creek. Here was a great abundance of wild-cherries, plums, gooseberries, and currants. The stream, however, like most of the others which we passed, was dried up with the heat, and we had to dig holes in the sand to find water for ourselves and our horses. Two days after, we left the banks of the creek, which we had been following for some time, and began to cross the high dividing ridge which separates the waters of the Platte from those of the Arkansas. The scenery was altogether changed. In place of the burning plains, we passed through rough and savage glens, and among hills crowned with a dreary growth of pines. We encamped among these solitudes on the night of the sixteenth of August. A tempest was threatening. The sun went down among volumes of jet-black

cloud, edged with a bloody red. But in spite of these portentous
signs we neglected to put up the tent, and being extremely
fatigued, lay down on the ground and fell asleep. The storm broke
about midnight, and we pitched the tent amid darkness and confusion. In the morning all was fair again, and Pike's Peak, white
with snow, was towering above the wilderness afar off.

We pushed through an extensive tract of pine woods. Large
black-squirrels were leaping among the branches. From the farther
edge of this forest we saw the prairie again, hollowed out before
us into a vast basin, and about a mile in front we could discern
a little black speck moving upon its surface. It could be nothing
but a buffalo. Henry primed his rifle afresh and galloped forward.
To the left of the animal was a low rocky mound, of which Henry
availed himself in making his approach. After a short time we
heard the faint report of the rifle. The bull, mortally wounded
from a distance of nearly three hundred yards, ran wildly round
and round in a circle. Shaw and I then galloped forward, and
passing him as he ran, foaming with rage and pain, discharged our
pistols into his side. Once or twice he rushed furiously upon us,
but his strength was rapidly exhausted. Down he fell on his
knees. For one instant he glared up at his enemies, with burning
eyes, through his black, tangled mane, and then rolled over on
his side. Though gaunt and thin, he was larger and heavier than
the largest ox. Foam and blood flew together from his nostrils
as he lay bellowing and pawing the ground, tearing up grass and
earth with his hoofs. His sides rose and fell like a vast pair of
bellows, the blood spouting up in jets from the bullet-holes.
Suddenly his glaring eyes became like a lifeless jelly. He lay
motionless on the ground. Henry stooped over him, and making an
incision with his knife, pronounced the meat too rank and tough
for use; so, disappointed in our hopes of an addition to our
stock of provisions, we rode away and left the carcass to the
wolves.

In the afternoon we saw the mountains rising like a gigantic
wall at no great distance on our right. *'Des sauvages! des sauvages!'*
exclaimed Deslauriers, looking round with a frightened face, and
pointing with his whip towards the foot of the mountains. In fact,
we could see at a distance a number of little black specks, like
horsemen in rapid motion. Henry Chatillon, with Shaw and myself galloped towards them to reconnoitre, when to our amusement we saw the supposed Arapahoes resolved into the black

tops of some pine-trees which grew along a ravine. The summits of these pines, just visible above the verge of the prairie, and seeming to move as we ourselves were advancing, looked exactly like a line of horsemen.

We encamped among ravines and hollows, through which a little brook was foaming angrily. Before sunrise in the morning the snow-covered mountains were beautifully tinged with a delicate rose color. A noble spectacle awaited us as we moved forward. Six or eight miles on our right, Pike's Peak and his giant brethren rose out of the level prairie, as if springing from the bed of the ocean. From their summits down to the plain below they were involved in a mantle of clouds, in restless motion, as if urged by strong winds. For one instant some snowy peak, towering in awful solitude, would be disclosed to view. As the clouds broke along the mountain, we could see the dreary forests, the tremendous precipices, the white patches of snow, the gulfs and chasms as black as night, all revealed for an instant, and then disappearing from the view.

On the day after, we had left the mountains at some distance. A black cloud descended upon them, and a tremendous explosion of thunder followed, reverberating among the precipices. In a few moments everything grew black, and the rain poured down like a cataract. We got under an old cotton-wood tree, which stood by the side of a stream, and waited there till the rage of the torrent had passed.

The clouds opened at the point where they first had gathered, and the whole sublime congregation of mountains was bathed at once in warm sunshine. They seemed more like some vision of eastern romance than like a reality of that wilderness; all were melted together into a soft delicious blue, as voluptuous as the sky of Naples or the transparent sea that washes the sunny cliffs of Capri. On the left the sky was still of an inky blackness; but two concentric rainbows stood in bright relief against it, while far in front the ragged clouds still streamed before the wind, and the retreating thunder muttered angrily.

Through that afternoon and the next morning we were passing down the banks of the stream, called 'Boiling Spring Creek,' from the boiling spring whose waters flow into it. When we stopped at noon, we were within six or eight miles of the Pueblo. Setting out again, we found by the fresh tracks that a horseman had just been out to reconnoitre us; he had circled half round the camp, and then galloped back at full speed for the Pueblo. What made him so shy of us we could not conceive. After an hour's ride we reached the edge of a hill, from which a welcome sight greeted us. The Arkansas ran along the valley below, among woods and groves, and closely nestled in the midst of wide corn-fields and green meadows, where cattle were grazing, rose the low mud walls of the Pueblo.

21. The Pueblo and Bent's Fort

We approached the gate of the Pueblo. It was a wretched species of fort, of most primitive construction, being nothing more than a large square inclosure, surrounded by a wall of adobe, miserably cracked and dilapidated. The slender pickets that surmounted it were half broken down, and the gate dangled on its wooden hinges so loosely that to open or shut it seemed likely to fling it down altogether. Two or three squalid Mexicans, with their broad hats, and their vile faces overgrown with hair, were lounging about the bank of the river in front of it. They disappeared as they saw us approach; and as we rode up to the gate, a light, active little figure came out to meet us. It was our old friend Richard. He had come from Fort Laramie on a trading expedition to Taos; but finding when he reached the Pueblo that the war would prevent his going farther, he was quietly waiting till the conquest of the country should allow him to proceed. He seemed to feel bound to do the honors of the place. Shaking us warmly by the hand, he led the way into the area.

Here we saw his large Santa Fé wagons standing together. A few squaws and Spanish women, and a few Mexicans, as mean and miserable as the place itself, were lazily sauntering about. Richard conducted us to the state apartment of the Pueblo, a small mud room, very neatly finished, considering the material, and garnished with a crucifix, a looking-glass, a picture of the Virgin, and a rusty horse-pistol. There were no chairs, but instead of them a number of chests and boxes ranged about the room. There was another room beyond, less sumptuously decorated, and here three or four Spanish girls, one of them very pretty, were baking cakes at a mud fireplace in the corner. They brought out a poncho, which they spread upon the floor by way of table-cloth. A supper, which seemed to us luxurious, was soon laid out upon it, and folded buffalo-robes were placed around it to receive the guests. Two or three Americans besides ourselves were present. We sat down in Turkish fashion, and began to ask the news. Richard told us that, about three weeks before, General Kearney's army had left Bent's Fort to march against Santa Fé; that when last heard from they were approaching the defiles that led to the city. One of the Americans produced a dingy newspaper, containing an account of the battles of Palo Alto and Resaca de la Palma. While we were discussing these matters the doorway was darkened by a tall, shambling fellow, who stood with his hands in his pockets taking a leisurely survey of the premises before he entered. He wore brown homespun trousers, much too short for his legs, and a pistol and bowie-knife stuck in his belt. His head and one eye were enveloped in a huge bandage of linen. Having completed his observations, he came slouching in, and sat down on a chest. Eight or ten more of the same stamp followed, and very coolly arranging themselves about the room began to stare at the company. We were forcibly reminded of the Oregon emigrants, though these unwelcome visitors had a certain glitter of the eye, and a compression of the lips which distinguished them from our old acquaintances of the prairie. They began to catechise us at once, inquiring whence we had come, what we meant to do next, and what were our prospects in life.

The man with the bandaged head had met with an untoward

accident a few days before. He was going down to the river to bring water, and was pushing through the young willows which covered the low ground, when he came unawares upon a grizzly bear, which, having just eaten a buffalo-bull, had lain down to sleep off the meal. The bear rose on his hind legs, and gave the intruder such a blow with his paw that he laid his forehead entirely bare, clawed off the front of his scalp, and narrowly missed one of his eyes. Fortunately he was not in a very pugnacious mood, being surfeited with his late meal. The man's companions, who were close behind, raised a shout, and the bear walked away, crushing down the willows in his leisurely retreat.

These men belonged to a party of Mormons, who, out of a well-grounded fear of the other emigrants, had postponed leaving the settlements until all the rest were gone. On account of this delay, they did not reach Fort Laramie until it was too late to continue their journey to California. Hearing that there was good land at the head of the Arkansas, they crossed over under the guidance of Richard, and were now preparing to spend the winter at a spot about half a mile from the Pueblo.

When we took leave of Richard it was near sunset. Passing out of the gate, we could look down the little valley of the Arkansas; a beautiful scene, and doubly so to our eyes, so long accustomed to deserts and mountains. Tall woods lined the river, with green meadows on either hand; and high bluffs, quietly basking in the sunlight, flanked the narrow valley. A Mexican on horseback was driving a herd of cattle towards the gate, and our little white tent, which the men had pitched under a tree in the meadow, made a pleasing feature in the scene. When we reached it we found that Richard had sent a Mexican to bring us an abundant supply of green corn and vegetables and invite us to help ourselves to whatever we wanted from the fields around the Pueblo.

The inhabitants were in daily apprehension of an inroad from more formidable consumers than we. Every year, at the time when the corn begins to ripen, the Arapahoes, to the number of several thousands, come and encamp around the Pueblo. The handful of white men, who are entirely at the mercy of this swarm of barbarians, choose to make a merit of necessity; they come forward very cordially, shake them by the hand, and tell them that the harvest is entirely at their disposal. The Arapahoes take them at their word, help themselves most liberally, and usually turn their horses into the cornfields afterwards. They have the foresight, however, to leave enough of the crops untouched to serve as an inducement for planting the fields again for their benefit in the next spring.

The human race in this part of the world is separated into three divisions, arranged in the order of their merits: white men, Indians, and Mexicans; to the latter of whom the honorable title of 'whites' is by no means conceded.

In spite of the warm sunset of that evening, the next morning was a dreary and cheerless one. It rained steadily, clouds resting upon the very tree-tops. We crossed the river to visit the Mormon settlement. As we passed through the water several trappers on horseback entered it from the other side. Their buckskin frocks were soaked through by the rain, and clung fast to their limbs with a most clammy and uncomfortable look. The water was trickling down their faces, and dropping from the ends of their rifles and from the traps which each carried at the pommel of his saddle. Horses and all, they had a disconsolate and woe-begone appearance, which we could not help laughing at, forgetting how often we ourselves had been in a similar plight.

After half an hour's riding we saw the white wagons of the Mormons drawn up among the trees. Axes were sounding, trees falling, and log-huts rising along the edge of the woods and upon the adjoining meadow. As we came up the Mormons left their work, seated themselves on the timber around us, and began earnestly to discuss points of theology, complain of the ill-usage they had received from the 'Gentiles,' and sound a lamentation over the loss of their great temple of Nauvoo. After remaining with them an hour we rode back to our camp, happy that the settlements had been delivered from the presence of such blind and desperate fanatics.

On the following morning we left the Pueblo for Bent's Fort. The conduct of Raymond had lately been less satisfactory than before, and we had discharged him as soon as we arrived at the former place, so that the party, ourselves included, was now reduced to four. There was some uncertainty as to our future course. The trail between Bent's Fort and the settlements, a distance computed at six hundred miles, was at this time in a dangerous state; for since the passage of General Kearney's army, great numbers of hostile Indians, chiefly Pawnees and Camanches, had gathered about some parts of it. They became soon after so numerous and audacious that scarcely a single party, however large, passed between the fort and the frontier without some token of their hostility. The newspapers of the time sufficiently display this state of things. Many men were killed, and great numbers of horses and mules carried off. Not long since I met with a young man, who, during the autumn came from Santa Fé to Bent's Fort, where he found a party of seventy men, who thought themselves too weak to go down to the settlements alone, and were waiting there for a reinforcement. Though this excessive timidity proved the ignorance of the men, it may also evince the state of alarm which prevailed in the country. When we were there in the month of August, the danger had not become so great. There was nothing very attractive in the neighborhood. We supposed, moreover, that we might wait there half the winter without finding any party to go down with us; for Sublette and the others whom we had relied upon had, as Richard told us, already left Bent's Fort. Thus far on our journey Fortune had kindly befriended us. We resolved therefore to take advantage of her gracious mood, and trusting for a continuance of her favors, to set out with Henry and Deslauriers, and run the gauntlet of the Indians in the best way we could.

Bent's Fort stands on the river, about seventy-five miles below the Pueblo. At noon of the third day we arrived within three or four miles of it, pitched our tent under a tree, hung our looking-glasses against its trunk, and having made our primitive toilet, rode towards the fort. We soon came in sight of it, for it is visible from a considerable distance, standing with its high clay walls in the midst of the scorching plains. It seemed as if a swarm of locusts had invaded the country. The grass for miles around was cropped close by the horses of General Kearney's soldiery. When we came to the fort we found that not only had the horses eaten up the grass, but their owners had made way with the stores of the little trading post; so that we had great difficulty in procuring the few articles which we required for our homeward journey. The army was gone, the life and bustle passed away, and the fort was a scene of dull and lazy tranquillity. A few invalid officers and soldiers sauntered about the area, which was oppressively hot; for the glaring sun was reflected down upon it from the high white walls around. The proprietors were absent, and we were received by Mr Holt, who had been left in charge of the fort. He invited us to dinner, where to our admiration, we found a table laid with a white cloth, with casters in the middle, and chairs placed around it. This unwonted repast concluded, we rode back to our camp.

Here, as we lay smoking round the fire after supper, we saw through the dusk three men approaching from the direction of the fort. They rode up and seated themselves near us on the ground. The foremost was a tall, well-formed man, with a face and manner such as inspire confidence at once. He wore a broad hat of felt, slouching and tattered, and the rest of his attire consisted of a frock and leggings of buckskin, rubbed with the yellow clay found among the mountains. At the heel of one of his moccasins was buckled a huge iron spur, with a rowel five or six inches in diameter. His horse, which stood quietly looking over his head, had a rude Mexican saddle, covered with a shaggy bear-skin, and furnished with a pair of wooden stirrups of preposterous size. The next man was a sprightly, active little fellow, about five feet and a quarter high, but very strong and compact. His face was swarthy as a Mexican's, and covered with a close, curly, black beard. An old, greasy, calico handkerchief was tied round his head, and his close buckskin dress was blackened and polished by grease and hard service. The last who came up was a large, strong man, dressed in the coarse homespun of the frontiers, who dragged his long limbs over the ground as if he were too lazy for the effort. He had a sleepy gray eye, a retreating chin, an open mouth, and a protruding upper lip, which gave him an air of exquisite indolence and helplessness. He was armed with an old United States yager, which redoubtable weapon, though he could never hit his mark with it, he was accustomed to cherish as the very sovereign of firearms.

The first two men belonged to a party who had just come from California, with a large band of horses, which they had sold at Bent's Fort. Munroe, the taller of the two, was from Iowa. He was an excellent fellow, open, warm-hearted, and intelligent. Jim Gurney, the short man, was a Boston sailor, who had come in a trading vessel to California, and taken the fancy to return across the continent. The journey had already made him an expert 'mountain-man' and he presented the extraordinary phenomenon of a sailor who understood how to manage a horse. The third of our visitors, named Ellis, was a Missourian, who had come out with a party of Oregon emigrants; but having got as far as Bridger's Fort, he had fallen homesick, or as Jim averred, lovesick. He thought proper, therefore, to join the California men, and return homeward in their company.

They now requested that they might unite with our party, and make the journey to the settlements in company with us. We readily assented, for we liked the appearance of the first two men, and were very glad to gain so efficient a reinforcement. We told them to meet us on the next evening at a spot on the riverside, about six miles below the fort. After we had smoked a pipe together, our new allies left us, and we lay down to sleep.

22. Tête Rouge, the Volunteer

The next morning, having directed Deslauriers to repair with his cart to the place of meeting, we came again to the fort to make some arrangements for the journey. After completing these we sat down under a sort of porch, to smoke with some Cheyenne Indians whom we found there. In a few minutes we saw an extraordinary little figure approach us in a military dress. He had a small, round countenance, garnished about the eyes with the kind of wrinkles commonly known as crow's feet, and surmounted by an abundant crop of red curls, with a little cap resting on the top of them. Altogether, he had the look of a man more conversant with mint-juleps and oyster suppers than with the hardships of prairie service. He came up to us and entreated that we would take him home to the settlements, saying that unless he went with us he should have to stay all winter at the fort. We liked our petitioner's appearance so little that we excused ourselves from complying with his request. At this he begged us so hard to take pity on him, looked so disconsolate, and told so lamentable a story, that at last we consented, though not without many misgivings.

The rugged Anglo-Saxon of our new recruit's real name proved utterly unmanageable on the lips of our French attendants; and Henry Chatillon, after various abortive attempts to pronounce it, one day coolly christened him Tête Rouge, in honor of his red curls. He had at different times been clerk of a Mississippi steamboat, and agent in a trading establishment at Nauvoo, besides filling various other capacities, in all of which he had seen much more of 'life' than was good for him. In the spring, thinking that a summer's campaign would be an agreeable recreation, he had joined a company of St Louis volunteers.

'There were three of us,' said Tête Rouge, 'me and Bill Stevens and John Hopkins. We thought we would just go out with the army, and when we had conquered the country, we would get discharged and take our pay, you know, and go down to Mexico. They say there 's plenty of fun going on there. Then we could go back to New Orleans by way of Vera Cruz.'

But Tête Rouge, like many a stouter volunteer, had reckoned without his host. Fighting Mexicans was a less amusing occupation than he had supposed, and his pleasure trip was disagreeably interrupted by brain fever, which attacked him when about half-way to Bent's Fort. He jolted along through the rest of the journey in a baggage wagon. When they came to the fort he was taken out and left there, with the rest of the sick. Bent's Fort does not supply the best accommodations for an invalid. Tête Rouge's sick-chamber was a little mud room, where he and a companion, attacked by the same disease, were laid together, with nothing but a buffalo-robe between them and the ground. The assistant-surgeon's deputy visited them once a day and brought them each a huge dose of calomel, the only medicine, according to his surviving victim, with which he was acquainted.

Tête Rouge woke one morning, and turning to his companion saw his eyes fixed upon the beams above with the glassy stare of a dead man. At this the unfortunate volunteer lost his senses outright. In spite of the doctor, however, he eventually recovered; though between the brain fever and the calomel, his mind,

originally none of the strongest, was so much shaken that it had
not quite recovered its balance when we came to the fort. In spite
of the poor fellow's tragic story, there was something so ludicrous
in his appearance, and the whimsical contrast between his military dress and his most unmilitary demeanor, that we could not
help smiling at them. We asked him if he had a gun. He said
they had taken it from him during his illness, and he had not seen
it since; but 'perhaps,' he observed, looking at me with a beseech-
ing air, 'you will lend me one of your big pistols if we should meet
with any Indians.' I next inquired if he had a horse; he declared
he had a magnificent one, and at Shaw's request, a Mexican led
him in for inspection. He exhibited the outline of a good horse,
but his eyes were sunk in the sockets, and every one of his ribs
could be counted. There were certain marks too about his shoulders, which could be accounted for by the circumstance that,
during Tête Rouge's illness, his companions had seized upon the
insulted charger, and harnessed him to a cannon along with the
draft horses. To Tête Rouge's astonishment we recommended him
by all means to exchange the horse, if he could, for a mule. Fortunately the people at the fort were so anxious to get rid of him
that they were willing to make some sacrifice to effect the object,
and he succeeded in getting a tolerable mule in exchange for the
broken-down steed.

A man soon appeared at the gate, leading in the mule by a
cord, which he placed in the hands of Tête Rouge, who, being
somewhat afraid of his new acquisition, tried various flatteries
and blandishments to induce her to come forward. The mule,
knowing that she was expected to advance, stopped short in
consequence, and stood fast as a rock, looking straight forward
with immovable composure. Being stimulated by a blow from
behind, she consented to move, and walked nearly to the other
side of the fort before she stopped again. Hearing the bystanders
laugh, Tête Rouge plucked up spirit and tugged hard at the rope.
The mule jerked backward, spun herself round, and made a dash
for the gate. Tête Rouge, who clung manfully to the rope, went
whisking through the air for a few rods, when he let go and stood
with his mouth open, staring after the mule, which galloped away
over the prairie. She was soon caught and brought back by a
Mexican, who mounted a horse and went in pursuit of her with his
lasso.

Having thus displayed his capacities for prairie travelling,

Tête Rouge proceeded to supply himself with provisions for the journey, and with this view applied to a quartermaster's assistant, who was in the fort. This official had a face as sour as vinegar, being in a state of chronic indignation because he had been left behind the army. He was as anxious as the rest to get rid of Tête Rouge. So, producing a rusty key, he opened a low door which led to a half-subterranean apartment, into which the two disappeared together. After some time they came out again, Tête Rouge greatly embarrassed by a multiplicity of paper parcels containing the different articles of his forty days' rations. They were consigned to the care of Deslauriers, who about that time passed by with the cart, on his way to the appointed place of meeting with Munroe and his companions.

We next urged Tête Rouge to provide himself, if he could, with a gun. He accordingly made earnest appeals to the charity of various persons in the fort, but totally without success,—a circumstance which did not greatly disturb us, since, in the event of a skirmish, he would be more apt to do mischief to himself or his friends than to the enemy. When all these arrangements were completed we saddled our horses, and were preparing to leave the fort, when, looking round, we discovered that our new associate was in fresh trouble. A man was holding the mule for him in the middle of the fort, while he tried to put the saddle on her back, but she kept stepping sideways and moving round and round in a circle until he was almost in despair. It required some assistance before all his difficulties could be overcome. At length he clambered into the black war-saddle on which he was to have carried terror into the ranks of the Mexicans.

'Get up,' said Tête Rouge; 'come now, go along, will you?'

The mule walked deliberately forward out of the gate. Her recent conduct had inspired him with so much awe that he never dared to touch her with his whip. We trotted forward toward the place of meeting, but before we had gone far, we saw that Tête Rouge's mule, who perfectly understood her rider, had stopped and was quietly grazing, in spite of his protestations, at some distance behind. So getting behind him, we drove him and the contumacious mule before us, until we could see through the twilight the gleaming of a distant fire. Munroe, Jim, and Ellis were lying around it; their saddles, packs, and weapons were scattered about, and their horses picketed near them. Deslauriers was there too with our little cart. Another fire was soon blazing. We invited our new allies to take a cup of coffee with us. When both the others had gone over to their side of the camp, Jim Gurney still stood by the blaze, puffing hard at his little black pipe, as short and weather-beaten as himself.

'Well,' he said, 'here are eight of us; we 'll call it six—for them two boobies, Ellis over yonder and that new man of yours, won't count for anything. We 'll get through well enough, never fear for that, unless the Camanches happen to get foul of us.'

23. Indian Alarms

We began our journey for the settlements on the twenty-seventh of August, and a more ragamuffin cavalcade never was seen on the banks of the Upper Arkansas. Of the large and fine horses with which we had left the frontier in the spring, not one remained: we had supplied their place with the rough breed of the prairie, as hardy as mules and almost as ugly; we had also with us a number of the latter detestable animals. In spite of their strength and hardihood, several of the band were already worn down by hard service and hard fare, and as none of them were shod, they were fast becoming footsore. Every horse and mule had a cord of twisted bull-hide coiled about his neck, which by no means added to the beauty of his appearance. Our saddles and all our equipments were worn and battered, and our weapons had become dull and rusty.

The dress of the riders corresponded with the dilapidated furniture of our horses, and of the whole party none made a more disreputable appearance than my friend and I. Shaw had for an upper garment an old red flannel shirt, flying open in front, and belted round him like a frock; while I, in absence of other clothing, was attired in a time-worn suit of buckskin.

Thus, happy and careless as so many beggars, we crept slowly from day to day along the monotonous banks of the Arkansas. Tête Rouge gave constant trouble, for he could never catch his mule, saddle her, or indeed do anything else without assistance. Every day he had some new ailment, real or imaginary, to complain of. At one moment he would be woe-begone and disconsolate, and at the next he would be visited with a violent flow of spirits, to which he could only give vent by incessant laughing, whistling, and telling stories. When other resources failed, we used to amuse ourselves by tormenting him; a fair compensation for the trouble he cost us. Tête Rouge rather enjoyed being laughed at, for he was an odd compound of weakness, eccentricity, and good-nature. He made a figure worthy of a painter as he paced along before us, perched on the back of his mule, and enveloped in a huge buffalo-robe coat, which some charitable person had given him at the fort. This extraordinary garment, which would have contained two men of his size, he chose, for some reason best known to himself, to wear inside out, and he never took it off even in the hottest weather. It was fluttering all over with seams and tatters, and the hide was so old and rotten that it broke out every day in a new place. Just at the top of it a large pile of red curls was visible, with his little cap set jauntily upon one side, to give him a military air. His seat in the saddle was no less remarkable than his person and equipment. He pressed one leg close against his mule's side, and thrust the other out at an angle of forty-five degrees. His trousers were decorated with a military red stripe, of which he was extremely vain; but being much too short, the whole length of his boots was usually visible below them. His blanket, loosely rolled up into a large bundle, dangled at the back of his saddle, where he carried it tied with a string. Four or five times a day it would fall to the ground. Every few minutes he would drop his pipe, his knife, his flint and steel, or a piece of tobacco, and scramble down to pick them up. In doing this he would contrive to get in everybody's way; and as most of the party were by no means remarkable for a fastidious choice of language, a storm of anathemas would be showered upon him, half in earnest and half in jest, until Tête Rouge would declare that there was no comfort in life, and that he never saw such fellows before.

Only a day or two after leaving Bent's Fort Henry Chatillon rode forward to hunt, and took Ellis along with him. After they had been some time absent we saw them coming down the hill driving three dragoon horses, which had escaped from their owners on the march, or perhaps had given out and been abandoned. One of them was in tolerable condition, but the others were much emaciated and severely bitten by the wolves. Reduced as they were, we carried two of them to the settlements, and Henry exchanged the third with the Arapahoes for an excellent mule.

On the day after, when we had stopped to rest at noon, a long train of Santa Fé wagons came up and trailed slowly past us in their picturesque procession. They belonged to a trader named Magoffin, whose brother, with a number of other men, came and sat down with us on the grass. The news they brought was not of the most pleasing complexion. According to their accounts, the trail below was in a very dangerous state. They had repeatedly detected Indians prowling at night around their camps; and the large party which had left Bent's Fort a few weeks before us had been attacked, and a man named Swan, from Massachusetts, had been killed. His companions had buried the body; but when Magoffin found his grave, which was near a place called 'The Caches,' the Indians had dug up and scalped him, and the wolves had shockingly mangled his remains. As an offset to this intelligence, they gave us the welcome information that the buffalo were numerous at a few days' journey below.

On the next afternoon, as we moved along the bank of the river, we saw the white tops of wagons on the horizon. It was some hours before we met them, when they proved to be a train of clumsy ox-wagons, quite different from the rakish vehicles of the Santa Fé traders, and loaded with government stores for the troops. They all stopped, and the drivers gathered around us in a crowd. Many of them were mere boys, fresh from the plough. In respect to the state of the trail, they confirmed all that the Santa Fé men had told us. In passing between the Pawnee Fork and the Caches, their sentinels had fired every night at real or imaginary Indians. They said also that Ewing, a young Kentuckian in the party that had gone down before us, had shot an Indian who was prowling at evening about the camp. Some of them advised us to turn back, and others to hasten forward as fast as we could; but they all seemed in such a state of feverish anxiety, and so little capable of cool judgment, that we attached slight weight to what they said. They next gave us a more definite piece of intelligence: a large village of Arapahoes was encamped on the river below. They represented them to be friendly; but some distinction was to be made between a party of thirty men, travelling with oxen, which are of no value in an Indian's eyes, and a mere handful like ourselves, with a tempting band of mules and horses.

Early in the afternoon of the next day, looking along the horizon before us, we saw that at one point it was faintly marked with pale indentations like the teeth of a saw. The distant lodges of the Arapahoes, rising between us and the sky, caused this singular appearance. It wanted still two or three hours of sunset when we came opposite their camp. There were full two hundred lodges standing in the midst of a grassy meadow at some distance beyond the river, while for a mile around on both banks of the Arkansas were scattered some fifteen hundred horses and mules, grazing together in bands, or wandering singly about the prairie. The whole were visible at once, for the vast expanse was unbroken by hills, and there was not a tree or a bush to intercept the view.

Here and there walked an Indian, engaged in watching the horses. No sooner did we see them than Tête Rouge begged Deslauriers to stop the cart and hand him his military jacket, which was stowed away there. In this he invested himself, having for once laid the old buffalo-coat aside, assumed a martial posture in the saddle, set his cap over his left eye with an air of defiance, and earnestly entreated that somebody would lend him a gun or a pistol only for half an hour. Being called upon to explain these proceedings, Tête Rouge observed that he knew from experience what effect the presence of a military man in his uniform always has upon the mind of an Indian, and he thought the Arapahoes ought to know that there was a soldier in the party.

Meeting Arapahoes here on the Arkansas was a very different thing from meeting the same Indians among their native mountains. There was another circumstance in our favor. General Kearney had seen them a few weeks before as he came up the river with his army, and, renewing his threats of the previous year he told them that if they ever again touched the hair of a white man's head he would exterminate their nation. This placed them for the time in an admirable frame of mind, and the effect of his menaces had not yet disappeared. I wished to see the village and its inhabitants. We thought it also our best policy to visit them openly, as if unsuspicious of any hostile design; and Shaw and I, with Henry Chatillon, prepared to cross the river. The rest of the party meanwhile moved forward as fast as they could, in order to get as far as possible from our suspicious neighbors before night came on.

The Arkansas at this point, and for several hundred miles below, is in August nothing but a broad sand-bed over which glide a few scanty threads of water, now and then expanding into wide shallows. At several places, during the autumn the water sinks into the sand and disappears altogether. At this season, were it not for the numerous quicksands, the river might be forded almost anywhere without difficulty, though its channel is often a quarter of a mile wide. Our horses jumped down the bank, and wading through the water, or galloping freely over the hard sand-beds, soon reached the other side. Here, as we were pushing through the tall grass, we saw several Indians not far off; one of them waited until we came up, and stood for some moments in perfect silence before us, looking at us askance with his little snake-like eyes. Henry explained by signs what we wanted, and the Indian, gathering his buffalo-robe about his shoulders, led the way towards the village without speaking a word.

The language of the Arapahoes is so difficult, and its pronunciation so harsh and guttural, that no white man, it is said, has ever been able to master it. Even Maxwell, the trader who has been most among them, is compelled to resort to the curious sign-language common to most of the prairie tribes. With this sign-language Henry Chatillon was perfectly acquainted.

Approaching the village, we found the ground strewn with piles of waste buffalo-meat in incredible quantities. The lodges were pitched in a circle. They resembled those of the Dakota in everything but cleanliness. Passing between two of them, we entered the great circular area of the camp, and instantly hundreds of Indians, men, women, and children, came flocking out of their habitations to look at us; at the same time the dogs all around the village set up a discordant baying. Our Indian guide walked towards the lodge of the chief. Here we dismounted; and loosening the trail-ropes from our horses' necks, held them fast as we sat down before the entrance, with our rifles laid across our laps. The chief came out and shook us by the hand. He was a mean-looking fellow, very tall, thin-visaged, and sinewy, like the rest of the nation, and with scarcely a vestige of clothing. We had not been seated a moment before a multitude of Indians came crowding around us from every part of the village, and we were shut in by a dense wall of savage faces. Some of our visitors crouched about us on the ground; others sat behind them; others, stooping, looked over their heads; while many more stood behind, peering over one another's shoulders, to get a view of us. I looked in vain among this throng of faces to discover one manly or generous expression; all were wolfish, sinister, and malignant, and their complexions, as well as their features, unlike those of the Dakota, were exceedingly bad. The chief, who sat close to the entrance, called to a squaw within the lodge, who soon came out and placed a wooden bowl of meat before us. To our surprise, however, no pipe was offered. Having tasted of the meat as a matter of form, I began to open a bundle of presents,—tobacco, knives, vermilion, and other articles which I had brought with me. At this there was a grin on every countenance in the rapacious crowd; their eyes began to glitter, and long thin arms were eagerly stretched towards us on all sides to receive the gifts.

The Arapahoes set great value upon their shields, which they transmit carefully from father to son. I wished to get one of them; and displaying a large piece of scarlet cloth, together with some tobacco, and a knife, I offered them to any one who would bring me what I wanted. After some delay a tolerable shield was produced. They were very anxious to know what we meant to do with it, and Henry told them that we were going to fight their enemies the Pawnees. This instantly produced a visible impression in our favor, which was increased by the distribution of the presents. Among these was a large paper of awls, a gift appropriate to the women; and as we were anxious to see the beauties of the Arapahoe village, Henry requested that they might be called to receive them. A warrior gave a shout, as if he were calling a pack of dogs together. The squaws, young and old, hags of eighty and girls of sixteen, came running with screams and laughter out of the lodges; and as the men gave way for them, they gathered round us and stretched out their arms, grinning with delight, their native ugliness considerably enhanced by the excitement of the moment.

Mounting our horses, which during the whole interview we had held close to us, we prepared to leave the Arapahoes. The crowd fell back on each side, and stood looking on. When we were half across the camp an idea occurred to us. The Pawnees were probably in the neighborhood of the Caches; we might tell the Arapahoes of this, and instigate them to send down a war-party and cut them off, while we ourselves could remain behind for a while and hunt the buffalo. At first thought, this plan of setting our enemies to destroy one another seemed to us a masterpiece of policy; but we immediately recollected that should we meet the Arapahoe warriors on the river below, they might prove quite as dangerous as the Pawnees themselves. So rejecting our plan as soon as it presented itself, we passed out of the village on the farther side. We urged our horses rapidly through the tall grass, which rose to their necks. Several Indians were walking through it at a distance, their heads just visible above its waving surface. It bore a kind of seed, as sweet and nutritious as oats; and our hungry horses, in spite of whip and rein, could not resist the temptation of snatching at this unwonted luxury as we passed along. When about a mile from the village, I turned and looked back over the undulating ocean of grass. The sun was just set; the western sky was all in a glow, and sharply defined against it, on the extreme verge of the plain, stood the clustered lodges of the Arapahoe camp.

Reaching the bank of the river, we followed it for some distance farther, until we discerned through the twilight the white covering of our little cart on the opposite bank. When we reached it we found a considerable number of Indians there before us. Four or five of them were seated in a row upon the ground, looking like so many half-starved vultures. Tête Rouge, in his uniform, was holding a close colloquy with another by the side of the cart. Finding his signs and gesticulation of no avail, he tried to make the Indian understand him by repeating English words very loudly and distinctly again and again. The Indian sat with his eye fixed steadily upon him, and in spite of the rigid immobility of his features, it was clear at a glance that he perfectly understood and despised his military companion. The exhibition was more amusing than politic, and Tête Rouge was directed to finish what he had to say as soon as possible. Thus rebuked, he crept under the cart and sat down there; Henry Chatillon stooped to look at him in his retirement, and remarked in his quiet manner that an Indian would kill ten such men and laugh all the time.

One by one our visitors arose and stalked away. As the darkness thickened we were saluted by dismal sounds. The wolves are incredibly numerous in this part of the country, and the offal around the Arapahoe camp had drawn such multitudes of them together that several hundreds were howling in concert in our immediate neighborhood. There was an island in the river, or rather an oasis in the midst of the sands, at about the distance of a gunshot, and here they seemed to be gathered in the greatest numbers. A horrible discord of low, mournful wailings, mingled with ferocious howls, arose from it incessantly for several hours after sunset. We could distinctly see the wolves running about the prairie within a few rods of our fire, or bounding over the sand-beds of the river and splashing through the water. There was not the slightest danger from them, for they are the greatest cowards on the prairie.

In respect to the human wolves in our neighborhood, we felt much less at our ease. That night each man spread his buffalo-robe upon the ground with his loaded rifle laid at his side or clasped in his arms. Our horses were picketed so close around us that one of them repeatedly stepped over me as I lay. We were not in the habit of placing a guard, but every man was anxious and watchful: there was little sound sleeping in camp, and some one of the party was on his feet during the greater part of the night. For myself, I lay alternately waking and dozing until midnight. Tête Rouge was reposing close to the river bank, and about this time, when half asleep and half awake, I was conscious that he shifted his position and crept on all-fours under the cart. Soon after I fell into a sound sleep, from which I was roused by a hand shaking me by the shoulder. Looking up, I saw Tête Rouge stooping over me with a pale face and dilated eyes.

'What's the matter?' said I.

Tête Rouge declared that as he lay on the river bank something caught his eye which excited his suspicions. So creeping under the cart for safety's sake, he sat there and watched, when he saw two Indians, wrapped in white robes, creep up the bank, seize upon two horses, and lead them off. He looked so frightened and told his story in such a disconnected manner that I did not believe him, and was unwilling to alarm the party. Still it might be true, and in that case the matter required instant attention. So directing Tête Rouge to show me which way the Indians had gone, I took my rifle, in obedience to a thoughtless impulse, and left the camp. I followed the river bank for two or three hundred yards, listening and looking anxiously on every side. In the dark prairie on the right I could discern nothing to excite alarm; and in the dusky bed of the river, a wolf was bounding along in a manner which no Indian could imitate. I returned to the camp, and when within sight of it, saw that the whole party was aroused. Shaw called out to me that he had counted the horses, and that every one of them was in his place. Tête Rouge, being examined as to what he had seen, only repeated his former story with many asseverations, and insisted that two horses were certainly carried off. At this Jim Gurney declared that he was crazy; Tête Rouge indignantly denied the charge, on which Jim appealed to us. As we declined to give our judgment on so delicate a matter, the dispute grew hot between Tête Rouge and his accuser, until he was directed to go to bed, and not alarm the camp again if he saw the whole Arapahoe village coming.

24. The Chase

The country before us was now thronged with buffalo, and a sketch of the manner of hunting them will not be out of place. There are two methods commonly practised,—'running' and 'approaching.' The chase on horseback, which goes by the name of 'running,' is the more violent and dashing mode of the two, that is to say, when the buffalo are in one of their wild moods; for otherwise it is tame enough. A practised and skilful hunter, well mounted, will sometimes kill five or six cows in a single chase, loading his gun again and again as his horse rushes through the tumult. In attacking a small band of buffalo, or in separating a single animal from the herd and assailing it apart from the rest, there is less excitement and less danger. In fact, the animals are at times so stupid and lethargic that there is little sport in killing them. With a bold and well-trained horse the hunter may ride so close to the buffalo that as they gallop side by side he may touch him with his hand; nor is there much danger in this as long as the buffalo's strength and breath continue unabated; but when he becomes tired and can no longer run with ease, when his tongue lolls out and the foam flies from his jaws, then the hunter had better keep a more respectful distance; the distressed brute may turn upon him at any instant, and especially at the moment when he fires his gun. The horse then leaps aside, and the hunter has need of a tenacious seat in the saddle, for if he is thrown to the ground there is no hope for him. When he sees his attack defeated the buffalo resumes his flight, but if the shot is well directed he soon stops; for a few moments he stands still, then totters and falls heavily upon the prairie.

The chief difficulty in running buffalo, as it seems to me, is that of loading the gun or pistol at full gallop. Many hunters, for convenience' sake, carry three or four bullets in the mouth; the powder is poured down the muzzle of the piece, the bullet dropped in after it, or spit from the mouth into the barrel, the stock struck hard upon the pommel of the saddle, and the work is done. The danger of this is obvious. Should the blow on the pommel fail to send the bullet home, or should the bullet, in the act of aiming, start from its place and roll towards the muzzle, the gun would probably burst in discharging. Many a shattered hand and worse casualties besides have been the result of such an accident. To obviate it, some hunters make use of a ramrod, usually hung by a string from the neck, but this materially increases the difficulty of loading. The bows and arrows which the Indians use in running buffalo have many advantages over firearms, and even white men occasionally employ them.

The danger of the chase arises not so much from the onset of the wounded animal as from the nature of the ground which the hunter must ride over. The prairie does not always present a smooth, level, and uniform surface; very often it is broken with hills and hollows, intersected by ravines, and in the remoter parts studded by the stiff wild-sage bushes. The most formidable obstructions, however, are the burrows of wild animals,—wolves, badgers, and particularly prairie-dogs, with whose holes the ground for a great extent is frequently honey-combed. In the blindness of the chase the hunter rushes over it unconscious of danger; his horse, at full career, thrusts his leg deep into one of the burrows; the bone snaps, the rider is hurled forward to the ground and probably killed. Yet accidents in buffalo running happen less frequently than one would suppose; in the recklessness of the chase, the hunter enjoys all the impunity of a drunken man, and may ride in safety over gullies and declivities, where, should he attempt to pass in his sober senses he would infallibly break his neck.

The method of 'approaching,' being practised on foot, has many advantages over that of 'running;' in the former one neither breaks down his horse nor endangers his own life; he must be cool, collected, and watchful; must understand the buffalo, observe the features of the country and the course of the wind, and be well skilled in using the rifle. The buffalo are strange animals; sometimes they are so stupid and infatuated that a man may walk up to them in full sight on the open prairie, and even shoot several of their number before the rest will think it necessary to retreat. At another moment they will be so shy and wary that in order to approach them the utmost skill, experience, and judgment are necessary. Kit Carson, I believe, stands pre-eminent in running buffalo; in approaching, no man living can bear away the palm from Henry Chatillon.

After Tête Rouge had alarmed the camp, no farther disturbance occurred during the night. The Arapahoes did not attempt mischief, or if they did the wakefulness of the party deterred them from effecting their purpose. The next day was one of activity and excitement, for about ten o'clock the man in advance shouted the gladdening cry of 'Buffalo! buffalo!' and in the hollow of the prairie just below us, a band of bulls were grazing. The temptation was irresistible, and Shaw and I rode down upon them. We were badly mounted on our travelling horses, but by hard lashing we overtook them, and Shaw, running alongside a bull, shot into him both balls of his double-barrelled gun. Looking round as I galloped by, I saw the bull in his mortal fury rushing again and again upon his antagonist, whose horse constantly leaped aside, and avoided the onset. My chase was more protracted, but at length I ran close to the bull and killed him with my pistols. Cutting off the tails of our victims by way of trophy, we rejoined the party in about a quarter of an hour after we had left it. Again and again that morning rang out the same welcome cry of 'Buffalo! buffalo!' Every few moments, in the broad meadows along the river, we saw bands of bulls, who raising their shaggy

heads would gaze in stupid amazement at the approaching horsemen, and then breaking into a clumsy gallop, file off in a long line
across the trail in front, towards the rising prairie on the left. At
noon, the plain before us was alive with thousands of buffalo,
bulls, cows, and calves, all moving rapidly as we drew near; and
far off beyond the river the swelling prairie was darkened with
them to the very horizon. The party was in gayer spirits than
ever. We stopped for a nooning near a grove of trees by the river.

'Tongues and hump-ribs to-morrow,' said Shaw, looking with
contempt at the venison steaks which Deslauriers placed before
us. Our meal finished, we lay down to sleep. A shout from Henry
Chatillon aroused us, and we saw him standing on the cart-wheel,
stretching his tall figure to its full height while he looked towards
the prairie beyond the river. Following the direction of his eyes,
we could clearly distinguish a large dark object, like the black
shadow of a cloud, passing rapidly over swell after swell of the
distant plain; behind it followed another of similar appearance
though smaller, moving more rapidly, and drawing closer and
closer to the first. It was the hunters of the Arapahoe camp
chasing a band of buffalo. Shaw and I caught and saddled our best
horses, and went plunging through sand and water to the farther
bank. We were too late. The hunters had already mingled with
the herd, and the work of slaughter was nearly over. When we
reached the ground we found it strewn far and near with numberless carcasses, while the remnants of the herd, scattered in all
directions, were flying away in terror, and the Indians still
rushing in pursuit. Many of the hunters, however, remained upon
the spot, and among the rest was our yesterday's acquaintance,
the chief of the village. He had alighted by the side of a cow,
into which he had shot five or six arrows, and his squaw, who had
followed him on horseback to the hunt, was giving him a draught
of water from a canteen purchased or plundered from some
volunteer soldier. Recrossing the river, we overtook the party,
who were already on their way.

We had gone scarcely a mile when we saw an imposing spectacle.
From the river bank on the right, away over the swelling prairie
on the left, and in front as far as the eye could reach, was one vast
host of buffalo. The outskirts of the herd were within a quarter of
a mile. In many parts they were crowded so densely together that
in the distance their rounded hacks presented a surface of uniform blackness; but elsewhere they were more scattered, and

from amid the multitude rose little columns of dust where some of them were rolling on the ground. Here and there a battle was going forward among the bulls. We could distinctly see them rushing against each other, and hear the clattering of their horns and their hoarse bellowing. Shaw was riding at some distance in advance, with Henry Chatillon; I saw him stop and draw the leather covering from his gun. With such a sight before us, but one thing could be thought of. That morning I had used pistols in the chase. I had now a mind to try the virtue of a gun. Deslauriers had one, and I rode up to the side of the cart; there he sat under the white covering, biting his pipe between his teeth and grinning with excitement.

'Lend me your gun, Deslauriers.'

'Oui, Monsieur, oui,' said Deslauriers, tugging with might and main to stop the mule, which seemed obstinately bent on going forward. Then everything but his moccasins disappeared as he crawled into the cart and pulled at the gun to extricate it.

'Is it loaded?' I asked.

'Oui, bien chargé; you 'll kill, mon bourgeois; yes, you 'll kill—c'est un bon fusil.'

I handed him my rifle and rode forward to Shaw.

'Are you ready?' he asked.

'Come on,' said I.

'Keep down that hollow,' said Henry, 'and then they won't see you till you get close to them.'

The hollow was a kind of wide ravine; it ran obliquely towards the buffalo, and we rode at a canter along the bottom until it became too shallow; then we bent close to our horses' necks, and, at last, finding that it could no longer conceal us, came out of it and rode directly towards the herd. It was within gunshot; before its outskirts numerous grizzly old bulls were scattered, holding guard over their females. They glared at us in anger and astonishment, walked towards us a few yards, and then turning slowly round retreated at a trot which afterwards broke into a clumsy gallop. In an instant the main body caught the alarm. The buffalo began to crowd away from the point towards which we were approaching, and a gap was opened in the side of the herd. We entered it, still restraining our excited horses. Every instant the tumult was thickening. The buffalo, pressing together in large bodies, crowded away from us on every hand. In front and on either side we could see dark columns and masses, half hidden by clouds of dust, rushing along in terror and confusion, and hear the tramp and clattering of ten thousand hoofs. That countless multitude of powerful brutes, ignorant of their own strength, were flying in a panic from the approach of two feeble horsemen. To remain quiet longer was impossible.

'Take that band on the left,' said Shaw; 'I'll take these in front.'

He sprang off, and I saw no more of him. A heavy Indian whip, or 'quirt,' was fastened by a band to my wrist; I swung it into the air and lashed my horse's flank with all the strength of my arm. Away she darted, stretching close to the ground. I could see nothing but a cloud of dust before me, but I knew that it concealed a band of many hundreds of buffalo. In a moment I was in the midst of the cloud, half suffocated by the dust and stunned by the trampling of the flying herd; but I was drunk with the chase and cared for nothing but the buffalo. Very soon a long dark mass became visible, looming through the dust; then I could distinguish each bulky carcass, the hoofs flying out beneath, the short tails held rigidly erect. In a moment I was so close that I could have touched them with my gun. Suddenly, to my amazement, the hoofs were jerked upwards, the tail flourished in the air, and amid a cloud of dust the buffalo seemed to sink into the earth before me. One vivid impression of that instant remains upon my mind. I remember looking down upon the backs of several buffalo dimly visible through the dust. We had run unawares upon a ravine. At that moment I was not the most accurate judge of depth and width, but when I passed it on my return, I found it about twelve feet deep and not quite twice as wide at the bottom. It was impossible to stop; I would have done so gladly if I could; so, half sliding, half plunging, down went the little mare. She came down on her knees in the loose sand at the bottom; I was pitched forward against her neck and nearly thrown over her head among the buffalo, who amid dust and confusion came tumbling in all around. The mare was on her feet in an instant and scrambling like a cat up the opposite side. I thought for a moment that she would have fallen back and crushed me, but with a violent effort she clambered out and gained the hard prairie above. Glancing back I saw the huge head of a bull clinging as it were by the fore-feet at the edge of the dusty gulf. At length I was fairly among the buffalo. They were less densely crowded than before, and I could see nothing but bulls, who always run at the rear of a herd to

protect their females. As I passed among them they would lower
their heads, and turning as they ran, try to gore my horse; but as
they were already at full speed there was no force in their onset,
and as Pauline ran faster than they, they were always thrown
behind her in the effort. I soon began to distinguish cows amid
the throng. One just in front of me seemed to my liking, and I
pushed close to her side. Dropping the reins I fired, holding the
muzzle of the gun within a foot of her shoulder. Quick as lightning she sprang at Pauline; the little mare dodged the attack, and
I lost sight of the wounded animal amid the tumult. Immediately
after, I selected another, and urging forward Pauline, shot into
her both pistols in succession. For a while I kept her in view, but
in attempting to load my gun lost sight of her also in the confusion. Believing her to be mortally wounded and unable to keep
up with the herd, I checked my horse. The crowd rushed onwards.
The dust and tumult passed away, and on the prairie, far behind
the rest, I saw a solitary buffalo galloping heavily. In a moment
I and my victim were running side by side. My firearms were all
empty, and I had in my pouch nothing but rifle bullets, too
large for the pistols and too small for the gun. I loaded the gun,
however, but as often as I levelled it to fire, the bullets would roll
out of the muzzle and the gun returned only a report like a squib
as the powder harmlessly exploded. I rode in front of the buffalo
and tried to turn her back; but her eyes glared, her mane bristled,
and, lowering her head, she rushed at me with the utmost fierceness and activity. Again and again I rode before her, and again
and again she repeated her furious charge. But little Pauline was
in her element. She dodged her enemy at every rush, until at
length the buffalo stood still, exhausted with her own efforts, her
tongue lolling from her jaws.

Riding to a little distance, I dismounted, thinking to gather a
handful of dry grass to serve the purpose of wadding, and load the
gun at my leisure. No sooner were my feet on the ground than the
buffalo came bounding in such a rage towards me that I jumped
back again into the saddle with all possible despatch. After waiting
a few minutes more, I made an attempt to ride up and stab her
with my knife; but Pauline was near being gored in the attempt.
At length, bethinking me of the fringes at the seams of my buckskin trousers, I jerked off a few of them and, reloading the gun,
forced them down the barrel to keep the bullet in its place; then
approaching, I shot the wounded buffalo through the heart.

Sinking to her knees, she rolled over lifeless on the prairie. To my astonishment, I found that, instead of cow, I had been slaughtering a stout young bull. No longer wondering at his fierceness, I opened his throat, and cutting out his tongue tied it at the back of my saddle. My mistake was one which a more experienced eye than mine might easily make in the dust and confusion of such a chase.

Then for the first time I had leisure to look at the scene around me. The prairie in front was darkened with the retreating multitude, and on either hand the buffalo came filing up in endless columns from the low plains upon the river. The Arkansas was three or four miles distant. I turned and moved slowly towards it. A long time passed before, far in the distance, I distinguished the white covering of the cart and the little black specks of horsemen before and behind it. Drawing near, I recognized Shaw's elegant tunic, the red flannel shirt, conspicuous far off. I overtook the party, and asked him what success he had had. He had assailed a fat cow, shot her with two bullets, and mortally wounded her. But neither of us was prepared for the chase that afternoon, and Shaw, like myself, had no spare bullets in his pouch; so he abandoned the disabled animal to Henry Chatillon, who followed, despatched her with his rifle, and loaded his horse with the meat.

We encamped close to the river. The night was dark, and as we lay down we could hear, mingled with the howling of wolves, the hoarse bellowing of the buffalo, like the ocean beating upon a distant coast.

25. The Buffalo Camp

Nobody in the camp was more active than Jim Gurney, and nobody half so lazy as Ellis. Between these two there was a great antipathy. Ellis never stirred in the morning until he was compelled, but Jim was always on his feet before daybreak; and this morning as usual the sound of his voice awakened the party.

'Get up, you booby! up with you now, you 're fit for nothing but eating and sleeping. Stop your grumbling and come out of that buffalo-robe, or I 'll pull it off for you.'

Jim's words were interspersed with numerous expletives, which gave them great additional effect. Ellis drawled out something in a nasal tone from among the folds of his buffalo-robe; then slowly disengaged himself, rose into a sitting posture, stretched his long arms, yawned hideously, and, finally raising his tall person erect, stood staring about him to all the four quarters of the horizon. Deslauriers's fire was soon blazing, and the horses and mules, loosened from their pickets, were feeding on the neighboring meadow. When we sat down to breakfast the prairie was still in the dusky light of morning; and as the sun rose we were mounted and on our way again.

'A white buffalo!' exclaimed Munroe.

'I 'll have that fellow,' said Shaw, 'if I run my horse to death after him.'

He threw the cover of his gun to Deslauriers and galloped out upon the prairie.

'Stop, Mr Shaw, stop!' called out Henry Chatillon, 'you 'll run down your horse for nothing; it 's only a white ox.'

But Shaw was already out of hearing. The ox, which had no doubt strayed away from some of the government wagon trains, was standing beneath some low hills which bounded the plain in the distance. Not far from him a band of veritable buffalo bulls were grazing; and startled at Shaw's approach, they all broke into a run and went scrambling up the hillsides to gain the high prairie above. One of them in his haste and terror involved himself in a fatal catastrophe. Along the foot of the hills was a narrow strip of deep marshy soil, into which the bull plunged and hopelessly entangled himself. We all rode to the spot. The huge carcass was half sunk in the mud, which flowed to his very chin, and his shaggy mane was outspread upon the surface. As we came near, the bull began to struggle with convulsive strength; he writhed to and fro, and in the energy of his fright and desperation would lift himself for a moment half out of the slough, while the reluctant mire returned a sucking sound as he strained to drag his limbs from its tenacious depths. We stimulated his exertions by getting behind him and twisting his tail; nothing would do. There was clearly no hope for him. After every effort his heaving sides were more deeply imbedded and the mire almost overflowed his nostrils; he lay still at length, and looking round at us with a furious eye, seemed to resign himself to his fate. Ellis slowly dismounted, and, levelling his boasted yager, shot the old bull through the heart; then lazily climbed back again to his seat, pluming himself no doubt on having actually killed a buffalo. That day the redoubtable yager drew blood for the first and last time during the whole journey.

The morning was a bright and gay one, and the air so clear that on the farthest horizon the outline of the pale blue prairie was sharply drawn against the sky. Shaw was in the mood for hunting; he rode in advance of the party, and before long we saw a file of bulls galloping at full speed upon a green swell of the prairie at some distance in front. Shaw came scouring along behind them, arrayed in his red shirt, which looked very well in the distance; he gained fast on the fugitives, and as the foremost bull was disappearing behind the summit of the swell, we saw him in the act of assailing the hindmost; a smoke sprang from the muzzle of his gun and floated away before the wind like a little white cloud; the bull turned upon him, and just then the rising ground concealed them both from view.

We were moving forward until about noon, when we stopped by the side of the Arkansas. At that moment Shaw appeared riding slowly down the side of a distant hill; his horse was tired and jaded, and when he threw his saddle upon the ground, I observed that the tails of two bulls were dangling behind it. No sooner were the horses turned loose to feed than Henry, asking Munroe to go with him, took his rifle and walked quietly away. Shaw, Tête Rouge, and I sat down by the side of the cart to discuss the dinner which Deslauriers placed before us, and we had scarcely finished when we saw Munroe walking towards us along the river bank. Henry, he said, had killed four fat cows and had sent him back for horses to bring in the meat. Shaw took a horse for himself and another for Henry, and he and Munroe left the camp together. After a short absence all three of them came back, their horses loaded with the choicest parts of the meat. We kept two of the cows for ourselves, and gave the others to Munroe and his companions. Deslauriers seated himself on the grass before the pile of meat and worked industriously for some time to cut it into thin broad sheets for drying, an art in which he had all the skill of an Indian squaw. Long before night, cords of raw hide were stretched around the camp, and the meat was hung upon them to dry in the sunshine and pure air of the prairie. Our California companions were less successful at the work; but they accomplished it after their own fashion, and their side of the camp was soon garnished in the same manner as our own.

We meant to remain at this place long enough to prepare provisions for our journey to the frontier, which, as we supposed, might occupy about a month. Had the distance been twice as

great and the party ten times as large, the rifle of Henry Chatillon
would have supplied meat enough for the whole within two days;
we were obliged to remain, however, until it should be dry enough
for transportation; so we pitched our tent and made other arrangements for a permanent camp. The California men who had no
such shelter, contented themselves with arranging their packs
on the grass around their fire. In the meantime we had nothing to
do but amuse ourselves. Our tent was within a rod of the river, if
the broad sand-beds, with a scanty stream of water coursing here
and there along their surface, deserve to be dignified with the
name of river. The vast flat plains on either side were almost on
a level with the sand-beds, and they were bounded in the distance
by low, monotonous hills, parallel to the course of the stream. All
was one expanse of grass; there was no wood in view, except some
trees and stunted bushes upon two islands which rose from the
wet sands of the river. Yet, far from being dull and tame, the scene
was often a wild and animated one; for twice a day, at sunrise and
at noon, the buffalo came issuing from the hills, slowly advancing
in their grave processions to drink at the river. All our amusements were to be at their expense. An old buffalo-bull is a brute
of unparalleled ugliness. At first sight of him every feeling of pity
vanishes. The cows are much smaller and of a gentler appearance,
as becomes their sex. While in this camp we forebore to attack
them, leaving to Henry Chatillon, who could better judge their
quality, the task of killing such as we wanted for use; but against
the bulls we waged an unrelenting war. Thousands of them might
be slaughtered without causing any detriment to the species,
for their numbers greatly exceed those of the cows; it is the hides
of the latter alone which are used for the purposes of commerce
and for making the lodges of the Indians; and the destruction
among them is therefore greatly disproportionate.

Our horses were tired and we now usually hunted on foot.
While we were lying on the grass after dinner, smoking, talking,
or laughing at Tête Rouge, one of us would look up and observe,
far out on the plains beyond the river, certain black objects slowly
approaching. He would inhale a parting whiff from the pipe, then
rising lazily, take his rifle, which leaned against the cart, throw
over his shoulder the strap of his pouch and powder-horn, and
with his moccasins in his hand walk across the sand towards the
opposite side of the river. This was easy; for though the sands
were about a quarter of a mile wide, the water was nowhere more

than two feet deep. The farther bank was about four or five feet high and quite perpendicular, being cut away by the water in spring. Tall grass grew along its edge. Putting it aside with his hand, and cautiously looking through it, the hunter can discern the huge shaggy back of the bull slowly swaying to and fro, as, with his clumsy swinging gait, he advances towards the water. The buffalo have regular paths by which they come down to drink. Seeing at a glance along which of these his intended victim is moving, the hunter crouches under the bank within fifteen or twenty yards, it may be, of the point where the path enters the river. Here he sits down quietly on the sand. Listening intently, he hears the heavy monotonous tread of the approaching bull. The moment after, he sees a motion among the long weeds and grass just at the spot where the path is channelled through the bank. An enormous black head is thrust out, the horns just visible amid the mass of tangled mane. Half sliding, half plunging, down comes the buffalo upon the river-bed below. He steps out in full sight upon the sands. Just before him a runnel of water is gliding, and he bends his head to drink. You may hear the water as it gurgles down his capacious throat. He raises his head, and the drops trickle from his wet beard. He stands with an air of stupid abstraction, unconscious of the lurking danger. Noiselessly the hunter cocks his rifle. As he sits upon the sand, his knee is raised, and his elbow rests upon it, that he may level his heavy weapon with a steadier aim. The stock is at his shoulder; his eye ranges along the barrel. Still he is in no haste to fire. The bull, with slow deliberation, begins his march over the sands to the other side. He advances his foreleg, and exposes to view a small spot, denuded of hair, just behind the point of his shoulder; upon this the hunter brings the sight of his rifle to bear; lightly and delicately his finger presses the hair-trigger. The spiteful crack of the rifle responds to his touch, and instantly in the middle of the bare spot appears a small red dot. The buffalo shivers; death has overtaken him, he cannot tell from whence; still he does not fall, but walks heavily forward, as if nothing had happened. Yet before he has gone far out upon the sand, you see him stop; he totters; his knees bend under him, and his head sinks forward to the ground. Then his whole vast bulk sways to one side; he rolls over on the sand, and dies with a scarcely perceptible struggle.

Waylaying the buffalo in this manner, and shooting them as they come to water, is the easiest method of hunting them. They may also be approached by crawling up ravines, or behind hills, or even over the open prairie. This is often surprisingly easy; but at other times it requires the utmost skill of the most experienced hunter. Henry Chatillon was a man of extraordinary strength and hardihood; but I have seen him return to camp quite exhausted with his efforts, his limbs scratched and wounded, and his buckskin dress stuck full of the thorns of the prickly-pear, among which he had been crawling. Sometimes he would lie flat upon his face, and drag himself along in this position for many rods together.

On the second day of our stay at this place, Henry went out for an afternoon hunt. Shaw and I remained in camp until, observing some bulls approaching the water upon the other side of the river, we crossed over to attack them. They were so near, however, that before we could get under cover of the bank our appearance as we walked over the sands alarmed them. Turning round before coming within gun-shot, they began to move off to the right in a direction parallel to the river. I climbed up the bank and ran after them. They were walking swiftly, and before I could come within gun-shot distance they slowly wheeled about and faced me. Before they had turned far enough to see me I had fallen flat on my face. For a moment they stood and stared at the strange object upon the grass; then, turning away again, they walked on as before; and I, rising immediately, ran once more in pursuit. Again they wheeled about, and again I fell prostrate. Repeating this three or four times, I came at length within a hundred yards of the fugitives, and as I saw them turning again I sat down and levelled my rifle. The one in the centre was the largest I had ever seen. I shot him behind the shoulder. His two companions ran off. He attempted to follow, but soon came to a stand, and at length lay down as quietly as an ox chewing the cud. Cautiously approaching him, I saw by his dull and jelly-like eye that he was dead.

When I began the chase, the prairie was almost tenantless; but a great multitude of buffalo had suddenly thronged upon it, and, looking up, I saw within fifty rods a heavy, dark column stretching to the right and left as far as I could see. I walked towards them. My approach did not alarm them in the least. The column itself consisted almost entirely of cows and calves, but a great many old bulls were ranging about the prairie on its flank, and as I drew near they faced towards me with such a grim and

ferocious look that I thought it best to proceed no farther. Indeed
I was already within close rifle-shot of the column, and I sat down
on the ground to watch their movements. Sometimes the whole
would stand still, their heads all one way; then they would trot
forward, as if by a common impulse, their hoofs and horns
clattering together as they moved. I soon began to hear at a distance on the left the sharp reports of a rifle, again and again repeated; and not long after, dull and heavy sounds succeeded,
which I recognized as the familiar voice of Shaw's double-barrelled
gun. When Henry's rifle was at work there was always meat to be
brought in. I went back across the river for a horse, and, returning,
reached the spot where the hunters were standing. The buffalo
were visible on the distant prairie. The living had retreated from
the ground, but ten or twelve carcasses were scattered in various
directions. Henry, knife in hand, was stooping over a dead cow,
cutting away the best and fattest of the meat.

When Shaw left me he had walked down for some distance
under the river-bank to find another bull. At length he saw the
plains covered with the host of buffalo, and soon after heard the
crack of Henry's rifle. Ascending the bank, he crawled through
the grass, which for a rod or two from the river was very high
and rank. He had not crawled far before to his astonishment he
saw Henry standing erect upon the prairie, almost surrounded by
the buffalo. Henry was in his element. Quite unconscious that any
one was looking at him, he stood at the full height of his tall
figure, one hand resting upon his side, and the other arm leaning
carelessly on the muzzle of his rifle. His eye was ranging over the
singular assemblage around him. Now and then he would select
such a cow as suited him, level his rifle, and shoot her dead; then
quietly reloading, he would resume his former position. The
buffalo seemed no more to regard his presence than if he were one
of themselves; the bulls were bellowing and butting at each other,
or rolling about in the dust. A group of buffalo would gather
about the carcass of a dead cow, snuffing at her wounds; and
sometimes they would come behind those that had not yet fallen
and endeavor to push them from the spot. Now and then some
old bull would face towards Henry with an air of stupid amazement, but none seemed inclined to attack or fly from him. For
some time Shaw lay among the grass, looking in surprise at this
extraordinary sight; at length he crawled cautiously forward, and
spoke in a low voice to Henry, who told him to rise and come on.

Still the buffalo showed no sign of fear; they remained gathered about their dead companions. Henry had already killed as many cows as we wanted for use, and Shaw, kneeling behind one of the carcasses, shot five bulls before the rest thought it necessary to disperse.

The frequent stupidity and infatuation of the buffalo seems the more remarkable from the contrast it offers to their wildness and wariness at other times. Henry knew all their peculiarities; he had studied them as a scholar studies his books, and derived quite as much pleasure from the occupation. The buffalo were companions to him, and, as he said, he never felt alone when they were about him. He took great pride in his skill in hunting. He was one of the most modest of men; yet in the simplicity and frankness of his character, it was clear that he looked upon his pre-eminence in this respect as a thing too palpable and well established to be disputed. But whatever may have been his estimate of his own skill, it was rather below than above that which others placed upon it. The only time that I ever saw a shade of scorn darken his face was when two volunteer soldiers, who had just killed a buffalo for the first time, undertook to instruct him as to the best method of 'approaching.' Henry always seemed to think that he had a sort of prescriptive right to the buffalo, and to look upon them as something belonging to himself. Nothing excited his indignation so much as any wanton destruction committed among the cows, and in his view shooting a calf was a cardinal sin.

Henry Chatillon and Tête Rouge were of the same age; that is, about thirty. Henry was twice as large, and about six times as strong as Tête Rouge. Henry's face was roughened by winds and storms; Tête Rouge's was bloated by sherry-cobblers and brandy-toddy. Henry talked of Indians and buffalo; Tête Rouge of theatres and oyster-cellars. Henry had led a life of hardship and privation; Tête Rouge never had a whim which he would not gratify at the first moment he was able. Henry moreover was the most disinterested man I ever saw; while Tête Rouge, though equally good-natured in his way, cared for nobody but himself. Yet we would not have lost him on any account; he served the purpose of a jester in a feudal castle; our camp would have been lifeless without him. For the past week he had fattened in a most amazing manner; and, indeed this was not at all surprising, since his appetite was inordinate. He was eating from morning till

night; half the time he would be at work cooking some private
mess for himself, and he paid a visit to the coffee-pot eight or ten
times a day. His rueful and disconsolate face became jovial and
rubicund, his eyes stood out like a lobster's, and his spirits, which
before were sunk to the depths of despondency, were now elated
in proportion; all day he was singing, whistling, laughing, and
telling stories. Being mortally afraid of Jim Gurney, he kept close
in the neighborhood of our tent. As he had seen an abundance of
low fast life, and had a considerable fund of humor, his anecdotes
were extremely amusing, especially since he never hesitated to
place himself in a ludicrous point of view, provided he could raise
a laugh by doing so. Tête Rouge, however, was sometimes rather
troublesome; he had an inveterate habit of pilfering provisions at
all times of the day. He set ridicule at defiance; and would never
have given over his tricks, even if they had drawn upon him the
scorn of the whole party. Now and then, indeed, something worse
than laughter fell to his share; on these occasions he would exhibit
much contrition, but half an hour after we would generally observe
him stealing round to the box at the back of the cart, and slyly
making off with the provisions which Deslauriers had laid by for
supper. He was fond of smoking; but having no tobacco of his
own, we used to provide him with as much as he wanted, a small
piece at a time. At first we gave him half a pound together; but
this experiment proved an entire failure, for he invariably lost not
only the tobacco, but the knife intrusted to him for cutting it, and
a few minutes after he would come to us with many apologies and
beg for more.

We had been two days at this camp, and some of the meat was
nearly fit for transportation, when a storm came suddenly upon
us. About sunset the whole sky grew as black as ink, and the long
grass at the edge of the river bent and rose mournfully with the
first gusts of the approaching hurricane. Munroe and his two companions brought their guns and placed them under cover of our
tent. Having no shelter for themselves, they built a fire of drift-
wood that might have defied a cataract, and, wrapped in their
buffalo-robes, sat on the ground around it to bide the fury of the
storm. Delauriers ensconced himself under the cover of the cart.
Shaw and I, together with Henry and Tête Rouge, crowded into
the little tent; but first of all the dried meat was piled together,
and well protected by buffalo-robes pinned firmly to the ground.
About nine o'clock the storm broke amid absolute darkness; it

blew a gale, and torrents of rain roared over the boundless expanse of open prairie. Our tent was filled with mist and spray beating through the canvas, and saturating everything within. We could only distinguish each other at short intervals by the dazzling flashes of lightning, which displayed the whole waste around us with its momentary glare. We had our fears for the tent; but for an hour or two it stood fast, until at length the cap gave way before a furious blast; the pole tore through the top, and in an instant we were half suffocated by the cold and dripping folds of the canvas, which fell down upon us. Seizing upon our guns we placed them erect, in order to lift the saturated cloth above our heads. In this agreeable situation, involved among wet blankets and buffalo-robes, we spent several hours of the night, during which the storm would not abate for a moment, but pelted down with merciless fury. Before long the water gathered beneath us in a pool two or three inches deep; so that for a considerable part of the night we were partially immersed in a cold bath. In spite of all this, Tête Rouge's flow of spirits did not fail him; he laughed, whistled, and sang in defiance of the storm, and that night paid off the long arrears of ridicule which he owed us. While we lay in silence, enduring the infliction with what philosophy we could muster, Tête Rouge, who was intoxicated with animal spirits, cracked jokes at our expense by the hour together.

At about three o'clock in the morning, preferring 'the tyranny of the open night' to such a wretched shelter, we crawled out from beneath the fallen canvas. The wind had abated, but the rain fell steadily. The fire of the California men still blazed amid the darkness, and we joined them as they sat around it. We made ready some hot coffee by way of refreshment; but when some of the party sought to replenish their cups, it was found that Tête Rouge, having disposed of his own share, had privately abstracted the coffee-pot and drunk the rest of the contents out of the spout.

In the morning, to our great joy, an unclouded sun rose upon the prairie. We presented a rather laughable appearance; for the cold and clammy buckskin, saturated with water, clung fast to our limbs. The light wind and warm sunshine soon dried it again, and then we were all encased in armor of intolerable stiffness. Roaming all day over the prairie and shooting two or three bulls were scarcely enough to restore the stiffened leather to its usual pliancy.

Besides Henry Chatillon, Shaw and I were the only hunters in the party. Munroe this morning made an attempt to run a buffalo, but his horse could not come up to the game. Shaw went out with him, and being better mounted soon found himself in the midst of the herd. Seeing nothing but cows and calves around him, he checked his horse. An old bull came galloping on the open prairie at some distance behind; and turning, Shaw rode across his path, levelling his gun as he passed, and shooting him through the shoulder into the heart.

A great flock of buzzards was usually soaring about a few trees that stood on the island just below our camp. Throughout the whole of yesterday we had noticed an eagle among them; to-day he was still there; and Tête Rouge, declaring that he would kill the bird of America, borrowed Deslauriers's gun and set out on his unpatriotic errand. As might have been expected, the eagle suffered no harm at his hands. He soon returned, saying that he could not find him, but had shot a buzzard instead. Being required to produce the bird in proof of his assertion, he said he believed that he was not quite dead, but he must be hurt from the swiftness with which he flew off.

'If you want,' said Tête Rouge, 'I'll go and get one of his feathers; I knocked off plenty of them when I shot him.'

Just opposite our camp was another island covered with bushes, and behind it was a deep pool of water, while two or three considerable streams coursed over the sand not far off. I was bathing at this place in the afternoon when a white wolf, larger than the largest Newfoundland dog, ran out from behind the point of the island, and galloped leisurely over the sand not half a stone's-throw distant. I could plainly see his red eyes and the bristles about his snout; he was an ugly scoundrel, with a bushy tail, a large head, and a most repulsive countenance. Having neither rifle to shoot nor stone to pelt him with, I was looking after some missile for his benefit, when the report of a gun came from the camp, and the ball threw up the sand just beyond him; at this he gave a slight jump, and stretched away so swiftly that he soon dwindled into a mere speck on the distant sand-beds. The number of carcasses that by this time were lying about the neighboring prairie summoned the wolves from every quarter; the spot where Shaw and Henry had hunted together soon became their favorite resort, for here about a dozen dead buffalo were fermenting under the hot sun. I used often to go over the river and watch them at their meal. By lying under the bank it was easy to get a full view of them. There were three different kinds: the white wolves and the gray wolves, both very large, and besides these the small prairie wolves, not much bigger than spaniels. They would howl and fight in a crowd around a single carcass, yet they were so watchful, and their senses so acute, that I never was able to crawl within a fair shooting distance; whenever I attempted it, they would all scatter at once and glide silently away through the tall grass. The air above this spot was always full of turkey-buzzards or black vultures; whenever the wolves left a carcass they would descend upon it, and cover it so densely that a rifle bullet shot at random among the gormandizing crowd would generally strike down two or three of them. These birds would often sail by scores just above our camp, their broad black wings seeming half transparent, as they expanded them against the bright sky. The wolves and the buzzards thickened about us every hour, and two or three eagles also came to the feast. I killed a bull within rifle-shot of the camp; that night the wolves made a fearful howling close at hand, and in the morning the carcass was completely hollowed out by these voracious feeders.

After remaining four days at this camp we prepared to leave it. We had for our own part about five hundred pounds of dried meat, and the California men had prepared some three hundred more; this consisted of the fattest and choicest parts of eight or nine cows, a small quantity only being taken from each, and the rest abandoned to the wolves. The pack animals were laden, the horses saddled, and the mules harnessed to the cart. Even Tête Rouge was ready at last, and slowly moving from the ground, we resumed our journey eastward. When we had advanced about a mile, Shaw missed a valuable hunting-knife, and turned back in search of it, thinking that he had left it at the camp. The day was dark and gloomy. The ashes of the fires were still smoking by the river-side; the grass around them was trampled down by men and horses, and strewn with all the litter of a camp. Our departure had been a gathering signal to the birds and beasts of prey. Scores of wolves were prowling about the smouldering fires, while multitudes were roaming over the neighboring prairie; they all fled as Shaw approached, some running over the sand-beds and some over the grassy plains. The vultures in great clouds were soaring overhead, and the dead bull near the camp was completely blackened by the flock that had alighted upon it; they flapped their broad wings, and stretched upward their crested head and long skinny necks, fearing to remain, yet reluctant to leave their disgusting feast. As he searched about the fires he saw the wolves seated on the hills waiting for his departure. Having looked in vain for his knife, he mounted again, and left the wolves and the vultures to banquet undisturbed.

26. Down the Arkansas

In the summer of 1846 the wild and lonely banks of the Upper
Arkansas beheld for the first time the passage of an army. General
Kearney, on his march to Santa Fé, adopted this route in preference to the old trail of the Cimarron. When we were on the
Arkansas the main body of the troops had already passed on;
Price's Missouri regiment, however, was still on its way, having
left the frontier much later than the rest; and about this time we
began to meet one or two companies at a time moving along the
trail. No men ever embarked upon a military expedition with a
greater love for the work before them than the Missourians; but
if discipline and subordination are the criterion of merit, they
were worthless soldiers indeed. Yet when their exploits have rung
through all America, it would be absurd to deny that they were

excellent irregular troops. Their victories were gained in the teeth of every established precedent of warfare; and were owing to a combination of military qualities in the men themselves. Doniphan's regiment marched through New Mexico more like a band of free companions than like the paid soldiers of a modern government. When General Taylor complimented him on his success at Sacramento and elsewhere, the Colonel's reply very well illustrates the relations which subsisted between the officers and men of his command.

'I don't know anything of the manœuvres. The boys kept coming to me to let them charge; and when I saw a good opportunity, I told them they might go. They were off like a shot, and that's all I know about it.'

The backwoods lawyer was better fitted to conciliate the goodwill than to command the obedience of his men. There were many serving under him, who both from character and education could better have held command than he.

At the battle of Sacramento his frontiersmen fought under every disadvantage. The Mexicans had chosen their position; they were drawn up across the valley that led to their native city of Chihuahua; their whole front was covered by intrenchments and defended by batteries, and they outnumbered the invaders five to one. An eagle flew over the Americans, and a deep murmur rose along their lines. The enemy's batteries opened; long they remained under fire, but when at length the word was given, they shouted and ran forward. In one of the divisions, when mid-way to the enemy, a drunken officer ordered a halt; the exasperated men hesitated to obey.

'Forward, boys!' cried a private from the ranks; and the Americans rushed like tigers upon the enemy. Four hundred Mexicans were slain upon the spot and the rest fled, scattering over the plain like sheep. The standards, cannon, and baggage were taken, and among the rest a wagon laden with cords, which the Mexicans, in the fulness of their confidence, had made ready for tying the American prisoners.

Doniphan's volunteers, who gained this victory, passed up with the main army; but Price's soldiers, whom we now met were men from the same neighborhood, precisely similar in character, manners, and appearance. One morning, as we were descending upon a wide meadow, where we meant to rest for an hour or two, we saw a body of horsemen approaching at a distance. In order to

find water, we were obliged to turn aside to the river bank, a full
half-mile from the trail. Here we put up a kind of awning, and
spreading buffalo-robes on the ground Shaw and I sat down to
smoke.

'We are going to catch it, now,' said Shaw; 'look at those fellows; there 'll be no peace for us here.'

And in truth about half the volunteers had straggled away from
the line of march, and were riding over the meadow towards us.

'How are you?' said the first who came up, alighting from his
horse and throwing himself upon the ground. The rest followed
close, and a score of them soon gathered about us, some lying at
full length and some sitting on horseback. They all belonged to a
company raised in St Louis. There were some ruffian faces among
them, and some haggard with debauchery; but on the whole they
were extremely good-looking men, superior beyond measure to the
ordinary rank and file of an army. Except that they were booted
to the knees, they wore their belts and military trappings over the
ordinary dress of citizens. Besides their swords and holster pistols,
they carried slung from their saddles the excellent Springfield
carbines, loaded at the breech. They inquired the character of our
party, and were anxious to know the prospect of killing buffalo,
and the chance that their horses would stand the journey to
Santa Fé. All this was well enough, but a moment after a worse
visitation came upon us.

'How are you, strangers? whar are you going, and whar are you
from?' said a fellow who came trotting up with an old straw hat
on his head. He was dressed in the coarsest brown homespun
cloth. His face was rather sallow from fever-and-ague, and his tall
figure, though strong and sinewy, had a lean angular look, which,
together with his boorish seat on horseback, gave him an appearance anything but graceful. More of the same stamp were close
behind him. Their company was raised in one of the frontier counties, and we soon had abundant evidences of their rustic breeding;
they came crowding round by scores, pushing between our first
visitors, and staring at us with unabashed faces.

'Are you the captain?' asked one fellow.

'What 's your business out here?' asked another.

'Whar do you live when you 're to home?' said a third.

'I reckon you 're traders,' surmised a fourth; and to crown the
whole, one of them came confidentially to my side and inquired
in a low voice, 'What 's your partner's name?'

As each new-comer repeated the same questions, the nuisance
became intolerable. Our military visitors were soon disgusted at
the concise nature of our replies, and we could overhear them
muttering curses. While we sat smoking, not in the best imaginable humor, Tête Rouge's tongue was not idle. He never forgot
his military character, and during the whole interview he was incessantly busy among his fellow-soldiers. At length we placed him
on the ground before us, and told him that he might play the
part of spokesman. Tête Rouge was delighted, and we soon had
the satisfaction of seeing him gabble at such a rate that the torrent of questions was in a great measure diverted from us. A little
while after, a cannon with four horses came lumbering up behind
the crowd; and the driver, who was perched on one of the animals,
stretching his neck so as to look over the rest of the men, called
out,—

'Whar are you from, and what 's your business?'

The captain of one of the companies was among our visitors,
drawn by the same curiosity that had attracted his men. Unless
their faces belied them, not a few in the crowd might with great
advantage have changed places with their commander.

'Well, men,' said he, lazily rising from the ground where he had
been lounging, 'it 's getting late; I reckon we 'd better be moving.'

'I sha'n't start yet anyhow,' said one fellow, who was lying
half asleep with his head resting on his arm.

'Don't be in a hurry, Captain,' added the lieutenant.

'Well, have it your own way, we 'll wait a while longer,' replied
the obsequious commander.

At length, however, our visitors went straggling away as they
had come, and we, to our great relief, were left alone again.

No one was more relieved than Deslauriers by the departure of
the volunteers; for dinner was getting colder every moment. He
spread a well-whitened buffalo-hide upon the grass, placed in the
middle the juicy hump of a fat cow, ranged around it the tin plates
and cups, and then announced that all was ready. Tête Rouge,
with his usual alacrity on such occasions, was the first to take his
seat. In his former capacity of steamboat clerk, he had learned
to prefix the honorary *Mister* to everybody's name, whether of
high or low degree; so Jim Gurney was Mr Gurney, Henry was
Mr Henry, and even Deslauriers, for the first time in his life, heard
himself addressed as Mr Deslauriers. This did not prevent his con-
ceiving a violent enmity against Tête Rouge, who, in his futile

though praiseworthy attempts to make himself useful, always intermeddled with cooking the dinners. Deslauriers's disposition knew no medium between smiles and sunshine and a downright tornado of wrath; he said nothing to Tête Rouge, but his wrongs rankled in his breast. Tête Rouge had taken his place at dinner; it was his happiest moment; he sat enveloped in the old buffalo-coat, sleeves turned up in preparation for the work, and his short legs crossed on the grass before him; he had a cup of coffee by his side and his knife ready in his hand, and while he looked upon the fat hump ribs, his eyes dilated with anticipation. Deslauriers sat opposite to him, and the rest of us by this time had taken our seats.

'How is this, Deslauriers? You have n't given us bread enough.'

At this Deslauriers's placid face flew into a paroxysm of contortions. He grinned with wrath, chattered, gesticulated, and hurled forth a volley of incoherent words in broken English at the astonished Tête Rouge. It was just possible to make out that he was accusing him of having stolen and eaten four large cakes which had been laid by for dinner. Tête Rouge, confounded at this sudden attack, stared at his assailant for a moment in dumb amazement, with mouth and eyes wide open. At last he found speech, and protested that the accusation was false; and that he could not conceive how he had offended Mr Deslauriers, or provoked him to use such ungentlemanly expressions. The tempest of words raged with such fury that nothing else could be heard. But Tête Rouge, from his greater command of Engli h, had a manifest advantage over Deslauriers, who, after sputtering and grimacing for a while, found his words quite inadequate to the expression of his wrath. He jumped up and vanished, jerking out between his teeth one furious *Sacré enfant de garce!* a Canadian title of honor, made doubly emphatic by being usually applied, together with a cut of the whip, to refractory mules and horses.

The next morning we saw an old buffalo-bull escorting his cow with two small calves over the prairie. Close behind came four or five large white wolves, sneaking stealthily through the long meadow-grass, and watching for the moment when one of the children should chance to lag behind his parents. The old bull kept well on his guard, and faced about now and then to keep the prowling ruffians at a distance.

As we approached our nooning-place we saw five or six buffalo standing at the summit of a tall bluff. Trotting forward to the spot where we meant to stop, I flung off my saddle and turned my horse loose. By making a circuit under cover of some rising ground I reached the foot of the bluff unnoticed, and climbed up its steep side. Lying under the brow of the declivity, I prepared to fire at the buffalo, who stood on the flat surface above, not five yards distant. The gleaming rifle-barrel levelled over the edge caught their notice, and they turned and ran. Close as they were, it was impossible to kill them when in that position, and stepping upon the summit, I pursued them over the high, arid table-land. It was extremely rugged and broken; a great sandy ravine was channelled through it, with smaller ravines entering on each side like tributary streams. The buffalo scattered, and I soon lost sight of most of them as they scuttled away through the sandy chasms; a bull and a cow alone kept in view. For a while they ran along the edge of the great ravine, appearing and disappearing as they dived into some chasm and again emerged from it. At last they stretched out upon the broad prairie, a plain nearly flat and almost devoid of verdure, for every short grass-blade was dried and shrivelled by the glaring sun. Now and then the old bull would face towards me; whenever he did so I fell to the ground and lay motionless. In this manner I chased them for about two miles, until at length I heard in front a deep hoarse bellowing. A moment after, a band of about a hundred bulls, before hidden by a slight swell of the plain, came at once into view. The fugitives ran towards them. Instead of mingling with the band, as I expected, they passed directly through, and continued their flight. At this I gave up the chase, crawled to within gun-shot of the bulls, and sat down on the ground to watch them. My presence did not disturb them in the least. They were not feeding, for there was nothing to eat; but they seemed to have chosen the parched and scorching desert as their play-ground. Some were rolling on the ground amid a cloud of dust; others, with a hoarse rumbling bellow, were butting their large heads together, while many stood motionless, as if quite inanimate. Except their monstrous growth of tangled, grizzly mane, they had no hair; for their old coat had fallen off in the spring, and their new one had not as yet appeared. Sometimes an old bull would step forward, and gaze at me with a grim and stupid countenance; then he would turn and butt his next neighbor; then he would lie down and roll in the dust, kicking his hoofs in the air. When satisfied with this amusement, he would jerk his head and shoulders upward, and resting on his forelegs, stare at me in this position, half blinded by his mane, and his face covered with dirt; then up he would spring upon all fours, shake his dusty sides, turn half round, and stand with his beard touching the ground, in an attitude of profound abstraction, as if reflecting on his puerile conduct. 'You are too ugly to live,' thought I; and aiming at the ugliest, I shot three of them in succession. The rest were not at all discomposed at this; they kept on bellowing, butting, and rolling on the ground as before. Henry Chatillon always cautioned us to keep perfectly quiet in the presence of a wounded buffalo, for any movement is apt to excite him to make an attack; so I sat still upon the ground, loading and firing with as little motion as possible. While I was thus employed a spectator made his appearance: a little antelope came running up to within fifty yards; and there it stood, its slender neck arched, its small horns thrown back, and its large dark eyes gazing on me with a look of eager curiosity. By the side of the shaggy and brutish monsters before me, it seemed like some lovely young girl in a den of robbers or a nest of bearded pirates. The buffalo looked uglier than ever. 'Here goes for another of you,' thought I, feeling in my pouch for a percussion-cap. Not a percussion-cap was there. My good rifle was useless as an old iron bar. One of the wounded bulls had not yet fallen, and I waited for some time, hoping every moment that his strength would fail him. He still stood firm, look-ing grimly at me; and disregarding Henry's advice, I rose and walked away. Many of the bulls turned and looked at me, but the wounded brute made no attack. I soon came upon a deep ravine which would give me shelter in case of emergency; so I turned around and threw a stone at the bulls. They received it with the utmost indifference. Feeling myself insulted at their refusal to be frightened, I swung my hat, shouted, and made a show of running towards them; at this they crowded together and galloped off, leaving their dead and wounded upon the field. As I moved to-wards the camp I saw the last survivor totter and fall dead. My speed in returning was wonderfully quickened by the reflection that the Pawnees were abroad, and that I was defenceless in case of meeting with an enemy. I saw no living thing, however, except two or three squalid old bulls scrambling among the sand-hills that flanked the great ravine. When I reached camp the party were nearly ready for the afternoon move.

We encamped that evening at a short distance from the river bank. About midnight, as we all lay asleep on the ground, the man nearest me, gently reaching out his hand, touched my shoulder, and cautioned me at the same time not to move. It was bright starlight. Opening my eyes and slightly turning, I saw a large white wolf moving stealthily around the embers of our fire, with his nose close to the ground. Disengaging my hand from the blanket, I drew the cover from my rifle, which lay close at my side; the motion alarmed the wolf, and with long leaps he bounded out of the camp. Jumping up, I fired after him, when he was about thirty yards distant; the melancholy hum of the bullet sounded far away through the night. At the sharp report, so suddenly breaking upon the stillness, all the men sprang up.

'You 've killed him!' said one of them.

'No I have n't,' said I; 'there he goes, running along the river.'

'Then there 's two of them. Don't you see that one lying out yonder?'

We went out to it, and instead of a dead white wolf, found the bleached skull of a buffalo. I had missed my mark, and what was worse had grossly violated a standing law of the prairie. When in a dangerous part of the country, it is considered highly imprudent to fire a gun after encamping, lest the report should reach the ears of Indians.

The horses were saddled in the morning, and the last man had lighted his pipe at the dying ashes of the fire. The beauty of the day enlivened us all. Even Ellis felt its influence, and occasionally made a remark as we rode along; and Jim Gurney told endless stories of his cruisings in the United States service. The buffalo were abundant, and at length a large band of them went running up the hills on the left.

'Too good a chance to lose!' said Shaw. We lashed our horses and galloped after them. Shaw killed one with each barrel of his gun. I separated another from the herd and shot him. The small bullet of the rifle-pistol striking too far back did not immediately take effect, and the bull ran on with unabated speed. Again and again I snapped the remaining pistol at him. I primed it afresh three or four times, and each time it missed fire, for the touch-hole was clogged up. Returning it to the holster, I began to load the empty pistol, still galloping by the side of the bull. By this time he had grown desperate. The foam flew from his jaws and his tongue lolled out. Before the pistol was loaded he sprang upon me, and followed up his attack with a furious rush. The only alternative was to run away or be killed. I took to flight, and the bull, bristling with fury, pursued me closely. The pistol was soon ready, and then looking back I saw his head five or six yards behind my horse's tail. To fire at it would be useless, for a bullet flattens against the adamantine skull of a buffalo bull. Inclining my body to the left, I turned my horse in that direction as sharply as his speed would permit. The bull, rushing blindly on with great force and weight, did not turn so quickly. As I looked back, his neck and shoulder were exposed to view; and turning in the saddle, I shot a bullet through them obliquely into his vitals. He gave over the chase and soon fell to the ground. An English tourist represents a situation like this as one of imminent danger. This is a mistake; the bull never pursues long, and the horse must be wretched indeed that cannot keep out of his way for two or three minutes.

We were now come to a part of the country where we were bound in common prudence to use every possible precaution. We mounted guard at night, each man standing in his turn; and no one ever slept without drawing his rifle close to his side or folding it with him in his blanket. One morning our vigilance was stimulated by finding traces of a large Camanche encampment. Fortunately for us, however, it had been abandoned nearly a week. On the next evening we found the ashes of a recent fire, which gave us at the time some uneasiness. At length we reached the Caches, a place of dangerous repute; and it had a most dangerous appearance, consisting of sand-hills everywhere broken by ravines and deep chasms. Here we found the grave of Swan, killed at this place, probably by the Pawnees, two or three weeks before. His remains, more than once violated by the Indians and the wolves, were suffered at length to remain undisturbed in their wild burial-place.

For several days we met detached companies of Price's regiment. Horses would often break loose at night from their camps. One afternoon we picked up three of these stragglers quietly grazing along the river. After we came to camp that evening, Jim Gurney brought news that more of them were in sight. It was nearly dark, and a cold, drizzling rain had set in; but we all turned out, and after an hour's chase nine horses were caught and brought in. One of them was equipped with saddle and bridle; pistols were hanging at the pommel of the saddle, a carbine was slung at its side, and a blanket rolled up behind it. In the morning, as we resumed our journey, our cavalcade presented a much more imposing appearance than ever before. We kept on till the afternoon, when, far behind, three horsemen appeared on the horizon. Coming on at a hand-gallop, they soon overtook us, and claimed all the horses as belonging to themselves and others of their company. Proof of ownership being shown, they were of course given up, very much to the mortification of Ellis and Jim Gurney.

Our own horses now showed signs of fatigue, and we resolved to give them half a day's rest. We stopped at noon at a grassy spot by the river. After dinner Shaw and Henry went out to hunt; and while the men lounged about the camp, I lay down to read in the shadow of the cart. Looking up, I saw a bull grazing alone on the prairie more than a mile distant, and taking my rifle I walked towards him. As I came near, I crawled upon the ground until I approached to within a hundred yards; here I sat down upon the grass and waited till he should turn himself into a proper position to receive his death-wound. He was a grim old veteran. His loves and his battles were over for that season, and now, gaunt and war-worn, he had withdrawn from the herd to graze by himself and recruit his exhausted strength. He was miserably emaciated; his mane was all in tatters; his hide was bare and rough as an elephant's, and covered with dried patches of the mud in which he had been wallowing. He showed all his ribs whenever he moved. He looked like some grizzly old ruffian grown gray in blood and violence, and scowling on all the world from his misanthropic seclusion. The old savage looked up when I first approached and gave me a fierce stare; then he fell to grazing again with an air of contemptuous indifference. The moment after, as if suddenly recollecting himself, he threw up his head, faced quickly about, and to my amazement came at a rapid trot directly towards me. I was strongly impelled to get up and run, but this would have been very dangerous. Sitting quite still, I aimed, as he came on, at the thin part of the skull above the nose, hoping that the shot might have the effect of turning him. After he had passed over about three quarters of the distance between us, I was on the point of firing, when, to my great satisfaction, he stopped short. I had full opportunity of studying his countenance; his whole front was covered with a huge mass of coarse, matted hair, which hung so low that nothing but his two forefeet were visible beneath it; his short, thick horns were blunted and split to the roots in his various battles, and across his nose and forehead were two or three large white scars, which gave him a grim, and at the same time a whimsical appearance. It seemed to me that he stood there motionless for a full quarter of an hour staring at me through the tangled locks of his mane. For my part I remained as quiet as he, and looked quite as hard. I felt greatly inclined to come to terms with him. 'My friend,' thought I, 'if you 'll let me off, I 'll let you off.' At length he seemed to have abandoned any hostile design. Very slowly and deliberately he began to turn about; little by little his side came into view, all beplastered with mud. It was a tempting sight. I forgot my prudent intentions, and fired my rifle; a pistol would have served at that distance. The old bull spun round like a top, and galloped away over the prairie. He ran some distance, and even ascended a considerable hill, before he lay down and died. After shooting another bull among the hills, I went back to camp.

At noon, on the fourteenth of September, a very large Santa Fé caravan came up. The plain was covered with the long files of their white-topped wagons, the close black carriages in which the traders travel and sleep, large droves of mules and horses, and men on horseback and on foot. They all stopped on the meadow near us. Our diminutive cart and handful of men made but an insignificant figure by the side of their wide and bustling camp. Tête Rouge went to visit them, and soon came back with half a dozen biscuits in one hand, and a bottle of brandy in the other. I inquired where he got them. 'Oh,' said Tête Rouge, 'I know some of the traders. Dr Dobbs is there besides.' I asked who Dr Dobbs might be. 'One of our St Louis doctors,' replied Tête Rouge. For two days past I had been severely attacked by the same disorder which had so greatly reduced my strength when at the mountains; at this time I was suffering not a little from pain and weakness. Tête Rouge, in answer to my inquiries, declared that Dr Dobbs was a physician of the first standing. Without at all believing him, I resolved to consult this eminent practitioner. Walking over to the camp, I found him lying sound asleep under one of the wagons. He offered in his own person but indifferent evidence of his skill, for it was five months since I had seen so cadaverous a face. His hat had fallen off, and his yellow hair was all in disorder; one of his arms supplied the place of a pillow; his trousers were wrinkled half-way up to his knees, and he was covered with little bits of grass and straw upon which he had rolled in his uneasy slumber. A Mexican stood near, and I made him a sign to touch the doctor.

Up sprang the learned Dobbs, and sitting upright rubbed his eyes and looked about him in bewilderment. I regretted the necessity of disturbing him, and said I had come to ask professional advice.

'Your system, sir, is in a disordered state,' said he, solemnly, after a short examination.

I inquired what might be the particular species of disorder.

'Evidently a morbid action of the liver,' replied the medical man; 'I will give you a prescription.'

Repairing to the back of one of the covered wagons, he scrambled in; for a moment I could see nothing of him but his boots. At length he produced a box which he had extracted from some dark recess within, and, opening it, presented me with a folded paper. 'What is it?' said I. 'Calomel,' said the doctor.

Under the circumstances I would have taken almost anything. There was not enough to do me much harm. and it might possibly do good; so at camp that night I took the poison instead of supper.

That camp is worthy of notice. The traders warned us not to follow the main trail along the river, 'unless,' as one of them observed, 'you want to have your throats cut!' The river at this place makes a bend; and a smaller trail, known as 'the Ridge-path,' leads directly across the prairie from point to point, a distance of sixty or seventy miles.

We followed this trail, and after travelling seven or eight miles came to a small stream, where we encamped. Our position was not chosen with much forethought or military skill. The water was in a deep hollow, with steep, high banks; on the grassy bottom of this hollow we picketed our horses, while we ourselves encamped upon the barren prairie just above. The opportunity was admirable either for driving off our horses or attacking us. After dark, as Tête Rouge was sitting at supper, we observed him pointing, with a face of speechless horror, over the shoulder of Henry, who was opposite to him. Aloof amid the darkness appeared a gigantic black apparition solemnly swaying to and fro as it advanced steadily upon us. Henry, half-vexed and half-amused, jumped up, spread out his arms, and shouted. The invader was an old buffalo-bull, who, with characteristic stupidity, was walking directly into camp. It cost some shouting and swinging of hats before we could bring him first to a halt and then to a rapid retreat.

The moon was full and bright, but as the black clouds chased rapidly over it, we were at one moment in light and at the next in darkness. As the evening advanced, a thunder-storm came up and struck us with such violence that the tent would have been blown over if we had not interposed the cart to break the force of the wind. At length it subsided to a steady rain. I lay awake through nearly the whole night, listening to its dull patter upon the canvas above. The moisture, which filled the tent and trickled from everything in it, did not add to the comfort of the situation. About twelve o'clock Shaw went out to stand guard amid the rain and pitchy darkness. Munroe was also on the alert. When about two hours had passed, Shaw came silently in, and, touching Henry, called to him in a low, quick voice to come out. 'What is it?' I asked. 'Indians, I believe,' whispered Shaw; 'but lie still; I 'll call you if there 's going to be a fight.'

He and Henry went out together. I took the cover from my rifle, put a fresh percussion-cap upon it, and then, being in much pain, lay down again. In about five minutes Shaw returned. 'All right,' he said, as he lay down to sleep. Henry was now standing guard in his place. He told me in the morning the particulars of the alarm. Munroe's watchful eye had discovered some dark objects down in the hollow, among the horses, like men creeping on all fours. Lying flat on their faces, he and Shaw crawled to the edge of the bank, and were soon convinced that these dark objects were Indians. Shaw silently withdrew to call Henry, and they all lay watching in the same position. Henry's eye is one of the best on the prairie. He detected after a while the true nature of the intruders; they were nothing but wolves creeping among the horses.

It is very singular that, when picketed near a camp, horses seldom show any fear of such an intrusion. The wolves appear to have no other object than that of gnawing the trail-ropes of raw hide by which the animals are secured. Several times in the course of the journey my horse's trail-rope was bitten in two by these nocturnal visitors.

27. The Settlements

The next day was extremely hot, and we rode from morning till night without seeing a tree, a bush, or a drop of water. Our horses and mules suffered much more than we, but as sunset approached, they pricked up their ears and mended their pace. Water was not far off. When we came to the descent of the broad, shallow valley where it lay, an unlooked-for sight awaited us. The stream glistened at the bottom, and along its banks were pitched a multitude of tents, while hundreds of cattle were feeding over the meadows. Bodies of troops, both horse and foot, and long trains of wagons, with men, women, and children, were moving over the opposite ridge and descending the broad declivity before us. These were the Mormon battalion in the service of government, together with a considerable number of Missouri volunteers. The Mormons were to be paid off in California, and they were allowed to bring with them their families and property. There was something very striking in the half-military, half-patriarchal appearance of these armed fanatics, thus on their way, with their wives and children, to found, it might be, a Mormon empire in California. We were much more astonished than pleased at the sight before us. In order to find an unoccupied camping ground, we were obliged to pass a quarter of a mile up the stream, and here we were soon beset by a swarm of Mormons and Missourians. The United States officer in command of the whole came also to visit us, and remained some time at our camp.

In the morning the country was covered with mist. We were always early risers, but before we were ready, the voices of men driving in the cattle sounded all around us. As we passed above their camp, we saw through the obscurity that the tents were falling, and the ranks rapidly forming; and, mingled with the cries of women and children, the rolling of the Mormon drums and the clear blast of their trumpets sounded through the mist.

From that time to the journey's end, we met almost every day long trains of government wagons laden with stores for the troops, crawling at a snail's pace towards Santa Fé.

Tête Rouge had a mortal antipathy to danger, but one evening he achieved an adventure more perilous than had befallen any man in the party. The day after we left the Ridge-path we encamped close to the river, and at sunset saw a train of wagons encamping on the trail, about three miles off. Though we saw them distinctly, we and our little cart, as it afterward proved, entirely escaped their notice. For some days Tête Rouge had been longing for a dram of whiskey. So, resolving to improve the present opportunity, he mounted his horse 'James,' which he had obtained from the volunteers in exchange for his mule, slung his canteen over his shoulder, and set out in search of his favorite liquor. Some hours passed without his returning. We thought that he was lost, or perhaps that some stray Indian had snapped him up. While the rest fell asleep I remained on guard. Late at night a tremulous voice saluted me from the darkness, and Tête Rouge and James soon became visible, advancing towards the camp. Tête Rouge was in much agitation and big with important tidings. Sitting down on the shaft of the cart, he told the following story:—

When he left the camp he had no idea, he said, how late it was. By the time he approached the wagoners it was perfectly dark;

and as he saw them all sitting around their fires within the circle of wagons, their guns laid by their sides, he thought he might as well give warning of his approach, in order to prevent a disagreeable mistake. Raising his voice to the highest pitch, he screamed out in prolonged accents, 'Camp ahoy!' This eccentric salutation produced anything but the desired effect. Hearing such hideous sounds proceeding from the outer darkness, the wagoners thought that the whole Pawnee nation was upon them. Up they sprang, wild with terror. Each man snatched his gun; some stood behind the wagons; some threw themselves flat on the ground, and in an instant twenty cocked muskets were levelled full at the horrified Tête Rouge, who just then began to be visible through the gloom.

'Thar they come!' cried the master wagoner. 'Fire! fire! shoot that feller!'

'No, no!' screamed Tête Rouge, in an ecstasy of fright; 'don't fire, don't; I 'm a friend, I 'm an American citizen!'

'You 're a friend, be you?' cried a gruff voice from the wagons; 'then what are you yellin' out thar for like a wild Injun. Come along up here if you 're a man.'

'Keep your guns p'inted at him,' added the master wagoner; 'maybe he 's a decoy, like.'

Tête Rouge in utter bewilderment made his approach, with the gaping muzzles of the muskets still before his eyes. He succeeded at last in explaining his true character, and the Missourians admitted him into camp. He got no whiskey; but as he represented himself as a great invalid, and suffering much from coarse fare, they made up a contribution for him of rice, biscuit, and sugar from their own rations.

In the morning at breakfast Tête Rouge once more related this story. We hardly knew how much of it to believe, though after some cross-questioning we failed to discover any flaw in the narrative. Passing by the wagoner's camp, they confirmed Tête Rouge's account in every particular.

'I would n't have been in that feller's place,' said one of them, 'for the biggest heap of money in Missouri.'

A day or two after, we had an adventure of another sort with a party of wagoners. Henry and I rode forward to hunt. After that day there was no probability that we should meet with buffalo, and we were anxious to kill one, for a supply of fresh meat. They were so wild that we hunted all the morning in vain, but at noon as we approached Cow Creek we saw a large band feeding near its margin. Cow Creek is densely lined with trees which intercept the view beyond, and it runs, as we afterwards found, at the bottom of a deep trench. We approached by riding along the bottom of a ravine. When we were near enough, I held the horses while Henry crept towards the buffalo. I saw him take his seat within shooting distance, prepare his rifle, and look about to select his victim. The death of a fat cow seemed certain, when suddenly a great smoke and a rattling volley of musketry rose from the bed of the creek. A score of long-legged Missourians leaped out from among the trees and ran after the buffalo, who one and all took to their heels and vanished. These fellows had crawled up the bed of the creek to within a hundred yards of the game. Never was there a fairer chance for a shot. They were good marksmen; all cracked away at once, and yet not a buffalo fell. In fact the animal is so tenacious of life that it requires no little knowledge of anatomy to kill it, and it is very seldom that a novice succeeds in his first attempt at approaching. The balked Missourians were excessively mortified, especially when Henry told them that if they had kept quiet he would have killed meat enough in ten minutes to feed their whole party. Our friends, who were at no great distance, hearing the fusillade, thought that the Indians had fired the volley for our benefit. Shaw came galloping on to reconnoitre and learn if we were yet among the living.

At Cow Creek we found the welcome novelty of ripe grapes and plums, which grew there in abundance. At the Little Arkansas, not much farther on, we saw the last buffalo, a miserable old bull, roaming over the prairie melancholy and alone.

From this time forward the character of the country was changing every day. We had left behind us the great arid deserts, meagrely covered by the tufted buffalo-grass, with its pale-green hue, and its short, shrivelled blades. The plains before us were carpeted with rich herbage sprinkled with flowers. In place of buffalo we found plenty of prairie-hens, and bagged them by dozens without leaving the trail. In three or four days we saw before us the forests and meadows of Council Grove. It seemed like a new sensation as we rode beneath the resounding arches of these noble woods,—ash, oak, elm, maple, and hickory, festooned with enormous grape-vines, purple with fruit. The shouts of our scattered party, and now and then the report of a rifle, rang through the breathless stillness of the forest. We rode out again with regret into the broad light of the open prairie. Little more than a hundred miles now separated us from the frontier settlements. The whole intervening country was a succession of green prairies, rising in broad swells, and relieved by trees clustering like an oasis around some spring, or following the course of a stream along some fertile hollow. These are the prairies of the poet and the novelist. We had left danger behind us. Nothing was to be feared from the Indians of this region, the Sacs and Foxes, Kanzas and Osages. We had met with rare good fortune. Although for five months we had been travelling with an insufficient force through a country where we were at any moment liable to depredation, not a single animal had been stolen from us, and our only loss had been one old mule bitten to death by a rattlesnake. Three weeks after we reached the frontier the Pawnees and the Camanches began a regular series of hostilities on the Arkansas trail, killing men and driving off horses. They attacked, without exception, every party, large or small, that passed during the next six months.

Diamond Spring, Rock Creek, Elder Grove, and other 'camping places besides, were passed in quick succession. At Rock Creek we found a train of government provision-wagons under the charge of an emaciated old man in his seventy-first year. Some restless American devil had driven him into the wilderness at a time of life when he should have been seated at his fireside with his grandchildren on his knees. I am convinced that he never returned; he was complaining that night of a disease the wasting effects of which upon a younger and stronger man I myself had proved from severe experience. Long before this no doubt the wolves have howled their moonlight carnival over the old man's attenuated remains.

Not long after we came to a small trail leading to Fort Leavenworth, distant but one day's journey. Tête Rouge here took leave of us. He was anxious to go to the fort in order to receive payment for his valuable military services. So he and his horse James, after an affectionate farewell, set out together, with what provisions they could conveniently carry, including a large quantity of brown sugar. On a cheerless rainy evening we came to our last 'camping ground.

In the morning we mounted once more. In spite of the dreary rain of yesterday, there never was a brighter autumnal morning than that on which we returned to the settlements. We were passing through the country of the half-civilized Shawanoes. It was a beautiful alternation of fertile plains and groves just tinged with the hues of autumn, while close beneath them nestled the log-houses of the Indian farmers. Every field and meadow bespoke the exuberant fertility of the soil. The maize stood rustling in the wind, ripe and dry, its shining yellow ears thrust out between the gaping husks. Squashes and huge yellow pumpkins lay basking in the sun in the midst of their brown and shrivelled leaves. Robins and blackbirds flew about the fences, and everything betokened our near approach to home and civilization. The forests that border the Missouri soon rose before us, and we entered the wide tract of bushes which forms their outskirts. We had passed the same road on our outward journey in the spring, but its aspect was now totally changed. The young wild apple-trees then flushed with their fragrant blossoms, were hung thickly with ruddy fruit. Tall grass grew by the roadside in place of tender shoots just peeping from the warm and oozy soil. The vines were laden with purple grapes, and the slender twigs of the swamp maple, then tasselled with their clusters of small red flowers, now hung out a gorgeous display of leaves stained by the frost with burning crimson. On every side we saw tokens of maturity and decay where all had before been fresh with opening life. We entered the forest, checkered, as we passed along, by the bright spots of sunlight that fell between the opening boughs. On either side rich masses of foliage almost excluded the sun, though here and there its rays could find their way down, striking through the broad leaves and lighting them with a pure transparent green. Squirrels barked at us from the trees; coveys of young partridges ran rustling over the fallen leaves, and the golden oriole, the blue-jay, and the flaming red-bird darted among the shadowy branches. We hailed these sights and sounds of beauty by no means with unmingled pleasure. Many and powerful as were the attractions of the settlements, we looked back regretfully to the wilderness behind us.

At length we saw the roof of a white man's dwelling between the opening trees. A few moments after, we were riding over the miserable log-bridge that led into Westport. Westport had beheld strange scenes, but a rougher-looking troop than ours, with our worn equipments and broken-down horses, was never seen even there. We passed the well-remembered tavern, Boone's grocery, and old Vogel's dram-shop, and encamped on a meadow beyond.

Here we were soon visited by a number of people who came to purchase our horses and equipments. This matter disposed of, we hired a wagon and drove to Kanzas landing. Here we were again received under the hospitable roof of our old friend Colonel Chick, and seated under his porch we looked down once more on the eddies of the Missouri.

Deslauriers made his appearance in the morning strangely transformed by a hat, a coat, and a razor. His little log-house was among the woods not far off. It seems he had meditated giving a ball in honor of his return, and had consulted Henry Chatillon as to whether it would do to invite his *bourgeois*. Henry expressed his entire conviction that we would not take it amiss, and the invitation was now proffered accordingly, Deslauriers adding as a special inducement that Antoine Lajeunesse was to play the fiddle. We told him we would certainly come, but before evening the arrival of a steamboat from Fort Leavenworth prevented our being present at the expected festivities. Deslauriers was on the rock at the landing-place, waiting to take leave of us.

'Adieu! mes bourgeois, adieu! adieu!' he cried as the boat put off; 'when you go another time to de Rocky Montagnes I will go with you; yes, I will go!'

He accompanied this assurance by jumping about, swinging his hat, and grinning from ear to ear. As the boat rounded a distant point the last object that met our eyes was Deslauriers still lifting his hat and skipping about the rock. We had taken leave of Munroe and Jim Gurney at Westport, and Henry Chatillon went down in the boat with us.

The passage to St Louis occupied eight days, during about a third of which time we were fast aground on sand-bars. We passed the steamer 'Amelia' crowded with a roaring crew of disbanded volunteers, swearing, drinking, gambling, and fighting. At length one evening we reached the crowded levee of St Louis. Repairing to the Planters' House, we caused diligent search to be made for our trunks, which were at length discovered stowed away in the farthest corner of the store-room. In the morning, transformed by the magic of the tailor's art, we hardly recognized each other.

On the evening before our departure Henry Chatillon came to our rooms at the Planters' House to take leave of us. No one who met him in the streets of St Louis would have taken him for a hunter fresh from the Rocky Mountains. He was very neatly and simply dressed in a suit of dark cloth; for although since his sixteenth year he had scarcely been for a month together among the abodes of men, he had a native good taste which always led him to pay great attention to his personal appearance. His tall, athletic figure with its easy, flexible motions appeared to advantage in his present dress; and his fine face, though roughened by a thousand storms, was not at all out of keeping with it. He had served us with a fidelity and zeal beyond all praise. We took leave of him with regret; and unless his changing features, as he shook us by the hand, belied him, the feeling on his part was no less than on ours. Shaw had given him a horse at Westport. My rifle, an excellent piece, which he had always been fond of using, is now in his hands, and perhaps at this moment its sharp voice is startling the echoes of the Rocky Mountains. On the next morning we left town, and after a fortnight of railroads, coaches, and steamboats, saw once more the familiar features of home.